# A TIME TO STAND

## Book 3 of the Soup Trilogy

### Tom DeWitt

*To my friends and supporters, each is unique but collectively creates the mosaic of humanity.*

*"Reality is created by the mind, we can change our reality by changing our mind."*

PLATO

# CONTENTS

Title Page

Dedication

Epigraph

Chapter 1   1

Chapter 2   23

Chapter 3   29

Chapter 4   40

Chapter 5   47

Chapter 6   51

Chapter 7   58

Chapter 8   62

Chapter 9   65

Chapter 10   81

Chapter 11   84

Chapter 12   98

Chapter 13   101

Chapter 14   112

Chapter 15   116

Chapter 16   126

Chapter 17   131

Chapter 18   136

| | |
|---|---|
| Chapter 19 | 146 |
| Chapter 20 | 152 |
| Chapter 21 | 169 |
| Chapter 22 | 176 |
| Chapter 23 | 179 |
| Chapter 24 | 187 |
| Chapter 25 | 191 |
| Chapter 26 | 201 |
| Chapter 27 | 206 |
| Chapter 28 | 210 |
| Chapter 29 | 216 |
| Chapter 30 | 220 |
| Chapter 31 | 226 |
| Chapter 32 | 231 |
| Chapter 33 | 237 |
| Chapter 34 | 250 |
| Chapter 35 | 256 |
| Chapter 36 | 264 |
| Chapter 37 | 271 |
| Chapter 38 | 275 |
| Chapter 39 | 279 |
| Chapter 40 | 283 |
| Chapter 41 | 287 |
| Chapter 42 | 296 |
| Chapter 43 | 300 |
| Chapter 44 | 309 |
| Chapter 45 | 315 |
| Chapter 46 | 320 |

Chapter 47                                            325

Chapter 48                                            330

Epilogue                                              338

About The Author                                      343

Books In This Series                                  345

# CHAPTER 1

## *14 Years before the SOUP is Operational*

Army Captain Franklin Apoe felt the dirt and small rocks sliding up his back, biting into his skin as his mind struggled to understand what was happening in the world around him. He felt a pair of hands around his ankles release their grip, and he began a slow, effortless slide downward in the loose dirt and sand until stopping moments later. Internally assessing himself for injuries and finding none, the young officer opened his eyes. He was in a shallow crater, about three feet deep and to his left laid a man on his back, staring skyward and breathing heavily as if he'd just completed a hard sprint. Next to the man was his rucksack. From the top of the canvas bag, a small antenna protruded about two feet into the air. Apoe could hear heavy rifle and machine-gun fire about 200 yards away.

"Good, you're alive," the man said. "Are you hurt?" he asked.

"No, just the breath knocked out of me," Apoe said slowly, seeing the burning helicopter off to his left. "Thanks for pulling me out of the wreckage. What the hell happened?"

The man surveyed Apoe's uniform and identified the twin bars attached by Velcro on his outer jacket. "I guess I should say are you hurt, SIR?"

Apoe checked the rank of the man next to him. He was a Sergeant First Class. "No need for formalities out here, Sergeant. I'm a medical doctor," Apoe placed a finger in his ear and started turning it to clear out the sand.

"You're a long way from Kabul. What the hell are you doing out here, Captain? This is where the shooting happens."

Apoe's head was clearing. He was feeling much better

and was aware of his surroundings, which signaled a slight pain in his lower back. "We were medivacing some Afghan VIPs to Kabul. They needed inflight care, and a female nurse or doctor would not work for them, which is why I was on board."

The Sergeant nodded his head, understanding the cultural differences between the US and her allies.

"So, I volunteered to go," Apoe said, sounding like he did not have a choice.

"Didn't the Army teach you not to volunteer, Captain?"

Apoe let the comment slide and continued. "The pilot got the call that you were in contact and had wounded. We had room, and the pilot decided to head your way, thinking to do a quick pick-up. We were hovering at about 5 feet, waiting for your guys. That's the last I remember."

"You're lucky, Captain. That's all I'll say. Name is Ellis," the Sergeant said.

The sounds of combat stopped suddenly. Both men rolled quickly to their stomachs and kept as low a profile as possible. They focused their attention on their front, where a full-on firefight occurred moments before. All firing had ceased as though the soundtrack of war turned off, filling the late afternoon with silence.

Both men looked at each other, their facial expressions showing surprise at the immediate quiet. A slight breeze blew sand and bits of small dead shrubs around the field. Apoe stared to his front, where gunfire and swearing infantrymen had filled his world. Both men squinted through the sweat that trailed through their eyes to obscure their vision like a translucent descending veil; they saw nothing. Apoe looked at Ellis. The Sergeant slowly moved his left hand downward for Apoe to see. The message was clear; remain still and listen.

Moments passed, and the battlefield offered no clues to Apoe, huddled in his shallow ditch in the middle of bumfuck nowhere. And then he heard it. A voice broke the silence as though it were an orchestral instrument playing a hauntingly simple solo leading to an entire symphonic piece. It was a single, clear tenor voice that projected its message. The precision of the notes and word diction were perfect. "Allah Akbar."

The phrase traveled on the air, covering each corner of the battlefield with its call. The beauty of the voice contrasted with the ominous meaning. Apoe felt fear, and his body responded with goosebumps and cold sweat. Once again, the remarkable solo voice sang his message, piercing the morning stillness with precise clarity.

"Allah Akbar."

"Look!" Apoe said in as low a whisper as possible. A group of Taliban fighters emerged from the rock coverings on the edge of a ridge to his front. Apoe estimated this was the location of the American platoon and expected the firefight to begin again at any second. Each carried AK rifles, and several had rocket-propelled grenade launchers. Apoe observed them walking unopposed through the area where a platoon of grunts had fought minutes before.

"I see them." The Sergeant pulled his bag slowly up next to him and removed the radio handset from a side pouch.

"There's no firing from the platoon. They would have opened up by now. The bad guys are right on top of them," Ellis said. His voice was calm and unemotional.

Apoe nodded slightly to agree and squinted, his eyes already burning with sweat, trying to identify the growing threat from the enemy as they approached. He wiped his forehead and face to clear his vision as Apoe alternated between watching the enemy and Ellis's calm response. *"Closer, Closer. How much longer before Ellis does something?"* Apoe questioned but knew Ellis understood the situation better than he did.

Ellis paused, waiting for the ambush that never came. The silence of gunfire removed all doubt his men could continue the fight, and he quickly concluded, "They're all dead," Ellis said and acted on his instincts. The Sergeant brought the device to the side of his face.

He whispered into the handset, "Romeo Five Six, this is Xray Three, fire mission, over."

From the radio's low volume, a whispered calm voice said from inside the headset, "Three, this is six, fire mission over." The response was barely auditable by Apoe.

"From Target Reference Point Juliet Five," The Sergeant began his call for fire, slowly annunciating each piece of information while keeping his voice low. "100 Meters left, approximately 20 enemy troops in the open, HE, fire for effect, I say again, fire for effect."

"Roger three, 100 left from TRP Juliet five, HE copy all, fire for effect. Six rounds. Out."

"Time for some payback, Captain. When you hear the rounds fire, stay low and don't move."

Apoe gave Ellis a thumbs up. He did not need to hear these instructions repeated. As the Taliban soldiers moved forward, Apoe listened to the rising chants of "Allah Akbar" as the soldiers joined the solo voice in celebrating their victory. Despite the cheering Apoe heard, he felt the hollow-sounding 'wumps' in his chest as the 155mm munitions left their cannon barrels kilometers away. His heart pushed the limits of his body, pumping wildly; his fear caused him to expel a large breath. Moments later, the ground shook underneath him, lifting him slightly as the artillery impacted his immediate front.

Apoe heard the Sergeant say much louder into the headset over the din of the falling death, "Repeat over."

"Repeat out."

"Stay down!" the Sergeant yelled. "It ain't over yet."

Apoe felt the hollow 'wumps,' followed by the howling steel racing over his head, and once again, the ground shook violently underneath him, exploding upward in heaps of rock and dirt mixed with flashes of yellow.

"Rounds complete," a voice said from the headset.

The Sergeant looked to his front and saw no movement. The absence of weapons fire or screams from dying fighters told both men the artillery had found its target with lethality. He ducked his head below the slight berm to continue the conversation.

"Roger rounds complete."

"Did we get them?" the voice on the radio wanted to know.

"Wait out," the Sergeant said, looking up over the edge of their temporary shelter once more.

Apoe uncurled from his fetal position and followed Ellis' example. He looked to his front. The area was smoke-filled and started to clear as the cloudy remnants of the munitions blew slowly away, leaving behind small fires in the desert shrubs.

"Look!" Apoe pointed to a man on the ridge about 200 meters away stumbling on the downward slope.

"I see the bastard." The Sergeant reached for his rifle when suddenly the man fell face forward in the dirt and tumbled out of sight.

"Looks like we got him, too," Apoe concluded.

The radio spoke again in the hushed tones of the low volume emerging from the handset. "Three, this is five-six. Be advised that friendlies are inbound. Estimated time of arrival, one five mikes."

"Roger five-six. We'll stay put."

"Estimated friendly losses?"

Apoe looked at Ellis. He could tell it was bad by the expression on his face.

"Believe all are casualties five-six. Status unknown. Send medivac."

There was momentary silence on the radio, then the response, professional and curt but Apoe could not miss the sorrow in the voice on the other end. "Roger, medivac on its way. Out."

"If you think there are wounded, I'm going out there, Sergeant."

"Sit right here, Sir! The Cavalry is inbound. You have no medical supplies and don't know if all the bad guys are dead.

It's only 15 minutes."

Apoe thought momentarily, knew what he needed to do, and accepted the risk.

"That's why you'll come with me, Sergeant." Apoe stood up, expecting to draw fire. *"This was the moment,"* he thought. *"I'm a perfect target."*

No shots, just silence.

Renewed with confidence and driven by his instincts and medical training, he looked at his companion, said, "Get your gear, Sergeant. Let's go," and started walking forward.

Ellis scrambled to collect his belongings. He reached for his rifle and ruck, adjusted his helmet, and mumbled, "you've got a lot of balls for a doctor."

Apoe didn't wait for his companion nor hear his comment. He focused on being able to save a life or two in the next 15 minutes.

The 155s cratered the ground to resemble a moonscape. The artillery fell perfectly in almost duplicate rows from the firing guns. The target area was a heap of dead Taliban soldiers in various states of carnage. Weapons lay scattered around, mixed in with dismembered body parts and their accompanying gore.

The Sergeant whistled, more of an expelled breath that made a whistling sound. All around him, the earth had unnaturally heaved upward, ejecting its rock to mix with the fragmenting steel to create the carnage around them. Ellis directed Apoe's attention to a headless body lying on its back with its knees bent as though it were casually lying on a picnic blanket, watching the clouds. Ellis looked at Apoe and began to comment on how natural it looked or some other statement of soldier bravado. "Look at that guy, he...."

Apoe looked at him and said, "I don't want to hear it, Sergeant."

Thankfully, Ellis did not finish his thought.

Apoe had a duty to perform. Ellis' duty was to take lives, a necessary part of any soldier's job in war. His was to clean up the mess. Apoe looked at each Taliban fighter; none appeared to have survived. They walked to the edge of the ridge, each saying nothing, and looked down. Only one body, the one they observed falling, was below.

"I count 27 dead, including the stiff at the bottom of the ravine. Not bad shooting," Ellis remarked.

Apoe looked around, mystified by the situation unfolding before him. "Where are our guys?" Apoe asked. "All I see are Taliban."

The Sergeant stopped mumbling about how accurate his call for fire was and said, "What did you say?"

"I said, where are our guys? There's nothing here but Taliban."

The Sergeant lifted his head, removed his helmet, and scanned the area around them. "There!" he pointed. "Off to your right, about 70 meters."

Both men sprinted to where the Sergeant pointed and stopped abruptly. Stacked in front of them were approximately 20 American soldiers, all lying flat, each placed on top of the other in perfect rows, three bodies high. Their weapons were stacked in a heap as though they were deposited there by a Good Samaritan that policed the battlefield.

"What the hell?" the Sergeant asked as he walked around the men that comprised his platoon only thirty minutes ago. Apoe surveyed the dead Americans and started noticing the motionless faces, each with unique expressions captured on their face from their last moments of life. Most looked afraid or confused.

The Sergeant chose this moment to release his contained emotions from the last hour or so, shouting while looking at the lifeless men whose positions held no explanation. "Who would do this, Doc? It could not be the Taliban we just saw! There was no time for them...." Apoe raised his hand, a signal for silence. The Sergeant's voice transformed into a head shake and a face filled with confusion.

Ellis understood the Captain's need for silence and

remained quiet, observing the doctor at work, occasionally shaking his head and mumbling, "this is some real bull shit here."

Apoe walked around the morbid pile inspecting the dead. Each body looked flat, as though steamrolled, but each retained its facial features and outer appearance of being human. Apoe leaned in close to each soldier, lifting an arm, turning a head, or pushing against rib cages. There was no resistance as he twisted each member, just the flesh, giving way to the doctor's prodding.

Apoe saw very little blood except on the soldiers that had been wounded previous to their death. "There's no structure here," he said out loud while formulating his thoughts. It was Apoe's turn to shake his head.

Apoe examined the last soldier and stood backward. His expression was a conflicted mixture of disgust and professional curiosity.

"Sergeant, this is incredible! There are no fatal bullet wounds that I can see; just a couple of them took shots that would wound them. Look, see here," he said, sounding like he was lecturing in a classroom.

Ellis moved closer to see where he was pointing. "This soldier took a round to his shoulder, and this one," he said, pointing to another, "through the thigh. These are explainable wounds. Other than these two, there are no other signs that the rest of these men were in combat."

"Then why are they dead?"

Apoe paused momentarily, not believing what he had discovered in the bodies. The Captain stood straight, looked at Ellis, and said, "Every bone in their bodies is broken from the inside. These men died because their necks were snapped or they experienced some other INTERNAL trauma to cause death. I have no explanation for why almost every other bone is also broken."

"That's impossible. Everyone here was shooting and laying down fire. No one could sneak up on a whole platoon, snap their necks, and stack them up like this!" Ellis exclaimed.

"Yet here they are. That's exactly what happened. I can't say how it happened, but I can tell you, that's how these men died." Apoe sat down on the desert floor. He needed to think. *This made no sense!*

The Sergeant heard the relief helicopters approaching. "Maybe someone on those birds can figure this out. I'm not sure that I agree with your assessment, Captain." Ellis stood straight as if to regain his composure before the helicopters landed.

"Agree or not. Can you explain what you are seeing?"

Before he could answer, the radio handset came to life. "Okay, three, pop some smoke for us. Can you see us?"

Ellis looked at Apoe and spoke into his handset. "Fresh out of smoke," he replied. "Keep coming straight. I'll talk you in." Ellis ran to a level clearing that allowed the four Blackhawks to touch down without incident and started waving his arms.

Apoe had difficulty thinking while helicopter engines and rotor noise created temporary chaos. The birds landed and immediately discharged a fresh platoon of infantrymen that hurried to form a perimeter. A young, square-jawed Major jumped off the closest and walked towards the Sergeant.

"Who's left, Mike?" It was a very informal greeting, the type exchanged by two warriors who had spent several years sharing the grime of combat.

"Just me and the Captain over there," he said, pointing to Apoe.

"A Captain? What's he doing here?"

"He's a doctor, Sir. Pulled him from that downed Blackhawk burning back there." Ellis pointed his thumb over his shoulder and continued, "He was taking some VIPs to Kabul, and his pilot diverted here to pick up a couple of our wounded."

The major nodded. "Looks like this is not your normal firefight," he said, eyeing the stacked men near the Captain.

"Did you two do that?"

"No, Sir, and before you ask, neither of us can explain it."

"What do you mean?"

"Doc says no one died from a gunshot wound. They all had their bones and necks snapped."

The major stopped and looked at Ellis. "What?" the Major asked.

"You heard me, Sir. We can't determine what happened, only what we see now."

Undeterred by this latest information, the major said, "You and the Doc start pulling your story together. That's a tall tale, and you might want to ensure you have all the details correct." The major paused to let what he was saying make its impact.

Ellis understood the implied message. "It is what it is, Major. You can't make this shit up, and our guys will see the same thing when they look at the bodies."

"Okay, I'm not telling you to lie; just make sure you have your facts right, HUA?"

"HUA, Sir."

"Where are the dead Taliban?"

"Walk that way," he said, nodding to his left. "You can't miss them. They are the only thing here that makes sense. Oh yeah, there's a dead one at the bottom of that small ravine, too." The helicopter's engines had stopped, bringing an eerie peace to this place of death.

"Thanks," the Major said, placing his hand on his friend's shoulder and patting it twice. "Great job. Glad you made it, Mike."

The Major walked towards the area where the Taliban were lying. One of his NCOs approached.

"Sir, so far, no real intelligence on any of the bodies. We still have a few more to search." The Major nodded. The Sergeant continued, "Private Franks saw one in the gulley off the ridge. He says the guy moved and thinks he's still alive. He might have something on him of value." The NCO surveyed the carnage and offered his assessment, "The arty did a number on these guys. Pretty accurate shooting."

The Major dismissed the comment. He knew war was not something heroic or filled with romantic glory. No one who ever fought in one believed that crap. He saw the remains of the Taliban fighters. Thirty minutes ago, they were living people with their own lives or as close to people as you could let your enemy get. Now they were pieces of human flesh thrown about the desert. His thoughts returned to the one that might be alive. "Okay, take a couple of men and bring him up. He might be able to tell us something."

"HUA!" the Sergeant said and turned to his men and shouted, "Okay, Franks, so you think he's alive? Pick a buddy, and let's go get 'em!" The order was met by the typical soldier's response from Franks, "Oh man, always the one with the idea has to do the work." He was still bitching when he and one of his fire team disappeared over the edge of the small ridge with the Sergeant.

The Major turned to his Operations NCO standing about 50 feet away and motioned for him to come to him. When he closed the distance, he ordered, "Call in and let HQ know the ground is secure. Report the loss of our platoon."

"Yes, Sir. Any idea what happened to our guys?"

"No ideas at this time. You got your iPhone with you?"

The Sergeant nodded.

"Okay, get some pics of our soldiers so that we don't have to convince folks of what we saw, then start loading our KIAs on the number 4 bird."

"On it, Sir." The Sergeant sprinted back to the helicopter to get his phone and make his report.

The Major walked over to the Captain and his friend, sitting quietly on the ground cross-legged. The men were quiet. Both stood up as the Major approached. The Captain started to salute, but the Sergeant said, "Not out here, Captain. We don't like the bad guys to know who's in charge."

Apoe stopped his arm motion and let his hand drop to

his side. "I'm Captain Apoe, Major. I guess the Sergeant filled you in."

"Yeah, he did," he said, nodding. "Are you sure you did a complete exam on our guys?"

"I didn't check every one of them but saw enough to know they did not die by gunshot wounds. This leads me to believe all of them died roughly the same way. Their necks were snapped and not just turned." Apoe paused, trying to find the right words. "*Who or what could do this*?" he wanted to offer a cause but knew everyone was looking at him for answers, and a guess at this point might cause rumors or worse. He continued, "Every bone was broken in two from the inside. There was real violence in their deaths. Some of their heads are on only because the skin keeps them on. It's as though whoever did this was in an uncontrollable rage, utterly destroying everything that made our guys human."

"Any thoughts about what could cause something like this?" the Major asked.

"Short of brute force, no."

"And the men stacked. Any ideas?"

"Way out of my medical lane, Sir."

The Major shook his head, resigned that he had a hell of a mystery on his hands and that folks would want answers, and he had none.

"Sir!" It was a shout from the edge of the ridge. The Major looked in the direction of the call and saw Private Franks waving his hand to come to him.

All three walked briskly to the arm-waving soldier. When they got close, he said, "Sir, you need to see this."

"What's going on?"

"Something ain't right. This dude's messed up but not from the Arty."

Apoe looked at him and thought, "*Great, one more frickin' mystery on top of what I already have.*"

"Doctor, you come with me," the Major said. He looked at his friend and nodded, indicating that he should join them.

The four slid down into the ravine, bracing their steps by turning sideways and kicking up dirt and dust until reaching the two men grouped around the body at the bottom. Both were standing, looking down at the fighter. It was evident to Apoe that both men were startled by what they were observing, standing back from the body, arms over their mouths as though whatever the fighter had could also infect them.

As Apoe reached the body, he immediately understood. Laying on the ground, face-up, was their adversary. His turban and clothing were standard Taliban, but he had no weapons near or on him. No pistol, ammo belt, or even the gear worn for water and food. Apoe saw it first and gasped. He heard the Major say, "holy shit."

The man's face was wrinkled as though he were an older man that had aged poorly. As Apoe checked his arms and legs, they showed the same aging and beginning signs of decay. Apoe touched the man's forearm and felt his bones between his fingers. His arm diameter could not be more than an inch. *"What's this?"* he thought, seeing something resembling an image on the palm side of the man's wrist.

Looking more closely, Apoe noticed a brand had raised the skin, and despite the condition of the man's body, the pattern was unmistakable and prominent. It was an Egyptian Ankh. *"What the hell is an Egyptian symbol doing on a Taliban fighter?"*

"Strange," Apoe said out loud.

"Find something?" the Major asked.

"Just a tattoo or brand of some sort," Apoe replied.

"So, what," Ellis said. "Tattoos are common on soldiers."

"I've been told permanent tattoos are forbidden by the Islamic faith, Sergeant," Apoe responded calmly, continuing to examine the fighter for other clues.

"That's a dumb ass rule," Franks muttered.

"Just because you think it's dumb doesn't make it so Private," The Major said.

Franks looked at Ellis's face and knew not to offer any more opinions.

Apoe was thankful for the Major's comments. The minor distraction allowed him to keep the details of his examination to himself, reluctant to add more information to the growing mystery.

The fighter stirred and began mumbling something in a whisper.

"What's he saying?" the Major asked.

"He's been mumbling something since we arrived," Private Franks commented.

"What was it, Private?" the Major said, raising his voice.

"Sir, look at this guy! I'm not going anywhere near him to hear what he's saying. This guy is ate up with something, and it ain't like anything I've ever seen. My granddad lived to 98 and didn't look this wrinkled." Frank's two companions nodded their heads.

"I'll listen," Apoe said and leaned in closer to hear. It started as a faint hiss, as though a breath had escaped a dying man's lips and gradually became something that began to form sounds. "Salty an minha." He heard it again. "Salty an minha." A third time confirmed the phrase. "Salty an minha."

Apoe was startled and pulled his head back as the man grabbed his arm and used his remaining strength to pull himself closer to Apoe's face. Apoe stared into the man's eyes. They were solid black, offering no indication of a pupil or any other color to reveal any remnants of humanity. The man whispered one last time. Softly he said, "Salty an minha." while nodding his head slowly. The old man smiled and released his grip on Apoe, his strength evaporating. Apoe looked at the man and knew he was close to death.

"It sounds like Salty an minha or Satie minha. Any idea what it means?" he said, standing up.

Everyone shook their head. The Major considered this added information and made his decision.

"We're not hanging around here to figure it out. We'll get

it translated when we get back. Doc, is he going to make it?"

Apoe shook his head. "I'm surprised he has held on this long." Apoe knelt once more and put his ear to the man's mouth to listen for breathing. There was none. He reached over for a pulse on his spindly wrist and then to his scrawny neck. A very faint pulse in both places told Apoe he was still alive.

"Still alive, barely."

"Sir, I think the three of us can handle this," Ellis said.

The major looked at him and knew Ellis had more to say without the men around.

The soldiers stood by, waiting for their next orders. They came quickly. "Alright," he said, addressing the three who retrieved the body. "Head on up. Have someone bring down a body bag. We'll take it from here."

They nodded and began their ascent back to the ridge top.

"Okay, Mike, what do you want to tell me?"

"Sir, none of this adds up. Our guys are dead, not a deadly wound between them, but every bone broken and stacked like cordwood." Ellis paused, mulling over what he was about to reveal. "What I got to say next, I don't want taken out of context, and you, Doc," he said, looking at Apoe still kneeling, "You gotta promise not to think I'm crazy. Agreed?"

"Agreed." Apoe stood up to pay direct attention to Ellis.

"Okay, Mike, let's hear it," the Major said.

"Our guys were not the only thing 'not shot.'"

"What do you mean?" Apoe asked.

"Your chopper Doc. It never took a shot."

"I don't understand, Sergeant. We were shot down."

"No, Sir, you were knocked down."

"What are you talking about?" the Major asked, slightly angry.

"Our platoon was moving across the open area when we came under fire. A couple of guys, the ones you've examined, Doc, were hit in the initial exchange. At first, we thought it was a couple of snipers in the hills, and everyone went to ground. The Lieutenant used his radio and called for medivac. He ordered a squad to the ground over there," Ellis pointed left and up the ridge, "where the cover was better. The rest of us just stayed low. When the shooting started, I ended up online with everyone else, but as they moved forward, the El-Tee told me to stay back and guide the medivac into a flat place for landing." Ellis stopped, collected his thoughts, and appeared to grapple with what to say next.

"So, what happened?" the Major prompted.

"Everything got real quiet. There was no more shooting; the only real noise was the occasional yelling between squads maneuvering into position. Then even the squad leaders stopped yelling at their teams once in place. No one moved for about five minutes, wanting to make sure the snipers were gone and trying to look for any signal that they were still around. Then, I saw your helo coming in low. I grabbed my smoke and popped it for your pilot to show him where to land. He saw it and hovered over top. I fully expected your bird to take fire when you came in but knew the other guys would take care of the Taliban if they started shooting. Just as your pilot was setting down, your helicopter stopped moving forward," Ellis paused.

It was apparent to Apoe that Ellis was having difficulty recalling the events, as though Ellis was questioning what he saw. The Sergeant continued much more slowly, reflecting on each word, "as if a hand had grabbed the front of the bird and held it in place. I could see the pilot struggling with the controls. I think he was as surprised as me."

The Sergeant stopped again, took a couple of deep breaths, and looked at Apoe's and the Major's expressions.

Ellis' talking returned to its normal rhythm. "Doc, if I'm lying, then I'm dying. It was as though an invisible hand turned the helicopter on its side and shook it. You were about five feet off the ground, and I saw you come out the side door, all ass, and elbows and hit the ground like a sack of potatoes.

After you hit, the chopper tilted to the other side, and then, it looked like it was thrown down to the ground, just like a kid that didn't want to play with his toy anymore. It came down about 20 feet from where you fell. Your bird hit hard and blew up. It shouldn't have exploded right away, but it did. When it blew up, the platoon started laying down suppressive fire into the hills, shooting at everything in general, hoping to hit whoever just brought you down. I saw the guys bringing the wounded back to me hit the ground when the chopper exploded. I looked, and you were close to the burning metal and the fuel explosions. I ran over and started dragging you back to my hole. Still, our guys were shooting, but no fire was coming our way. I had drug you about halfway when I heard the guys carrying the wounded scream rise off the turf, then twist and fall back to the ground. Now I was sure we were taking fire. I kept my head low and pulled you the rest of the way, not looking at anything else around me as the firing increased. All of our guys were shooting. When you came to, there was sustained fire coming from our guys, then you and I both heard that stop suddenly too."

Apoe nodded and said to the major, "The last thing I remember in the helicopter was securing my patients for landing, getting tubes and equipment out of the doorway to take in the wounded. That's when I felt myself thrown out. I thought we had taken an RPG in the side or something."

"Nothing hit you. Nothing HIT you!" Ellis yelled.

The major interjected, "Are you sure, Mike? None of this is adding up. You and I have served a long time together. We've seen some crazy stuff,"

"But you don't believe me!"

"I didn't say that. You've been through something traumatic here, well beyond what we've experienced before, and I agree, nothing here is making sense. But Mike, helicopters being stopped midair and thrown around. It's hard for me to get my head around something like that."

"You don't need to, Sir. It happened whether you get your

head around it or not," Ellis exploded.

The Major's tone softened as if trying to indicate some belief in what was happening to his friend.

"Okay, let's say you did see something like that; do you have any ideas what could have caused that chopper to 'be stopped' in midair and shaken like that?"

"None, Sir. I just know what I saw."

The conversation was interrupted by the man on the ground, who groaned loudly. The three men turned their focus to him. His breathing was labored, and he appeared frightened, thrashing his body from side to side, using some unknown energy source in his dying body. His face contorted as though he was seeing something that caused fear and panic.

"Satie minha!" he exclaimed, lifting himself with his arms, eyes wild and uncomprehending of the world around him. "Satie minha," he said quietly as he lay his head back on the desert floor. He let out a long slow breath, and his head tilted to one side, eyes staring into oblivion.

Apoe reached down and felt for a pulse. There was none. "He's dead."

"One less of the bastards to have to kill tomorrow," Ellis said.

"Ellis, can't you have a little pity for these guys?" Apoe asked.

"No, Captain, I can't! This guy was responsible for killing some of my best friends today. I hope he rots in hell!" he yelled into Apoe's face.

"Okay – knock it off!" the Major ordered, aggressively moving between the two soldiers. "Mike, back off!" and looking at Apoe, said, "Captain, you have a lot to learn about this war."

Apoe started to formulate his defense when the Major said, "Now shut up. Both of you." The Major, still between the two men, looked around and stepped backward to address both. "Are you feeling this?"

The Major had noticed it first; a slight cold breeze, out of place in the heat of Afghanistan, started blowing through the bottom of the ravine. Apoe felt coolness on his face, a relief from moments before when he was sweating from every pore. The wind began to intensify, picking up strength with each second. Apoe looked around him. The Major and Ellis felt the temperature change as it turned to an unmistakable cold, slowly enveloping them. Despite the increase in wind speed, the dirt remained in place, untouched by the whirlwind moving around them. Apoe could feel the wind on his hands and face, but his uniform remained perfectly still as though he was a part of the wind circling him.

"Look!" Ellis yelled and pointed to the body of the dead fighter. Beneath him, a small light emerged. It began at the center of his back, and soon it was part of a kaleidoscope of colors and points of light, all swirling around the body.

Apoe saw their surroundings dim as darkness began to surround them. Within the night, different points of light combined and formed a figure eight around the dead man, each color accentuated and made brilliant by the black enveloping them. Each small point began to enlarge and become brighter, filling the space around them with an indescribable collage of colors and brilliance.

The major placed his hand over the body and guided the light to different places along the dead man's chest, only for the light to wrap around his hand and return to the growing figure eight.

"We have taken this one," Apoe heard the words deep into his mind. A simple, peaceful voice placed him at ease despite what he observed and the coolness he was feeling. "How will you live the rest of your life?" the voice asked.

The colors and lights enlarged and merged into one entity that exuded warmth and deep feelings of peacefulness as all three men watched the body on the ground slowly transform into small lights, like night embers rising from a campfire. Each ember turned silver and was carried away on the breeze that dissipated into the desert.

The body was gone. All three men stood motionless.

Apoe grasped for awareness, slowly felt his mind place him back into his desert surroundings, and felt the sun warm his face again. No one spoke.

Sergeant Ellis broke the silence and quietly said, "Add that to your list of impossibilities, Sir. Can you explain what just happened? Did anyone else hear somebody say something?"

The Major said nothing, still transitioning from the experience.

"Sir! What the hell?" It was Franks holding a body bag standing next to them.

The three had not seen the soldier's arrival and were startled by his proximity to them.

"What's the matter, Private?" Apoe asked, hoping to bring everyone back to reality and control the dialogue.

"Sir, where were you? I came back to the top of the ridge and looked down. There was no one here, Major." The private looked to Ellis and then Apoe, hoping one of the men would confirm what he was saying. "I ran down the hill to find you and you three," he stopped and paused, looking at the Major's face, "came out of nowhere. One minute you were gone. The next minute you're standing here."

"Did you see anything else?" Apoe asked calmly while struggling with his questions and doubts about his sanity.

"Nothing Doc. Nothing at all."

Ellis jumped into the conversation. "The sun's casting some long shadows. It plays tricks this time of day with seeing things in the desert. It probably just looked like we were gone, Private Franks."

"Sergeant," Franks began, "this is no sun trick. You... hey, where's the stiff?"

The Major, sensing more questions could follow, said with the direct firmness of command, "Private, what you saw and what you think you saw are two different things. There is nothing more here you need to know about as far as I'm concerned. You get me?"

"HUA, Sir."

"Let's get the hell out of here," the Major said, starting the walk back up the ridge. Sergeant Ellis followed close behind.

"What am I supposed to do with this Doc?" Franks said, holding up the body bag.

"Bring it with you."

The two lagged behind the major, whose quick stride made steady progress in getting out of the ravine. Ellis was keeping pace with his friend. The two were nearly at the top.

"Doc, I asked one of the guys on the choppers that speaks Arabic what Salty an minha meant."

"What did he say?"

"He said it meant Shiny Ones or Shiny Things. Does that mean anything to you?"

Apoe stopped and looked at Franks. "No," he answered honestly, then continued. "Do you understand what the Major said about not seeing anything?"

"Yes, Sir."

"Let's keep it that way, or I will personally order your visit to a shrink when you get back. Get my meaning?"

"I didn't see or hear shit, Sir."

"Good, let's keep walking. We've got some long days in front of us." The two soldiers climbed to the top of the ridge.

"You go ahead, Private Franks. I'll join everyone shortly."

Franks nodded his head and walked towards his squad. Apoe turned and looked at the sun as it reached the zenith, its warmth leaving his face hot in the desert sun. So much to consider and so many unexplained events to research. He heard the platoon preparing to go. The telltale helicopter engine sounds amplified, and the turning chopper rotors swirled and kicked up the desert dust. The dead were collected, the photos taken, and the battlefield stripped of its intelligence. Only the questions defining the day remained.

*"How will you live the rest of your life?"* This time, the question popped into Apoe's head by his own doing.

*"That's a hell of a question,"* he thought.

"Come on, Captain!" Ellis yelled. "We are leaving!"

Apoe turned and saw Ellis pointing to a seat next to him and sprinted for the aircraft.

# CHAPTER 2

*Present Day*

Sarah Anderson was in the cafeteria munching her lunch. She had no clue where she was but suspected the location was somewhere in the United States. She assumed it was in the US since everyone spoke English and occasionally overheard references to the CIA and Department of Defense.

Two weeks had passed since she was sedated and taken by men in the middle of the night. She assumed again that they also cleared out her IT gear, and her consulting business with the White House was now over. Sarah thought about her client, COL Baxter. She wondered if he was in a facility like this or even knew what had happened to her. "*Well, they can have my IT equipment, but I'll be pissed if they find out about my retirement accounts in the Caymans,*" she thought. She had taken great pains to hide her money offshore and counted on her abilities as a hacker to use techniques that secured her future.

She looked around the cafeteria, and no one knew she existed. To date, everyone was polite. There were the usual pleasantries when bumping into people in the hall, but no one was 'talking to her.' Everyone minded their own business. There were no guards on her door, but it made her uncomfortable to hear the electric click at 8 p.m. each night that signified her door had locked for the evening. So far, the same click would unlock her door at 6:30 a.m. Her host restricted her movement to this part of the facility. There were no bars or cells with rotting cots and flea-filled blankets, and someone cleaned her room every day while she went to eat. A newly issued facility jumpsuit appeared in her closet during her Friday lunch. She received instructions to leave her old garments on a chair on Saturday, and they disappeared like magic. Except for the circumstances of her visit and lack of windows, she could have been in a Marriott. Sarah was too smart to plan an escape without understanding where and why she was confined. There might be some advantage to her circumstances. *"Be patient,"* she told herself.

"Mind if I join you?" a woman's voice said, interrupting Sarah's thoughts. Sarah looked up into the smiling face of an aristocratic beauty queen. Her blue eyes, short-cut blonde hair, and professional dark blue suit slightly intimidated Sarah in a jumpsuit and with no make-up. The woman held a tray containing her lunch and motioned toward the table with her head. "May I?" she asked, sitting in one of the table's chairs.

The voice and invitation to have a direct conversation startled Sarah. She shifted to 'negotiation mode,' which consisted of a firm voice accompanied by a stern look and an 'I don't really care' attitude.

"Free Country. Or at least it was until I got here," Sarah replied curtly.

"You've been treated well, right?"

"Still a jail." Sarah watched the woman's reaction to her comment and saw her facial expression soften.

"My name is Dr. Marks. I want to discuss your future."

"This is all quite sudden," Sarah quipped. "I'm not sure I'm ready to talk about anything yet."

"That's fine," Dr. Marks replied while opening her Diet Peach Snapple. "I can come back in another two weeks if you want."

"So that's it. You let me cool off for a couple of weeks and did not tell me anything about where I am or why I was taken out of my house – rather abruptly, I might add. You know, there are laws against that kind of stuff."

Dr. Marks smiled and took a sip of her Snapple, maintaining eye contact with Sarah. She placed her drink slowly back on the tray. She sat back, continuing to stare at Sarah, saying nothing.

Sarah understood the body language. Be civil – or spend another two weeks wondering what the hell was going on.

Sarah turned off her attitude but kept her defenses in place. She asked Dr. Marks nicely, "So why did you bring me here?"

Dr. Marks leaned forward. "Sarah Anderson, 23 years old, used by the White House National Security Advisor's office to access hardened IT systems worldwide. Quite successful if the briefing material is correct. When I say hardened systems, that also includes our own. CIA, Defense, Transportation, and Industry. Why Ms. Anderson, you have quite the resume." Dr. Marks took another drink of her Snapple. Sarah said nothing, observing the woman's movements and facial features to find a weakness or some other indication of deception.

"How did you get so good at hacking computers? Our investigation shows that you attended William and Mary but left after two years. Other training, perhaps?"

"If you are implying that the Chinese or some other country taught me my skills, you would be wrong. I'm just a quick learner." Sarah smiled.

"Recently hacked CIA and DoD TOP SECRET systems, successfully, I might add."

"Not too successfully. I'm here, aren't I?"

"So, you are." It was Dr. Marks' turn to smile. She continued, "Quite ingenious to hack the business that had a copy of the Satellite Operating System we are using. If I read the reports correctly, you masqueraded your way in as a satellite instead of a direct hack of the main system."

"You read them correctly." It was a simple statement. Sarah knew her approach had rattled the agency. *"Why else,"* she thought, *"would she be here? Wherever here was."*

Dr. Marks paused, "Professionally, I am intrigued by your methods. I want to discuss them one day, but not today. Let's talk about what lies ahead."

"Ah yes, my future," Sarah said, implying she was ready to get down to business. "What will it be, salt mines in Africa? Sold into the escort business in Thailand?"

Dr. Marks genuinely laughed. Sarah, believing the laughter was to disarm her and build a connection between her and Dr. Marks, added her laughter to play the game. Sarah stopped quickly when others around her took notice of their levity and stared. "*Not much happiness in this place,*" Sarah thought.

Aware of the stares from the people in the cafeteria, Dr. Marks ended her joviality with a slight chuckle and continued. "No, I think not, Ms. Anderson. You may have other talents, but they are irrelevant to our discussion," she said, smiling from their little laugh. Dr. Marks composed herself after the brief lapse of professionalism and then continued. "The US Government would like to offer you a job."

Sarah sat still for a moment. She looked at the expressionless face Dr. Marks presented and thought, "*She's serious.*"

Sarah asked, "Is this the part where we laugh again?"

Sarah was in a battle of wills with a professional. She had to think about what she would say next. Instead, as it was prone to, her mouth preempted her mental analysis and said, "What do you want me to do?"

Dr. Marks responded immediately. "We have a special team of talented people like you. You would become part of that team. Your skills and techniques would be a definite asset to your government. We are asking you to serve."

"*This is overwhelming! How could I work for these bastards knowing some of the things they are doing in the world? And that's just the tip of the iceberg. The last assignment Baxter had me do, worried him that parts of our government were working against itself. Take this job, and you'll enter a VERY dark world.*"

Sensing Sarah's internal conversation, Dr. Marks continued to explain her offer, "Your pay would be pretty good, and you would have a chance to make a difference in the world. I don't need to tell you what a terrible place reality can sometimes be. You would start your skill evaluation here and move on to another assignment after about a month."

"*Skill evaluation? What the hell was a skill evaluation?*" Sarah needed to think about this. She needed to stall. "Will the new job have windows?" she asked, faking her laugh again.

"Possibly." Dr. Marks leaned forward and began to whisper, "This job is really not open for discussion. It's a long-term engagement. At your age, it could be very long. However, if you don't lose this little girl act, you will find that we have very little patience regarding indecision."

"Indecision?" Sarah whispered.

"You're a smart young lady. Haven't you figured it out yet?"

Sarah decided to test Dr. Marks one last time. "Tell me!" she whispered back.

Dr. Marks stared directly into Sarah's eyes, looking deep. Sarah stared back just as intently. "In this business, you are an asset or a liability. We spent the last two weeks discussing which one you were. I fought for you because I believe you have some genius buried under that tough façade you display. I told them you were worth the risk. If I hadn't, someone would have shown up and asked you to follow them outside." She stopped to make her point. "We don't offer these plush accommodations to liabilities," Dr. Marks said, moving her hands, palms up, pointing to her surroundings.

Sarah heard the message. "Why would you fight for me? I don't even know you."

"Because," Dr. Marks said. "I lead the team."

Sarah sat quietly.

"We'll have lunch tomorrow Ms. Anderson. I would like your answer then." Dr. Marks stood up, "Any more questions?"

Sarah looked up, "We're meeting at noon, right?"

***

The phone rang in the Director's underground office half a mile from the facility cafeteria. The Director looked away from his computer reports and picked up the phone. "Dr. Apoe," Apoe spoke his name curtly into the phone receiver.

"Franklin, this is Elizabeth."

"How did it go?" Dr. Apoe asked, softening his voice.

"She is a pain in the ass, but most brilliant people are. I

think she will take the job."

"You're positive you need her?"

"It's not her skills I want. It's her thinking. She approached this problem much differently than most hackers and, more importantly, made it work. Something about her is special. I need special."

"So, how long did you give her to decide?"

"She owes me an answer tomorrow at lunch. We are meeting at noon in the cafeteria. I thought a public place over lunch was appropriate."

"Okay. If she says 'yes,' I will give you the necessary resources."

"Thanks, Franklin. You'll be the second person to know." Dr. Marks hesitated a moment, then asked, "Meet you tonight around 9:00 to discuss?"

"See you then," Apoe replied. CLICK

Dr. Marks smiled. She hated shallow relationships but needed this one to grow her Team. In this age of computers, true power existed in information. Her team was the right mix of talent and skill to find and extract the digital artifacts hidden in other automated systems threatening the US government. Sarah Anderson would be a great addition to her group. "Besides," Marks mused, "she just might be developing feelings for Dr. Apoe."

# CHAPTER 3

A lec Richardson was standing in his life support container, known as the 'box,' looking at the room around him. He remembered being in this same space when the Supervisor asked him to write the story that would announce to the world that the SOUP existed. He never imagined that he would become part of the inmate population less than 300 feet down the hall.

"Where is the Supervisor?" he asked.

"A lot has changed while you've been in the SOUP Mr. Richardson," the Supervisor said. She stepped forward to assist Richardson with stepping out of his box and onto the concrete floor. UT stepped forward and provided a white warming jacket to Alec, who took it and wrapped it around his shoulders. He could feel the jacket's warmth immediately begin to elevate his temperature to normal.

Alec looked at the supervisor, realized his ability to look into her mind, and then corrected himself. Alec was not looking into her mind as much as he could understand the thoughts coming from her. If the Supervisor thought about anything, the electromagnetic energy that comprised each thought emanated into space around her. By his proximity, he could collect and understand them as though reading a book after you learn the language. Many thoughts were coming from her, and most were about him. So much new information!

She was the new supervisor. The old one – the one responsible for placing him in the SOUP was with the inmates as well – his name was Boyd. His mind was bombarded with the amount of information now pouring from the mind of Mr. UT. Alec could not think on his own. It was as if nature's barriers to human perception suddenly disappeared, and Alec could discern each sound in each frequency around him;

the higher frequencies that drive dogs to bark or the lower frequencies of skin mites scurrying across his arm. The noise was one continuous bombardment of ideas, questions, and the facility's operations, so many that he could no longer discern between them. They were just noise. He placed his hand on his ears and bent forward at the waist, causing the Supervisor and UT to grab him to prevent him from falling.

Alec instinctively created a visual representation of a volume control knob in his mind and turned it down until the thoughts around him ceased to be invasive. He turned it again, and Alec could no longer hear or detect the stream of sounds escaping into space.

The four walked in silence out of the cell block and into the administrative portion of the facility. The Supervisor and UT assisted Alec into the conference room. Alec sat in a chair, and the others took their seats.

Alec looked around, so many memories, old memories coming back to him in stark contrast to the reality where he left a loving wife, a young daughter, and a wonderful life. And now, white walls in a facility that he knew all too well and the purpose it served.

"What UT, no coffee? I'm surprised you didn't fill up a cup before setting me into my seat," Alec said.

"It's great to have you back again, Alec," UT said, acknowledging his quirk for coffee that he had shared during Alec's visit. "I have so many questions."

"I know!" Alec said, putting his hands back on his ears and smiling at everyone. "Yours came through the strongest UT."

UT smiled. Alec was back!

"You all do. I think it best we ease into all those questions. Don't you agree?"

The team nodded in agreement.

"Are you reading our thoughts now?" the Supervisor asked.

"No," Alec replied. "There was too much noise. I have

blocked everything. Until I learn to control this, let's do it old school and talk."

"Do you need to rest?" Dr. O'Neil asked. "This might be a crazy question, but are you hungry?"

"No thanks, and I'm not hungry. But I want to get out of this suit you have me in. Do we have anything else I can wear?"

"UT, can you find a jumpsuit for Alec?" The Supervisor asked.

UT nodded and walked out of the conference room.

"We'll give you some privacy, Alec. Then we can get together in about 15 minutes, okay?"

"Ms. Supervisor, I'd like to offer a recommendation."

"Go ahead, Dr. O'Neil."

"I believe, with all the noise that Alec is hearing and the difficulty sorting out who is who, etc., you and Alec should converse alone. It will make the conversation more focused."

The Supervisor looked at Alec, and he nodded in agreement. "It would make things easier for now."

"I'll let UT know before he gets back." Dr. O'Neil stood up, as did the Supervisor, and both walked to the door.

"Okay then. 15 minutes Alec. See you then." He was alone.

Alec stood up and stretched his arms above his head. Everything felt fine. As far as his body knew, he was never in a small container, living off a liquid diet in a completely different and artificially created world. This reality appeared natural and continuous. Only his memories provided information to indicate there was a second reality. Without these minds' images, he would deny he was ever in another artificial world and, in doing so, knew the life he chose to leave was not real. Adelle, Addie – so much to disregard. His life in the SOUP was nothing more than an outcome of probabilities created by a virtual reality system that responded to his desires and dreams. Alec felt remorse that his family would not be with him in this world as they were in the SOUP. His sadness was genuine.

The philosophers were right. The mind is the creator of your reality, and unfortunately for Alec, his virtual world provided more meaning to him than this one. The here and now is the only thing that is real, and this reality was void of his greatest happiness, stripped away quickly without any opportunity to resolve or understand. Plato was on to something. He needed to change his mental perception to comply with his new present. He disputed the past, created by combined memories of this world and his virtual one. They were one large group of experiences intertwined without reason. His past memories needed to resolve themselves with introspection and time. He was confused as he struggled to identify what was real, who he really was, and the strong emotions associated with both worlds.

UT walked into the conference room and placed the jumpsuit on the table. "Here you go. Welcome back, Alec. I guess I'll have to wait to talk with you. Here, let me get that back clip on the suit. It would be difficult doing it by yourself."

UT reached over and released a small clip above the small of Alec's back on the suit.

"Thanks for understanding about not being included in the questioning."

"No problem. It's great to have you back." UT embraced Alec in a deep bear hug, turned, and exited the conference room.

Alec undressed, put on the new jumpsuit, and placed his other garment on the floor in the corner of the room.

Alec remained standing, taking in the details of his surroundings. In what life did he sit in this conference room? Did he talk to the Supervisor about this incredible asset the Nation was about to inherit? Was the discussion part of his virtual life? An honest answer to crime. And now, through some act of fate, Alec had experienced that solution firsthand, leaving him with questions of his own.

"*Adelle!*" She and Grant were also in the SOUP with him. "*What is going on?*"

Alec felt overwhelmed. A big piece of his life was missing, but they were only images and memories. *"Was any part real?"*

Alec knew the answer but knowing an answer is nothing without resolution. Alec tapped into his previous philosophy books. Descartes, Locke, Berkeley. Reality was your mind's experiences, fed by the senses. He agreed with this. It was the truth that always tripped him up. Alec realized the cause of his initial confusion. Truth and reality were not always the same. His truth was in the daily reports that monitored his vital signs, his body's health, and his brain wave patterns. These reports verified his body was lying in a refurbished casket even though his mind was elsewhere. Where? A place where he created reality from his desires and the information accessible to him. He had seen all this data on the other inmates during his visit, their minds creating experiences built by a relationship between a complex machine and the human mind.

"Plato," Alec said aloud.

"Excuse me?" the Supervisor said, walking back into the conference room.

Alec looked at her and replied, "Plato's cave. It was a story in the book Plato's Republic."

"I'm sorry," the Supervisor smiled. I must have missed ancient philosophy in school."

"That's a shame. Philosophy has real relevance for you, given your profession now."

The Supervisor looked at Alec. She knew his life story before the SOUP and was impressed with the Pulitzer Prize-winning author and his bravery in Afghanistan.

"Go on, then. How about the short version."

Alec smiled. He liked this Supervisor. "A group of men were prisoners in a cave since childhood. Plato states these restrained men were forced to look only forward. The prisoners couldn't even see each other. Behind them was a fire casting shadows of activity of the real world, shown on a wall in front of them. Each of the shadows cast by the fire looks the same. They could hear the voices of people and, over time, thought the voices came from the shadows. Their reality was only a limited view of the truth."

The Supervisor thought a moment and connected the cave and the SOUP. "Very true, Alec. The SOUP, and even this world, work the same way. We only see a portion of the big picture, the portion our senses allow us to experience." Sensing more to the story, the Supervisor said, "Please go on."

"Here's where the story gets interesting. One day, one of the men is taken out of the cave and into the sunlight. The sun hurts his eyes, and he is temporarily blinded from living in the dark for so long. After a while, he adjusts to the light and see's the world in all its wonder. He sees colors, people, and landscapes, and each is different. Because of his new vision, his reality changes. For a time, he chooses to live in a world of light. One day, the man returns to the cave to share his findings with his fellow prisoners. Because he is unaccustomed to the dark, he can't see. He tells his fellow cave dwellers about the reality he's witnessed and encourages them to experience the real world. Instead of wanting to escape, they assume that leaving creates pain, blindness, and insanity, for how, could a place as he described exist? Plato concludes that if these men were not restrained, they would kill the man if he tried to take them into a world where they would suffer the pain, insanity, and blindness of their fellow prisoner when leaving their reality."

"Is that how you feel now, Alec? I know this must be difficult for you to reconcile your memories that cross between the SOUP and this world."

Alec acknowledged her statement with a nod. "I'm not sure. But to be honest, I would say I'm having second thoughts about leaving the SOUP. This feeling is something, Ms. Supervisor, I will have to resolve on my own. Anyway, on to matters at hand. I have many questions and would like to propose something different."

"I'm listening."

"I would like you to think about everything that has happened. It will be…"

"Much faster and as much of the situation as I remember it." the Supervisor finished. "I agree to this, Alec."

Both sat down at the conference table. Alec made himself comfortable in his chair and visualized his volume control. He turned it up and tuned the frequency to hear only the supervisor and her thoughts.

"*How are we going to do this*?" he heard.

He said, "Why don't you start chronologically and think about everything from when I entered the SOUP at BWI Airport? I know your mind will follow tangents and stray thoughts. I will be able to handle them."

The Supervisor smiled, aware that Alec was already receiving her thoughts and an audible conversation would be unnecessary. Both closed their eyes and relaxed.

Alec focused on the Supervisor's mental narrative as she worked through his entry into the SOUP. The chronology unfolded of how the Supervisor used him to validate the Cause-and-Effect Scenario technology and Matthew Boyd's SOUP Entry with the first use of Last Memory Reset. Alec absorbed the details of the development of the Elder Care industry by tailoring the SOUP's technology and was impressed with the idea. The Supervisor's thoughts shifted to the inmate Exit in Los Angeles and their gifts, the current crisis caused by the Vice President, and the purpose of Alec's Exit. There were so many entangled bits of information, a barrage of descriptive details weaving around a central theme, creating the DNA of the Supervisor's experienced helix. Each of these bits contained some relevant context and a connection to the next, manifesting the thoughts and visual images placed on an arrow of time, providing the context for her reality. Alec was surprised as he felt each event as she had and realized the Supervisor's history connected with her emotions, the coupling of emotion with experience completing each memory. As it swirled within his mind, all this information was effortlessly processed and cataloged by Alec's brain.

Alec sensed the end of the Supervisor's thoughts and opened his eyes.

"You've been busy since I've been gone," he said. Alec returned his 'telepathy knob' to close out all the thoughts around him but his own.

The Supervisor replied, sounding tired after having relived the emotional roller coaster of her experiences. "You don't know the half of it. Wait, I guess you do."

Alec smiled. "Yes, you were very thorough."

"Alec," the Supervisor began. "I have only one question for you. Do you have other gifts?"

Alec studied the Supervisor closely. Deep inside, Alec felt he could do more than interpret the thoughts of others. His feeling was real, primordial, and tied to a decision to use the power instead of using it by instinct. Alec felt control over his power but had yet to understand the source of that control.

"Let me try something," he said. Alec stood up from the table and brought both hands to his front, slightly above his belt line. He began to concentrate on bringing forth from him the sheer energy associated with his emotion. As he did so, Alec could feel warmth envelop his forearms and move down to his hands. Separating his hands slowly, a blue sphere of moving particles began to form, each particle rotating around an invisible center in a circular orbit. As he moved his hands closer, the outer portion of the sphere decreased in size, and the particles inside blazed with a new intensity.

Alec observed the Supervisor stand up, and as she did, each of the chairs in the room began to rise silently. The Supervisor stood back from the table as all the unattached objects in the room, elevated and without a sound, rose to the center of the ceiling creating one extensive collection of intertwined chairs, the conference room table, and other office items. Alec closed his eyes and imagined each item moving to their exact location when grounded. The items responded to his thoughts and slowly lowered back to their original places as silently as they had risen. Alec opened his arms wide, and the blue sphere disappeared.

"Are you Okay, Alec?"

Alec nodded. "I'm fine. As a matter of fact, I feel rejuvenated!"

"What did you feel?"

"There was much more energy available. I called upon only a small amount. I don't know how, but I could sense there was so much more. It felt infinite."

"I knew you would be able to defend us, Alec. I was unsure until seeing what you just did. What's next, Alec?"

Alec knew time was short before taking action to defend the program against the three that would be moving against the SOUP and its facilities, but he also sensed this was not as great a threat as the Supervisor and her team perceived. He was more concerned about testing the control he had over his power. To move furniture in an office was a parlor trick. The use of his absolute power would enable destruction. He could feel it. He needed to know he could stop when needed.

There was a second feeling as well. Inside were personal demons to be addressed if Alec were to avoid insanity, despite the gifts he possessed.

"I need to leave for a while. There are memories and other things that I still need to reconcile. Unlike the three that Exited in Los Angeles, my memories created in the SOUP conflict with my real life. I can't fix those memories here. I have them under control, but I need to reconcile them before using what I just showed you."

The Supervisor looked at the table. Alec could see the conflict in her expressions, fighting between his and the program's rising threats. "I understand. How long do you believe you will be gone?"

"Until things are sorted out. Sorry I can't be more specific."

"When will you leave?"

"Immediately."

The Supervisor nodded her head. She understood

"Do you know where you are going?"

Alec thought a moment. "Not yet. But I have a feeling I'm being directed somewhere. I plan to get into the car and follow my instincts."

"I would say, with your current gifts, your instincts will guide you to the right spot. Good luck, Alec."

The Supervisor had shared Adelle's and Grant's conditions as part of her disclosure to Alec. As much as Alec longed to see and be with Adelle again, he was unsure about their reunion or future.

"We can talk more about Adelle and Grant when I get back. Having them, Exit won't make sense if I can't sort myself out. You would bring more problems out of the SOUP instead of just me." Alec paused, feeling slightly embarrassed about his next request, then continued. "Can you provide me with a temporary wardrobe, credit card, and a car? You know, the basics." Alec smiled.

"I'll even throw in a cell phone. Head upstairs to the Funeral Director's office. The guard will meet you at the topside elevator. You know the drill. Stay in the office. Someone will come to get you when everything is ready."

Alec nodded his head and moved close to the Supervisor. "Thank you," he said, extending his hand. The Supervisor stepped forward and hugged him. It was the first human contact Alec had experienced in a long time. The Supervisor felt differently. Alec sensed her strong purpose to do what was right and her worry for the program's future. He looked into her eyes and saw her sincerity for his well-being. There was no doubt he would be back. Alec hoped when he returned, he could help.

"See you later, Ms. Supervisor."

The Supervisor smiled, and Alec exited the room.

The Supervisor picked up the conference room phone and pressed a single button. "We have a guest coming up.

Please escort him to the Director's office."

"Yes, ma'am."

The Supervisor hung up the phone and turned to see Dr. O'Neil and UT standing at the door.

"Did Alec just leave?" UT asked.

"Yes."

"Is that a wise choice Ms. Supervisor? We had him Exit so that he could help defend our facilities. Without further evaluation, we are not even sure he has the psychic gifts to do so or can control them."

"Trust me when I say UT, Alec possesses what we need. My assessment of his telekinesis and telepathic powers are both off the charts."

# CHAPTER 4

D r. Franklin Apoe hung up his phone, ended the conversation with Dr. Elizabeth Marks, and poured himself a bourbon. He was not sure he favored the CIA's efforts to build yet another cyber team to hack into networks worldwide and extract information used to "leverage" other countries into agreements with the United States. He was all in favor of taking nuclear facilities and centrifuges offline in terrorist countries. But spying on the country's closest allies left a bad taste in his mouth. While he disagreed with Dr. Marks, he had other problems to solve.

Six weeks ago, two men, Lincoln Harris and Frank Livingston, arrived at his facility. While national security needs prevented him from being briefed on all the details, he received most of the information about the men, or so he thought. Apoe was told both were convicts "released" from the nation's most secure prison system. The Secure Operational Unfenced Prison or SOUP was supposed to be more secure than Alcatraz in its day, but that changed with these two. These men found a way out. Actually, there were three that escaped. The actions of the third Apoe believed provided the reason for bringing these men to his facility. Both demanded to see the Director of the CIA so that they could make a deal in exchange for their freedom for future participation in the Agency's Remote Viewing program. While Apoe understood what they wanted and probably what others promised, their experiences in Los Angeles and Las Vegas produced body counts that made them too high a risk for bringing in as assets until studied further. He was told by no one less than the Secretary of Defense "Hook Nose" Wellsley himself, "Figure out how they do it." The decision sucked, but Apoe knew this was how things played out in these circumstances.

Apoe read the reports on their apprehension. It spelled

out with great detail that both men possessed telepathic gifts and capabilities that allowed them to move objects and, unfortunately, kill with lethality. The three had proven this in Los Angeles. The third, Julian Hoffman, Apoe read, was the most lethal of the three but had broken off from the other two after escaping their CIA escort in Los Angeles. Apoe had his doubts about Hoffman being the worst after reviewing the video of the capture outside Las Vegas. The Secretary of Defense's order delayed the transfer of the men to the CIA, which was to happen after their initial meeting. Instead, it directed them to be moved from Maryland to his facility. It seemed there was some real bad blood developing between the CIA and DoD, but his role did not allow him the luxury of being involved in emerging politics between the two organizations. Apoe was on the hook to find something. For now, he would have them sedated. Keeping them sedated would provide the time needed to think of how to approach this unique problem.

Apoe met with both men shortly after arrival and confirmed their abilities. During the meeting, he successfully tested the DoD's ability to block their telepathic gifts with specially modified equipment called 'blockers.' He understood that he was in the dark about how telepathy occurred between individuals. Fortunately, the agency and DoD had used equipment to jam frequencies on the battlefield. Apoe's team modified the equipment to block the psychic communication between the two men. However, telepathy was not Apoe's biggest worry. Both men possessed telekinetic abilities that posed the most significant risk to the facility's security.

For this reason, his hair was turning prematurely gray even though his colleagues felt the men would not use their gifts while interred. Regardless, he ordered the men sedated to impair their cognitive functions and isolate them from most of the 400 other inhabitants occupying his underground city until talking with the inmates several days later. Each of his team carried the blockers, which hid their intention to sedate the inmates. His team reported they did not have to use the equipment and that both men agreed to the sedation without incident. Livingston, it was reported, stated frankly, "I'm all in."

Apoe found their story fantastic. Neither man understood their Exit from the SOUP, only that the facility staff had somehow 'buried' memories of their past and replaced those with different ones. They emerged from the SOUP unaware of their real past until assisting the CIA with a 'special project,' inexplicably putting them into a deep sleep. When they awoke, they regained their original identities and understood they lived once in a Virtual World. As a medical doctor, he was impressed with their ability to separate the two realities of their existence and not go insane.

Apoe's understanding of his situation changed a week ago when Frank Livingston began talking in his sedated condition. The monitors notified his team, and Apoe immediately headed for Livingston's room. Apoe was unsure if Livingston could answer questions, but Apoe pressed forward, and Livingston responded to each. Livingston stated that Hoffman had initiated the escape from the CIA Van and slumped to his knees afterward. Harris had found him first. When Livingston arrived, Hoffman looked like he'd aged 50 years or more. Harris and Livingston had carried him to a Cigar shop close to the escape location, and it was here that Hoffman was "taken" from them. His experience in Afghanistan almost 15 years ago with the Mullah matched Livingston's description precisely. A steady breeze, the lifting body, figure eight lights, as though the body converted to light and floated away. "What will you do with the rest of your life?" Livingston had quietly said. "What will you do with the rest of your life?" Livingston repeated, and though sedated, Apoe felt that Livingston was looking into his soul, challenging him to find his own answer. Not knowing why and prompted by his own experience in Afghanistan, Apoe lifted the jumpsuit sleeve on Livingston's right arm and saw a symbol of an Ankh slightly below his skin. Apoe asked one last question before leaving Livingston that night, "Will you destroy this facility?" to which Livingston responded, "It is not my intent to take life. To do so would violate the law."

Could he believe him? Could he trust him? Is that why the Mullah was taken because the holy man attacked the infantry platoon and used his gifts to brutally murder 22 American soldiers? Was Apoe being set up now by these inmates? If he discontinued the sedation, what would happen? What were the risks? And then the question that had haunted him since that day in the desert again. "What will you do with the rest of your life?" That day had transformed his career!

He had reported his experience, and the chain of command thought he needed a psych evaluation. He was isolated and pulled off duty, detained on post in Kabul, awaiting a formal investigation. Then the Agency showed up, and he was pulled out of Kabul and flown stateside, assigned to a "special" classified paranormal investigative unit in the Pentagon, and never saw the inside of a hospital again. That was over 14 years ago, and his new mission was to make connections and find others like the Mullah in the world. He was successful one other time. Like Afghanistan, eyewitnesses reported seeing bodies fly through the air and all bones broken in a fit of rage. Witnesses confirmed the rapid aging and seeing a body disappear into the light. Apoe was the expert on this phenomenon through luck and not intent.

And now, just two weeks ago, the young woman that hacked the footage for the Whitehouse of the inmate's escape and Las Vegas destruction was grabbed and brought here. Apoe knew enough from the written reports and video that these men were powerful, and Sarah Anderson had stepped over the line in D.C. by finding the files. And now, Dr. Marks concluded her evaluation and wants Anderson on her team.

Apoe's thoughts returned to the question continuing to haunt him, "How will you live the rest of your life?" What had he done since that day in Afghanistan? Had he done what was right? Right for who? Right for the government?

Yes, he had served faithfully and with integrity. He had done as ordered; unfortunately, other people's lives were impacted or lost; but the government remained and showed its power. Did he do what was right for the country? What he did to support his government, he did for his country. He knew he was a patriot and a good citizen but could not reconcile the times when loyalty to his government did not directly serve the country's needs. He was smart enough to identify that many of his orders were about personal power and failed to see how the result strengthened the nation's fabric. He justified them as the same, so the country grew stronger through the power of its leaders. He could not accept his career as right for the people. He chose medicine for that very reason. As a medical doctor, he established a direct connection between his actions and what he could do to help people. Yet now, the exact meaning of his life shifted from helping those in need to sustaining a government that needed to project power to remain relevant. Something happened inside him, convincing him that each person's life mattered more than countries and government.

The secrecy, the parochialism, the self-serving need for power; these motivations have existed since the beginning of man. But in his own life's evaluation, he accepted these things as part of life. Apoe realized he had become part of what he despised. How had he strayed so far from the noble ambitions of his early years? While many men and women in his facility were honorable and exceptional, they lacked the experience of watching a man following his beliefs commit savage murder and disappear into light. And the question haunting him, from where? Up to this point, Apoe remained true to his life as a scientist, exploring the event, trying to find other data points, and searching for its meaning.

Now he decided these experiences were no longer something that had happened to him over the years and needed to be studied; each of the two events was something to teach him about his purpose. These new lessons were required

A TIME TO STAND

to be the focus of his life. He needed to begin to serve others again, and he could change his path immediately through the authority of his current position.

He thought about Dr. Marks. He was getting pressure from some in DC to make Anderson go away, but that was low-level background noise. Fortunately, Apoe still had discretion in his decision from the people that mattered but knew he would be accountable for the outcome if it backfired and something went wrong. Apoe thought, *"what if I begin with Anderson, not as an outcome of the situation but as the focus of his decision?"*

He knew the techniques used by Dr. Marks to convince Anderson to join her team. It was hard for him to believe that Anderson wanted to be in this facility and dedicate the remainder of her life to serving a government that she, too, saw focused on personal victories about power and not what was suitable for its people. What if his objective was to help her to exit the facility? It would piss some people off, but he would do what was right for her. Is this the point where he could answer the question posed so many years ago? Was this finally the moment to make his change? He played out the evening in front of him. Dr. Marks would arrive, make small talk and then push her agenda for Anderson forward. He would be pensive in his decision. She would make her move and lead him to the bedroom like always. Afterward, she would bring the subject up again, hoping sex would prompt him to offer his decision. Marks was good at her job. She was creating an emotional bond that trumped his analytical rationale. He knew he was being used for her objectives, not his. He decided to support Marks with her team and help Anderson more than Marks understood.

Apoe picked up his phone and dialed his deputy. "John, I want the sedation to stop for Livingston and Harris immediately. I am convinced that neither is a threat to the facility."

"I am glad to hear you say that, boss. You know that was

my assessment when we first met them."

"I know, and you were right. I want the two of them moved to the regular guest quarters of the facility tomorrow in section three and want to meet Livingston for lunch around noon. Have him escorted by one of the security team. I have a lot to talk with him about. I will start with him since he will be the hardest to communicate with."

"That's moving kind of quick. I'm not sure the effects of the sedation will be completely gone. You could be talking with someone still in a confused state."

"Without further injections, the effects of the drugs will dissipate in 12 hours. I'm not concerned about his comprehension. He's proven he can provide reliable information while sedated."

"That's true. But don't you want them at least still confined? Let me set up something private in your office."

"I feel like if we want to make these two assets for the country, we need to get their trust back. They need to hear that from me and be in normal surroundings. Nothing like a public place to ensure they feel like it's all in the open."

Silence. "Okay, but this part is a little high risk."

"John, just make it happen."

"Okay – it's just that I've never been worried about a lunch appointment before."

"Me neither, John. We must start building trust. We start tomorrow."

"You're the boss."

# CHAPTER 5

Sarah Anderson saw Dr. Marks stand by her chair and give a half-hearted wave as Sarah walked into the facility cafeteria. Sarah was intentionally ten minutes late, a clear signal to Dr. Marks that she would be in charge of the conversation. As she approached the table where Dr. Marks stood, she could see the tight smile and frustration on her host's face.

Sarah knew that Dr. Marks would make the sales pitch and that getting Sarah to join her team was very important to her. Sarah reasoned that if she seemed indifferent to the offer, Dr. Marks might reveal more information than she would typically disclose to get Sarah to say 'yes.' At this point, Sarah had weighed her options within her circumstances and knew her only alternative was to agree to the offer. There had to be another way out other than selling your soul, but Sarah acknowledged her position and knew Dr. Marks held the leverage. There was, however, that defiant streak within her that wanted Dr. Marks to have to work for it. Sarah reasoned that Dr. Marks may have the advantage now, but eventually, the leverage would return to her.

"Glad you could make it, Sarah." Her tight smile had disappeared, and her eyes twinkled with warmth like seeing an old friend. "Do you want to go through the line or talk first?"

In response, Sarah pulled out her chair and took a seat.

Sarah began, "So, are you expecting this to be a yes or no answer, or do we talk through the details first?"

"I'll answer any questions you have."

"Even the classified ones?" Sarah asked.

"Sure– up to a point, if that helps you with your decision."

The two women looked deep into each other's eyes, again looking for clues indicating weakness or that the other was lying. Sarah observed none and felt respect for the professional across the table. *"Let's get this started."*

"How many are on the team?"

"You would make 12, 13 if you include me," Dr. Marks answered.

"Who calls the shots on what we do?"

"Dr. Apoe runs this facility and provides the team funding, so he is my immediate boss."

Sarah looked at Dr. Marks. "That's not what I meant, Dr. Marks. Who controls the team?"

"Let's say those requirements come from higher up and are sent directly to me. I work the operational elements for missions and deployments."

"Why not let you control the funding too?"

Dr. Marks smiled briefly, then continued, "Some people believe that would give me too much leeway to do what I wanted with no accountability. Imagine that, right?" she laughed slightly.

*"Thank God for that,"* Sarah thought. Sarah knew her capabilities. She could only imagine what someone like Dr. Marks could do with a team of 11 like her if no one kept her checked.

Before Sarah could ask her next question, Dr. Mark's expression changed. She had turned her gaze away from Sarah and was looking at the entry door to the cafeteria. Sarah watched Dr. Marks regain her composure, and the tight smile reappear.

"Why there's Dr. Apoe now," Dr. Marks said. "Funny, he never comes to lunch here."

Sarah turned and saw the man Dr. Marks had identified as Dr. Apoe. Several others in the cafeteria were also staring at Dr. Apoe, who raised his hand and waived to the lunch crowd as if to acknowledge his rare appearance. Dr. Apoe had a man next to him who was part of the facility security team trying to act like any other scientist. And then Sarah saw him. She recognized him immediately. It was one of the men from the videos she had hacked for COL Baxter, and <u>that man</u> was with Dr. Apoe in this cafeteria located where? There could be no doubt about his identity. She'd watched each of the videos numerous times after downloading them, sickened by the scenes of carnage but unable to pull away from the strange events captured in the bits of data on her monitor.

*"What the hell is he doing here?"* she thought.

Dr. Apoe looked in her direction as if to answer her question. He instructed the guard to take the man through the line and started walking toward their table. As he approached, Dr. Marks stood up. Sarah did as well.

"Good afternoon, Dr. Marks," he said, stopping at the table. He turned and looked at Sarah, "Is this Ms. Anderson?"

"Why yes, it is Dr. Apoe," Sarah responded, not waiting for Dr. Marks to enter the conversation.

Apoe seemed to appreciate Sarah's assertiveness and extended his hand. "Very nice to meet one of Dr. Mark's best and brightest."

"Is that what I am?" Sarah replied, trying to sound like a young girl meeting a rock star for the first time. She started fanning her face with her hand to exaggerate her statement. "Dr. Marks, I'm flattered." Dr. Marks turned to look at Sarah as she feinted false gratitude.

Sarah extended her hand, and the two shook. She felt a small item transfer from his hand to hers, much like COL Baxter had exchanged thumb drives with her many times before. Despite the surprise exchange, Sarah maintained her false humility and said, "I wasn't aware that Dr. Marks owned me yet." She felt her heart skip a beat as she realized the impact of what had just transpired without knowing the contents in her hand.

"We're still discussing the job, Dr. Apoe," Dr. Marks quickly added, turning her attention to him. "I was hoping we were getting close to wrapping up just before you came over."

Sarah slowly slid the item she'd received into her

jumpsuit pants pocket.

Dr. Apoe noticed the move. He looked at Sarah.

"Well, Ms. Anderson? Will you be joining the team?"

Dr. Marks had turned her attention back to her potential new team member.

Sarah looked at Dr. Marks. Sarah sensed Dr. Marks seemed genuinely interested in Sarah's decision to join.

Sarah looked at both professionals and said, "Yes, Dr. Marks, I think we have an agreement. After all, what choice do I have?"

# CHAPTER 6

Lincoln Harris was sitting cross-legged on his bed, considering the recent changes in his life. The men were in a simple room consisting of two twin beds, a shared bathroom, a couple of dressers, and matching nightstands with lamps containing a lone digital clock. Nothing fancy but livable. It was a welcome change after being in a less austere cell, drugged to the point between reality and insanity.

Harris could not help but notice the change in their living conditions and the decision to stop the daily injections that solidified their minds into reality. Something was going on, and changes were coming. He concluded that the government must no longer view them as a threat. There could be no other reason to stop the daily injections. That was a wrong assumption for the staff of this facility. He and Livingston were both pretty pissed about the way things had transpired.

*"What was their next step?"*

After their surrender in Las Vegas, both men expected to be 'reintegrated into society' in exchange for using their gifts to serve as remote viewers for the CIA or Defense Department. He and Liv had let their guard down and trusted Dr. Apoe to help them. Instead of setting them up in their new lives, Apoe used a device to impede their telepathy, and without knowing the motives of those around them, he and Livingston were quickly administered the drugs that took them to Lala land. Their ability to use their other gifts to free themselves ended with those first, well-timed injections. Neither knew how long they had existed in the world between reality and illusion.

Harris knew that the facility was still using the device that prevented them from telepathically talking or listening to those around them, despite being free of the drug's hallucinatory effects.

*"Fool me once but not twice,"* Harris thought.

Harris opened his eyes from meditating as his cellmate Frank Livingston walked through the door with two security guards behind him.

Harris looked at Livingston. "So, how was lunch with the boss, dear?" Harris asked, sitting on his bed.

"Smart ass," was Livingston's curt reply as the guards left the room and secured the door behind them.

Harris asked again, this time seriously, "Well?"

"I don't know," Livingston said, sitting on his bed next to Harris'.

"What do you mean you don't know?"

"Apoe was different, alright? He seemed changed. He said some things that took me by surprise."

"Okay, Liv, I'm not following here. How about starting by telling me what he said to you."

Livingston put his head down, shook it slightly, then raised it slowly, finding Harris's eyes and locked on that place. "I'm not sure I can remember."

Harris stayed patient. "Give it a try, just the main things Apoe said."

"Okay, let me think." Livingston paused to sort his thoughts, then continued, "He said, be ready. You're both leaving tonight."

"That's great! If it's true," Harris said, rubbing his hands together. "Do you think we can trust him? I mean, did he sound like he was telling the truth?"

"I don't know, Harris. I'm not a fricking polygraph. With all they have done to us over who knows how long, how can we trust what the SOB says?"

"Okay, Liv. Don't get pissed with me, but I want to ask you some questions, and then we can talk this out, sound good?"

"Whatever, professor," Livingston responded.

"How did he start the conversation?" Harris began.

Harris could see that his friend was physically

uncomfortable. "Still feeling the drugs, Liv?"

"That's part of it. But there is something else. Somewhere in my mind," Livingston said, tapping his head, "I feel pain and suffering. I think there's more to this facility than just us having a sleepover. My head still feels cloudy."

Harris felt the same emotions about the facility but not with the same intensity that Livingston seemed to be experiencing.

"Parts of my life are starting to come back into focus," Livingston continued. "There are other parts that I know are real, like what happened before the SOUP, and I don't know how to deal with them. God Harris, I murdered a woman because I couldn't get laid in an alley." Livingston stopped and buried his head into his hands, leaning forward on the bed. "There is so much guilt, and I feel I need to act on these feelings, but I'm lost. I don't know what to do."

"Are you in pain?" Harris asked, thinking his friend may be experiencing some form of withdrawal after being abruptly pulled off his daily fix. Harris put a hand on his friend's shoulder.

Livingston pulled away from Harris' gesture of comfort and sat up straight. "No," his friend said, "but I have never felt this. I always kept it..."

"Tucked away," Harris finished.

"Yes, and now it is stuck right here," Livingston said, slapping his forehead with an open palm, "and I can't get it out. It was the first thing I thought about as the drugs started to wear off." Unexpectantly, Livingston started to cry. "How could I be so stupid?"

Harris had never seen tears from Livingston and realized his friend was experiencing a different return to reality than him. Something had focused Livingston on his past and attuned him to this facility. Harris was unsure how to help.

"Do you feel guilty about Las Vegas or when we escaped the van in LA?"

Livingston wiped his eyes with his jumpsuit sleeve. "No. Those guys deserved to die. What we did to them was our way of protecting ourselves. The guys in choppers near Vegas killed the girls, and they would kill us too if we did not defend ourselves!"

"Okay, let's focus on what's happened to us. One minute we're in the SOUP, next minute we are out and can do, frankly, some bizarre things, like read minds and focus energy on our thoughts to move and break," Harris stopped, the thought of his actions tied to breaking men like tree twigs entered his mind. He had to push through this. "*Strength*," he thought, and the images of carnage and his actions in creating death diminished, allowing him to continue.

He began his sentence slowly, "After working with the Supervisor at the facility on that 'special project,' we all remembered our real selves before the SOUP."

Harris stopped and looked at Livingston. "Look, Liv. We've all done something terrible, or else we wouldn't have been in the SOUP." Livingston looked up, locking eyes with Harris, and nodded his head. A slight sniffle signaled the end of the tears trailing down Livingston's cheeks. Harris had his attention again.

"Do you remember what happened when we escaped the CIA Van?" Harris asked.

"Hoffman in the cigar shop. Something took him because he murdered the driver of the van."

"Right, we saw it happen. Hoffman told us at the end that he'd broken some law – he said crazy things. But I am beginning to believe they were not so crazy."

"Then the light show," Livingston said. "And then the voice and the question, 'What will you do with the rest of your life?'"

Harris nodded in agreement and repeated, "What will you do with the rest of your life?"

"But what does it mean?" Livingston asked.

Harris thought for a moment, unsure how to answer a

question that also confused him. Harris decided to provide his answer, knowing it was as far off as any other solution.

"It means that despite the messed-up stuff we did before the SOUP, we get a do-over, a second chance to live differently. It's called redemption, and for some crazy reason, we have these gifts to help us do it." Harris said.

"That's what Apoe said to me! He was looking for redemption!" Livingston exclaimed.

Harris felt a rush of energy move through his mind, sharpening his thoughts and removing the haze left by the drugs.

Livingston continued. "Apoe said we are all given a second chance. He said that giving us ours was the way for Apoe to get his."

"Why would he say that?"

Even as Harris asked the question, he sensed Apoe was the answer. He remembered what his lawyer told him as the judge ordered him to Virtual Life for killing his parents, "Life knocks you down. It's not the fall that matters but how you get back up. Change your mind about how you want to live when you get back up, and life will follow that decision." Harris had no idea what being sentenced to Virtual Life meant but suspected that his lawyer might. Harris knew his past decisions had brought him to this exact point in his life, and he was not happy with those decisions. He also believed everything going forward from this moment was up to him. It was time to change. A different decision today would change his life's direction. Was that the meaning of the question he and Liv were asked when Hoffman disappeared? He could sense that it was and smiled. It's a shame he did not understand this years ago when he thought of himself as a victim of abusive parents and not empowered as an individual.

Livingston's excitement brought Harris back to the conversation. "Okay, my mind is starting to focus, Harris. Oh, this is good. He said that this place, this facility, had done some bad things to people, all in the name of science and National

Security. I think that's all this other shit I'm feeling and can't get out of my head." he said, "Harris, I want a second chance. It's time to change my life. I want to fix this facility. So much pain here."

Harris reached into his mind and sensed the pain of others in the building. There was something here, but Harris's mind was not sharply focused like Livingston's to make anything out of his feelings. Harris began to understand what was happening. Apoe had figured it out, too, and was taking action to fix his life for his reasons. He and Liv were part of helping Apoe with his change.

"Our conversation is starting to come back much clearer now." Livingston continued, "He said to be ready to move quickly tonight. Apoe said we are leaving, and he will make sure it happens for us."

"So, Dr. Apoe will help us get out of here?"

"That's what he said. He did not have much time to explain a lot."

Harris nodded. He got it. The explanation and reason were now clear.

"Did he say anything else, Liv? Was there anyone else with you when he told you this?"

"No, he asked my escort to get him another drink or something. He only had like a minute to tell me stuff." The information was pouring from Livingston, and Harris' mind quickly processed the remarks considering his current understanding.

"Oh, and he said someone was coming with us and to make sure we did not leave without her."

"Her? Who is her?"

Livingston shrugged his shoulders. "Beats the hell outta me. He said to stay in the room until she showed up."

"Did he say how we were going to get out?"

"Nothing."

Harris thought for a moment and felt his mind was much more precise than an hour ago. Harris looked at the lamp on his night table stand.

*"Move!"* he commanded with his mind. The lamp flew across the room and smashed into the wall opposite the nightstand. As the light flew, the cord pulled from the wall plug sent sparks into the darkness created by the absent light. Harris and Livingston looked at the lamp's broken stem and the small pieces of glass from the exploded lightbulb.

Livingston looked at Harris with a grin, "Well, I'm not cleaning that up."

Harris' face reflected the satisfaction of using his gift successfully, despite the lamp's current condition. The sarcasm of Livingston's comment felt normal and stirred the feelings shared between two competing brothers. Harris turned to his friend and said, "Welcome back, Liv."

Dr. Apoe watched the conversation between Livingston and Harris. Only Apoe had access to the data from the miniature bug hidden in the room's overhead light. He had placed the bug there while the rest of his team was bringing Harris and Livingston from the holding facility to their new temporary quarters. By placing the device himself, he kept the bug off the facility network, where his security team was free to roam in and out of accounts owned by each lab employee. The bug's extremely low energy signature would mean it would be at least two hours before the facility scanners detected its presence, and by then, he would be long gone.

He sat in his office, transfixed on the conversation, when it abruptly stopped. Without warning, a lamp flew across the room and shattered on the wall. Apoe smiled and said, *"They're ready."*

# CHAPTER 7

Sarah Anderson sat in her room and stared at the two pieces of paper Dr. Apoe gave her. She had to admit that she loved figuring out encrypted ciphers. At least, she suspected that's what this message was. Sarah reflected on the remainder of the lunch with Dr. Marks and was not sure she heard a single word Marks said after her introduction to Dr. Apoe.

Now, it was 7:50 p.m., and she was finally free from the orientation tour of her training facility and rolling assignments that Marks added on after lunch. She was pleased with herself. Sarah was able to remember the fire escape route out of the facility. The whole situation was unexpected, and she realized there was more to Dr. Apoe than she thought. *"Was he trying to warn her about the job with Marks and her team, or would the message just be another test of her skills,"* she wondered.

The first piece of paper contained two expressions that read:

"How far do you travel until you arrive where you started?" The second was an equation. She'd seen it before but was not able to recall it immediately.

Solve for D the paper said:  D = R*T

The second paper contained a string of figures:

C L D S H G S D L I T I X C D
I T R P A E G J T C X C

*"Very smart,"* she murmured, *"to keep the key separate from the actual message."*

"So, let's see what you are trying to tell me?" Sarah said aloud. She had pulled out the courtesy paper pad in the top desk drawer and a government-issued pen. She leaned back in the chair to think.

"How far do you travel," she read and drew a line after the word travel separating the first portion of the sentence from the second.

"Until you arrive where you started," Sarah recited aloud, hoping that hearing the words in her ears would give her a clue.

She circled the word 'travel,' underlined 'arrive,' and drew a box around 'started,' an old trick she learned about isolating the action words. "Okay," she said, "arrive and started. If I were to reflect this message in a mirror, would it show me something?" Sarah started to feel the giddiness that came with the challenge of hacking into a network.

"No, it would just turn the characters around. That won't work. Let me focus on the equation."

Sarah's mind searched the organized boxes of memories she maintained in her brain. She learned at an early age to categorize information into discrete chunks and then use a memory trick to remember to find the information again, much like saying the name of the person she had just met numerous times when talking with them. She would use the name throughout her conversation to remember the person the next time she met them and then develop a mental association to help her remember. Sarah tried using her techniques but could not remember the equation. Then it hit her. "Travel!" she exclaimed.

"How far do you travel? This equation is about travel! Distance is equal to Rate multiplied by Time." Memories of traveling with her parents opened her memory box. The equation answered an age-old question when she traveled with her parents, "Are we there yet, and how much longer?" She immediately recalled how her father had shown her the algebra to move the variables to different sides of the equal sign to solve depending upon the information she had during the trip. If traveling at 60 miles per hour for one hour, what was the distance, and if they covered 70 miles in 80 minutes, what was their rate? She recalled loving to figure out the answer. As she grew into a teenager, she suspected her father would ask her to solve the equation on trips more to keep her engaged in the math and not ask questions while he was driving. She had not thought about her parents in years. Funny, she mused; they were the key to her current challenge.

Sarah looked at the second piece of paper. There were no numbers. *"How could she solve for distance if there were no numbers?"*

"Think, think," she encouraged herself. "Solve for D. Solve for D." She wrote the equation down on the pad and said to herself, "Distance is equal to rate multiplied by time."

Sarah stared at the equation. "Solve for D, solve for D." Then she saw it. "Wait a minute," she said aloud. "This is not about finding the distance but solving for the letter D. This equation has an asterisk between the R and T. Equations never use the asterisk and are written without the multiplication symbol. The asterisk is D! The letters are R and T. In the alphabet, it would flow R-S-T. D equals S! Could it be that simple? An alphabet cipher with S as the key."

Sarah ripped off the top sheet of paper with the equation and wrote down the side of the page the alphabet starting with the letter D. In a column next to the first, she wrote the letter S next to the letter D and completed the alphabet a second time, with E matched to T and so forth.

$$D = S$$
$$E = T$$
$$F = U$$
$$G = V$$

"Now for the words 'arrive and started.' Do I reverse the letters now or decipher and then reverse the letters?"

Sarah translated the letters as they were written on the second piece of paper and then reversed her result. It was gibberish.

"Nope, it's got to be the other way," she said, smiling

broadly. She wrote the letters in reverse, arriving at the characters:

C X C T J G E A P R T I D C X
I T I L D S G H S D L D

"Here goes, cross your fingers," she said to herself. She quickly deciphered the word 'nine.'

"I got you, Apoe!" Her hand moved quickly, translating the letters. She had her message and drew lines between the words. It read:

Nine UR place tonight. Two drs down.

"Nine, your place tonight. Two doors down," Sarah said triumphantly, tossing the pen on top of the pad resting on the desk. She leaned back in her chair again, satisfied with her efforts.

She looked at the clock on her nightstand. Sarah had no idea what it meant, but she knew something would happen in less than an hour.

# CHAPTER 8

Alec Richardson drove out of Washington, D.C., and headed west on Interstate 66. He was unsure of his destination but confident he was being led to it. When Alec reached the Gainesville exit, he turned south and ended up in Sperryville, one of many small and quaint Virginia towns tucked into the bosom of the Blue Ridge Mountains. He continued driving a short distance until reaching an entry point to Skyline Drive at Thornton Gap, at which point he joined a caravan of several cars heading south on the two-lane highway.

Shortly en route, he saw a mileage sign listing Big Meadows, among other places on the mountain road. He felt this was his destination. He was comfortable now, knowing that his journey contained an endpoint. Alec set aside the unknown of his future and focused on his present. As he drove along the scenic highway, he stopped at the overviews. He admired the physical structure of the Shenandoah Valley sprawled beneath him, its boundaries extending to the Ridge and Valley Appalachian Mountains on the opposite side.

Despite the beauty he witnessed, his thoughts focused on how the SOUP would portray something as majestic as this scenery. One day, he would need to bring Adelle here. She would appreciate the beauty and not be interested in how the system rendered the scene. Alec laughed at the thought of Adelle, focusing him on the grandeur of natural creation and not the reason for the valley's existence. He had not taken a drive such as this in that reality, as best as he could remember. Dr. O'Neil mentioned to him when she appeared as a Quantum Persona that everything that made up the background in his world was an elaborate façade, a 'Hollywood set,' she had said. Storefronts with nothing inside. Her actions to change the reality he observed convinced him he was not in the real world. Real-world, he pondered. Was this reality the same as the SOUP? Alec published an article several years ago on the existence of political issues and how they took on a life of their own. In doing the research, he stumbled on several essays by prominent scientists that made a case for this reality being a simulation. He had shrugged it off as mere nonsense, but his frame of reference had changed, his experience in the SOUP casting doubt on everything he saw.

*"Don't go down that rabbit hole Alec. You'll never climb out."*

True enough, he concluded. Up ahead, he saw his turn-off for the lodge. Alec pulled into the Big Meadows parking lot and turned off the car. He sat for a moment, feeling overwhelmed by what lay before him. Why was he at such an obscure place, and more importantly, who wanted him here? Alec looked up at the lodge. Its stone and wood construction perfectly complemented the woods around him.

"You won't find out sitting here," Alec said aloud and exited his vehicle. As he walked through the front door, he overheard the conversations in the lobby, reminding him to turn down his mental volume control. He did so, blocking all the forms of electromagnetic small talk exchanged by the lodge's guests.

He was the only person in line at the reception desk and was joined soon after by a young man behind the counter. "Hello, may I help you?"

Alec explained that he was unsure, but the young man stopped him.

"Last name please," was all he said.

"Richardson," Alec replied without thinking.

The young man looked at his desk computer, moving magic fingers across the keyboard. Up arrow, left arrow, up again, and then three Enter key presses. "Aw, here you are. Would you like one key or two?"

"One is fine." *"How the hell does he have a reservation for me?"*

"Good." The clerk provided Alec with his key and pulled a Big Meadows map with listed guest services from under the counter. The young man laid the sheet flat on the desktop. "You are here," he started, drawing a circle around the lodge location, and here is your room." He scrawled another ring on the map.

"Anything else I can answer for you?"

"Noooo," Alec said slowly. "It appears everything is taken care of."

"Excellent, Mr. Richardson. Enjoy your stay."

"Thanks." Alec turned and walked out. A sizeable line of people stretched outside and formed in the short time he talked during check-in.

"Where did they come from so quickly? That's very odd," he said aloud. Alec walked to his car and sat down inside.

"I feel like Scrooge on Christmas Eve."

# CHAPTER 9

Sarah Anderson sat on her bed and watched the digital display show 8:59 for what felt like an eternity. As the clock display changed to 9:00, she heard the door click and buzz. It was open!

*"Now what? Do Marines bust in and take me out of this place?"*

She stood up and walked to the door, opening it slowly while checking for anyone in the hallway that might detect her and sound an alarm. All clear.

*"Now what? I know cameras in the hall will pick me up when I walk out. What are you going to do here, Sarah? Make a decision."* She chose to trust Apoe. Taking a deep breath, she moved into the hallway and instantly saw the hallway cameras. *"Gotta move quick!"*

She focused her attention on the second door down and closed the distance. As she reached for the door handle, it pulled away from her and was replaced by two gentlemen, filling the doorway. She assessed them rapidly, one was cute, and the other looked grumpy. She recognized both from the videos and the grumpy one from the cafeteria with Apoe.

"Well," she said. "No time for formal introductions. I've seen you guys in the movies. I'll get autographs later. Now, we need to move with a purpose."

"Do you know where you are going?" the grumpy one asked.

"I know the way out if that's what you mean. Got the big tour today."

"Good enough for me," the cute one said. "Lead the way."

Sarah headed down the hall on her way to the cafeteria. The first confinement door barred their exit. She pushed, and it opened.

"Look, Harris," the grumpy one said. "Security cameras!"

"I know, Liv. We are heading into a big trap, or we trust Apoe. The doors are open. I think we can conclude that the cameras are not showing live feeds or not working."

"I'll take care of that anyway," Livingston said and focused on fusing the components of the facility cameras. The cameras glowed red momentarily, signaling that the devices in the group's immediate surroundings no longer functioned.

"A little less chatter, ladies, please. I gotta think," Sarah stated.

"What the hell?" Livingston said, looking at Harris and pointing his thumb at Sarah.

"She knows the way out. Let's go!" Harris whispered to Liv.

The three rounded a corner, and Livingston immediately recognized the cafeteria. Sarah stopped and motioned them to come close. "Okay, we're at the cafeteria. There's a good chance folks are inside getting coffee for their shifts etc. Let's pass the doors one at a time."

Both men nodded. "How far are we from the exit?" the cute one asked.

"Two doors and about 300 yards. There's a security checkpoint near the main door, and it opens into a bigger room at the exit. Most likely, two or three guards manning the point."

"Once we pass the exit door, what can we expect?" the grumpy one asked.

"I didn't get that far on my tour, and my crystal ball wouldn't show me," Sarah replied.

"So, then what do we do?" the grump persisted.

"Liv, take it easy. We'll figure it out. Let's get past these doors first," Harris said.

Livingston agreed but did not appear happy about taking orders from a curt woman. Harris smiled at the irony, having reached the same conclusion about Livingston leading them out in California. "Karma," Harris mumbled.

"I'll go first," Sarah stated. No one disagreed.

The three slowly worked their way up to the double

doors of the cafeteria. Sarah looked briefly inside. "Okay, it looks like twenty or so people, some in line and some eating. Someone is bound to see us, and these orange jumpsuits will give us away."

"I've got an idea," Harris said.

"Let's hear it but make it quick." Sarah prompted.

Harris stood and placed his back against the wall but closed his eyes rather than speak.

"What are you doing?" Sarah whispered.

"Okay, done," Harris said, opening his eyes.

"What's done?" Livingston asked.

"Check the cafeteria," Harris said.

Sarah was unsure what she would see after watching these two men and their performance in the videos. She turned her head around and looked through the double doors. She could no longer see inside! The glass panes were transformed from clear to translucent, as though someone had installed the doors to allow light to pass through while also providing privacy. Seeing the details of people on either side of the door would be impossible through the new glass.

"Smart!" Sarah whispered. "Let's go." Sarah moved across the opening first, followed by Harris.

Security Officer Jansen enjoyed his meatloaf inside the dining facility before starting his shift. Like most officers in law enforcement, he did not like sitting with his back to any door for fear of some bad guy getting the drop on him. As Jansen spooned up a healthy portion of mashed potatoes and brown gravy, the doors to the cafeteria appeared to change before his eyes from crystal-clear glass to a nice, tight diamond shape pattern that obscured his vision outside the door. Jansen dropped his spoon and moved toward the door to investigate. Reaching the door, he opened it to examine if the same effect on the glass prevented people from looking in from the outside. He opened the door at the exact moment that Livingston was crossing. The two men bumped into each other unceremoniously, and Jansen, recognizing Livingston's orange jumpsuit, immediately yelled, 'freeze!' while reaching for his sidearm.

Livingston 'pushed' the man inside with a reactive thought and sent him flying across the cafeteria, colliding with tables and chairs, which slid haphazardly into various positions with loud scraping noises. Jansen landed in a gray lump on the floor among the furniture, rose slowly to his feet in a daze, yelled, 'inmate, escape!' and collapsed to his knees.

Livingston had the presence of mind to close and lock the door by visualizing a weld of the locking mechanism, forgetting the cafeteria entry was made of glass. It would not hold long.

"Come on!" Sarah yelled just as the facility alarm sounded.

The three sprinted down the hall, reaching their next door. It was locked. "Shit!" Sarah exclaimed, "now what?"

Harris stared into her eyes. "I guess this is where Livingston and I contribute."

Sarah nodded. "Okay. Don't blow up or kill anything."

Harris placed his hand on the locked door. Sarah heard a loud buzz and watched Harris push it open. In front of them was another long hallway filled with facility staff offices, labs, two military police security guards, and numerous scientists, all coming from their respective offices to investigate the alarm in their secure area. Some were armed, and others, dressed in lab coats, scurried back into nearby offices when seeing the three.

Sarah watched Harris look down the hall. He closed his eyes, and each armed military police officer dropped to the floor.

"What did you do?" she asked, fearful she would be walking through a hallway of corpses. She recognized several of the staff from her orientation tour that were to be her new colleagues on the team. She liked them, and the thought of them dying because of her was unnerving.

Hearing her question's true meaning, Harris replied,

"they're sleeping, not dead."

Assured by his response, Sarah looked at the two men and said, "This way!"

"Liv, lock the door behind us!" Harris shouted.

Livingston could hear the crash of the cafeteria door glass. As the door closed behind him, he placed his hand over the locking mechanism and felt the heat from the seal he had just created. He pushed against the door to confirm his work.

"Done," Livingston yelled down the hall. "Nothing is getting through this way unless they blow the door."

"Which they might just do," Sarah yelled. "Let's keep moving!"

"How much further?" Harris asked.

"Through this door," she said, touching their newest barrier to freedom. "Then through a large area which is the security checkpoint. They bring all their cargo and supplies in through this point." Sarah chose not to ask how they would pass through the security barrier, knowing it was reinforced with more military police from the main facility.

"What lies beyond that?" Harris prodded.

Sarah looked at him, *"What kind of man is this? He knows we're outnumbered but not giving up."* she thought.

"Is that all there is to getting out of here?" Harris continued.

"No, we enter the main ring once we go through that checkpoint." Sensing the next question, she continued, "The main ring is like an underground highway that circles the whole complex. The ring has multiple access points to the outside world. The ring facilitates resupply, personnel changes, and the like, all outside the work areas. It's pretty smart if you think about it."

Sarah saw the look on Harris' face. His expression belonged to a man looking to escape the facility, not admire it. "Sorry, professional props to the builders, I guess." Sarah continued, "Anyway, once we cross the highway ring, just another security station on the other side, and then I'm not sure. I'm positive that we will be close to the outside."

Harris nodded. "Okay, one obstacle at a time."

Sarah looked into Harris' face, this time locking with his eyes. "No one gets killed," she said bluntly.

Livingston had caught up in the brief moments from locking the back door. "We might have to defend ourselves, Lady. No guarantees!"

"Liv, we can put them to sleep. No killing. We know how to defend ourselves. No more Las Vegas carnage. Agreed?"

"Harris," he started.

"Redemption Liv, remember?"

Livingston nodded his head. "Yes, you're right. It starts today."

"What starts today?" Sarah asked.

"A second chance," Harris said, looking at Livingston. "What's behind this door?"

"A workout room and more living quarters," Sarah stood back from the door. "Okay, boys. Do your magic. You have the lead now."

Harris touched the door, and it opened, surprising him since he expected the alarm to lock them all. "It's open! Let's go!"

The three moved into the space filled with the gym and living quarters. Only one staff member was in the workout room. Livingston looked in his direction, and the unfortunate man fell to the floor, releasing his grip on the pulldown bar used to work his lat muscles. The metal plates came crashing down, making a loud clattering sound on the weights below them, spinning the pulldown bar in the air without its user.

"Did you blow something up?" Sarah exclaimed, fearing the worst and looking at Livingston.

"No, lady. Will you just trust us?" Livingston yelled.

The rest of the area was clear. The last remaining door between the three and freedom loomed in front of them, and what would be a significant security force was anticipated on the other side.

"Liv," Harris said. "If this area is as large as Sarah believes, we won't be able to influence the security forces until we are closer." Livingston nodded in agreement.

"Okay, Sarah, you stay behind us," Harris directed, "we should be able to protect you when the shooting starts."

Remembering the video she saw of their fight and apprehension in Las Vegas, she had no doubts that these men had some rare, indescribable way that they would use to keep her safe.

"Okay," she replied.

"Ready, Liv," Harris said, his hand on the door.

"Let's do it!"

Harris thought quickly and melted the locking hasp in the door. He pushed it open and was immediately met by the command, 'Freeze!' and the sound of rounds moving into the chamber of numerous rifles.

Harris did a quick evaluation. About 30 men with small arms, each equipped with body armor and helmets. To his immediate front was the security checkpoint with scanners for pedestrians. About ten feet to its left was a large, closed cargo door that Harris felt would lead to the facility's traffic ring, as Sarah had explained. The security force looked to be protecting the pedestrian egress as the logical way out for the three.

Harris looked at Livingston, who said, "no one ever freezes."

Harris stepped out, followed by Livingston.

"Let's head for the cargo door. I don't think they expect us to do that." Harris announced. There were no objections.

Both men positioned themselves shoulder to shoulder with Sarah directly behind them. The three began walking towards the assembly of security forces, looking like a reversed Greek phalanx ready for combat. The command 'Freeze!' was yelled once more, but the three continued toward the cargo door and the way out. The forces were about 50 yards away. Harris tried to force them to sleep, but the troops remained unaffected.

"Last chance!" a man yelled.

The three continued walking. The man nodded to his forces, and the room erupted into an explosion of gunfire. Instantly, Harris and Livingston observed a blue light surround them.

"Harris, help!" Sarah yelled. "I'm not protected."

Harris turned and saw Sarah's face, a small trickle of blood running down her temple from an apparent ricochet.

"Get closer, Sarah," Harris directed.

She stepped forward, and the blue light covered her immediately with the extended protection of the two men. Inside the light, Harris observed that the bullets hit the outer boundary of the shield but never penetrated. It looked to him as though the rounds were 'disappearing' into the light.

The three continued through the chaos of bullets and ejected brass, cluttering the floor as shot after shot tried to penetrate their shield, and each rifle shot merged into one giant, loud, swirling noise.

They were getting closer to the cargo door, and the bullets stopped as quickly as the shooting began. Each soldier dropped, rifles clattering and bouncing off the concrete floor. It looked to Harris like some unseen hand unplugged a video game from a wall socket. The blue light surrounding them disappeared. Sarah dropped to her knees, aware of her miraculous survival. Harris saw her drop and moved close to her.

"Are you Okay, Sarah?"

"My God," Sarah whispered, barely able to talk.

"So, Liv and I believe it is," Harris responded.

"What?"

Avoiding her question, he knelt and looked into her eyes. "Here, let me look at the side of your face," he said, turning her head slightly with his hand. Harris surveyed the wound and saw a slight scrape at the top of her head and the telltale blood trail from the injury. There was no bullet entry.

"As expected, just a scratch that bled a lot. You'll be fine."

Sarah smiled, acknowledging his kindness. "Thank you."

Livingston disrupted their conversation standing near the cargo door, surveying its construction.

"Time's ticking away. We gotta keep moving."

A calm voice from the officer's communication device broke the stillness, "Team A leader. Are the suspects in custody or neutralized?"

Livingston walked about 20 feet to the radio, still in the hands of the sleeping officer. He picked it up and spoke into the device. "Neither."

"Who is this," the voice demanded.

"You'll know soon enough." Livingston dropped the device, which bounced off the floor and onto the sleeping officer's back. Livingston rejoined the two standing by the door.

"Okay, let's lift the door and get out of here. I think we're close."

"Harris, I need to talk with you a minute."

"Liv, we really don't have time."

"Sure, we do. What can they do to us?"

Harris realized his friend was right. There should be no urgency for either of them. At this point, there was little the facility staff could do to stop them.

Sarah was standing close. Livingston looked at her. "A moment with my friend, please."

"Don't you think we should be leaving?" she asked. Harris looked at her, and she realized what Harris had just concluded with Livingston. They were just going to walk out. She gave the two men their distance to talk.

"What now, Liv? What's so important that it can't wait?"

Livingston looked at Harris and said, "We've been through a lot since leaving LA. When I say a lot, I mean a lot that we can't even understand."

"I get that," Harris said, nodding in agreement.

"In the last twelve hours, since my mind cleared, I've had time to think about what I've made of my life. You know, 'what will I do with the rest of my life'? Even Apoe asked me that question."

Harris thought Livingston was beginning to experience a collision between his two realities. *"Damn, not now."* He saw his friend's face and instantly knew.

*"He's not leaving."*

Livingston read his thoughts. "Good, you can hear me again. You got it, Harris. This place, right now, is going to be my moment of redemption."

Harris opened his mind and connected it to Livingston's thoughts. He immediately understood what his friend wanted to do and, most importantly, why he wanted to do it. Harris experienced for himself the memories of the murder that night of Livingston's girl at the bar so long ago; each emotion and the guilt his friend felt and the feelings sickened him. Harris understood why Livingston wanted to free himself of these memories. His friend wanted to atone for his murder in his final moments, with the facility's destruction. The gifts would give him the necessary energy to accomplish the task.

"Liv, you can't do this!"

"I can, professor. This place is evil. I figure I'm pretty bad myself. It's a good trade-off to not live with what I've done."

"Liv, you're going to murder again! There are hundreds in the facility. How do you justify that?"

"I've talked with them, Harris."

"Who have you talked to?" Harris asked.

"THEM, Harris. The Shiny Ones, the same ones that talked with Hoffman. They told me this was what I should do. I agreed to do this. Trust me when I say I am the right person at the right place. I've felt, no experienced, through the dead and suffering, the darkness here. Even we were lab rats in someone's experiment. You haven't sensed this as I have! That means there is another path for you."

Harris felt his friend's strength begin to electrify the

space around them, charging the air with small pops of errant energy, rising to a level Harris had seldom recognized in his use of their skills. He knew Livingston would not deter from the path he was creating around him but had to try to convince him to leave.

"Liv, stop this. Let's go!"

"I was naïve to think we could work for the agency and they would give us our freedom. Apoe gave our freedom to us. You need to thank him for that if you ever see him again. He pulled us off the drugs so we could think and see our world clearly and bring us to this point. This is what I want to do for the rest of my life. Can you feel the energy that is swirling around us? Whatever my future will be, it starts here. Go find yours. The way out is clear. I have taken care of everything."

"You are going to die, or worse!"

"Death is just a doorway we all pass through to another place, professor. They told me that too."

"Jesus, Liv. Please reconsider!"

"Time to go, professor. Take good care of that shrew you are with. Even she has a great amount of light inside."

As Livingston spoke, the cargo door began to rise. Harris could see vehicles thrown around beyond the door, some burning. Security personnel were lying around them – Harris could see they were not sleeping. The air in the room began to swirl, reminiscent of the tobacco shop where Hoffman disappeared. A breeze started that would soon join with the swirl. In the center of the wind was Livingston, looking serene and at peace with his arms extended.

"Wait, THEY asked you to do this?" Harris yelled above the blowing wind. Livingston had blocked that part of his thinking. Harris could not read what was happening in his friend's mind. Livingston was becoming more powerful with each new moment, and the air was becoming charged with the electricity he was producing, increasing the swirl and the popping.

Sarah approached Harris, now frightened by the wind

and noise. "What are you two doing? This place is starting to make my skin crawl, literally. The air is electrified. Are we leaving?"

"You and I are, and please don't ask any more questions. We have got to get out of here."

"You have time, Harris," Livingston yelled. "It's a long way out. I'll wait until you are safe."

"How will you know."

"I just will. But you gotta get started."

Harris reached for Sarah's hand, and the two exited the cargo door. The wind inside did not leave the room with them. "Over there!" Sarah yelled, pointing at the exit sign across the ring road.

While Sarah was scanning up high for an exit indicator, Harris surveyed the scene directly in front of them.

"Don't look; close your eyes, hold my hand and let's go."

She stopped suddenly and pulled her hand away. "Bullshit!" she yelled, surveying the destruction and grossly shaped figures around her. "Liv killed them! He murdered every one of them! Were you part of this?"

"No! But if we don't get out of here, we're gonna join them. There is too much to explain now, so move it, damn it!"

Sarah was transfixed, and her feet would not move. Her face was a mixture of pure fear, anger, and disgust. Harris grabbed her hand again, and she did not recoil. The two moved quickly across the ring road to the opposite side near the exit marker. The road appeared as the way out for facility vehicles, and a passage door existed for pedestrians. Harris pushed open the pedestrian door and entered a long lighted concrete walkway that continued for some distance. The walkway lights seemed to rise and arch over its horizon and out of sight from Harris. "Let's go." Harris retook Sarah's hand and said, "this way."

The two walked for what seemed like hours without speaking. Signs appeared on the wall periodically indicating this was an emergency exit path in the event the vehicle tunnel access was unavailable.

Harris was reluctant to listen to Sarah's thoughts – believing that this would jeopardize his future with Sarah and in some strange way, with Livingston.

Harris began to sense a change in the walkway and felt they were no longer moving parallel to the tunnel access but were walking away from the vehicle tunnel and heading for another exit. They traveled about another mile before the tunnel came to a dead end with two elevator doors and a stairway that led upward. Sarah collapsed on the floor. Harris stepped over to the stairs and looked up, seeing a switchback about every 20 feet. The staircase's construction indicated to him this was a way out. It would be a hell of a climb if they needed to go this way, one he was not interested in making.

Harris walked over and pushed the up button. The elevator bell signaled the car was on their floor, and the doors opened, ready for the riders going to the surface. He lifted Sarah off the concrete floor and led her into the lift. He pressed the button that was marked 'exit.' The doors closed, and Harris sensed the familiar feeling in his stomach that the elevator was rising. He watched the display above the door show different levels, none of which made sense to him. After the fourth level, 'Exit' appeared. The doors opened into another entry control point operated by military police slumped over their duty positions, victims of Livingston's final gesture to clear the way for Harris.

Harris was moving out of the elevator, looking at what he hoped to be the final exit. He felt Sarah pull her hand out of his. "I can take it from here," she said, pushing by him. He could see her expression had transitioned from terror to rage. She moved by the police officers quickly and pushed open a metal door that stuck open. The room filled slowly with the emerging outside sunlight. It looked to Harris like it was just rising above the horizon. *"Had they been walking all night?"*

Harris moved quickly through the control point and out the door, where Sarah was on her knees, vomiting in the grass. He dropped to his knees next to her and pulled her hair back. She didn't shake away. Harris looked at his surroundings and noticed the outside entrance had the structure of a small wooden shed, much like where a gardener might keep their tools. Around them on three sides were short berms covered with grass and domestic plants hemmed in with a chicken wire fence attached to long split rails connected by intermittent posts. In the middle of the fenced area was a tilled area containing a garden. He only recognized the tomato plants with tiny buds among the variety of other vegetables that had not grown beyond their green stems. There was a small path made with gray flagstone from the small fence gate to the shed's entrance.

*"It must be late spring, he thought."* He breathed in the fresh air deeply, let it fill his lungs, and then let it out slowly. He retook a deep breath, smelling brackish water at low tide. He was somewhere near salt water and felt relieved that he was not in the middle of some remote desert. He turned his attention to Sarah. Her color was returning to her face. She wiped her mouth with her jumpsuit and said, standing up, "Any idea where we are?"

Harris stood as well. "No, but I think it's somewhere near the ocean or another saltwater body. West or East Coast, you have your pick."

"Glad it's not the desert. I hate the desert," Sarah remarked.

"I share your opinion about the desert." Harris looked around from his new vantage point. "We should be able to find a town nearby. We should also put some distance between this facility and us."

Harris looked at their orange jumpsuits. "We're going to generate a lot of questions and attention dressed like this. We got to get the uniforms from those military guys in there." He pointed back into the facility. "I'm not sure what's going to happen with Liv, but we have to move quickly."

Sarah nodded in agreement. "Okay."

The two headed back inside and approached the dead sentries. Both heads were hanging limply on their bodies. Harris observed their necks were snapped and was not surprised by his finding. As Sarah started to unbutton the outer blouse of the soldier closest in size to her, the body fell onto the floor.

"Shit!" she gasped. "These bodies are like putty."

"Don't think about it. Just grab the shirt and pants, and let's get out of here." Harris commented.

*"These people look like every other one that Liv and I killed in Vegas and Los Angeles; bodies snapped like twigs."* His fingers trembled as he undid the last shirt button and pulled it off his corpse, causing the body to slump off the chair, fall with a sliding noise, making a quiet thud when landing on the floor.

*"Livingston had cleared the way for them, but at what price? Did he have to kill them? So many living people until Liv just thought about their deaths. Thoughts caused by anger and fear. Was it self-defense? Was it justified as it had been with his parents after years of abuse?"* Lincoln remembered them all – at least the ones he watched personally die, their faces contorted into agony and disbelief as his special skills worked to snap each bone until their lives were extinguished.

*"How will I ever be whole? How can I ever live with what I've done?"*

"Harris, are you ready to go?" Sarah shouted.

Lincoln looked at his hands, surprisingly shaking, holding the soldier's uniform.

Harris looked at Sarah and allowed himself to hear what was in Sarah's mind. She had regained her cool-headed thinking, focusing now on what lay in front of them. *"Escape, run – to where?"*

Harris removed the pants from his policeman and said, "Done." There was no indication in his voice of his internal turmoil and doubts.

With one last pull of the pant legs, Sarah caused her police officer to stretch its arms over its head on the floor.

She turned her head, unwilling to see the gruesome sight any longer than necessary, and declared, "me too."

Outside, they inhaled the air again. Clean, salty, with no death. Harris pointed to the gate and motioned Sarah to exit.

Sarah reached the gate and lifted the latch. As the gate swung open, they stopped as a cold breeze struck them in the back with a slight shove. "Did you feel that?" Sarah asked.

"Sure did."

Both turned around to find the source of the quick temperature change.

"What the hell?" Harris uttered

Sarah gasped. "I don't understand."

The shed and garden were gone. Nothing was left to prove there was ever an entry point to the facility. Deep inside Harris' mind, he heard a familiar voice, *How will you live the rest of your life?*" and knew that Livingston was gone.

# CHAPTER 10

Vice President of the United States Trip Morrison took the secure cell phone from his aid. He was standing outside the closed door, waiting to enter the Oval Office for his 9:00 a.m. meeting with POTUS. The incoming call was from Mike Thompson, the CIA's Director.

"What's going on, Mike? Your timing is bad. I'm getting ready to go into the Oval."

"Sorry, Mr. Vice President, but this can't wait." Without pausing, he continued, "Site 35 is gone."

Morrison's hesitated a moment to let the short phrase register. While short, it was a straightforward statement that conveyed a crisis and loss of critical assets. Site 35 was the premier research and development facility for 'special projects' involving highly classified topics that even the President did not know existed. Generations of continuous effort and millions of dollars had produced experimental capabilities and irreplaceable infrastructure, not to mention the nearly 400 people that staffed its facility.

His response was emotionless. "How could that be?"

"Still sorting it out, sir."

"What the hell do you mean gone? Facilities just don't walk away or disappear." Morrison could hear his voice rise. He looked around, and his conversation attracted stares from the office staff, not for its content but for Morrison's volume. Realizing he was creating a distraction, the VP walked into the hallway away from the president's administrative staff.

"Okay, Mike, tell me, how do you know it's gone?"

"One of our teams showed up to deliver a couple of items and could not find the vehicular access tunnel. They said it was just," Thompson paused, "gone."

"How far away from the facility is the access tunnel?" Morrison asked.

"The entry point is about ten miles away, located at a construction equipment storage site we own. The tunnel access was in a large building we used to obscure vehicle access. When the driver entered the building, there was no elevator or other way to drop the vehicle down to the tunnel. It's like we never built it."

Morrison let that statement rattle around, knowing what Thompson was saying could not be the actual situation. Morrison moved on to more practical, verifiable subjects.

"Did we lose any of the data?"

Thompson understood precisely what the VP was asking. The facility utilized very secure fiber optic connections that connected the facilities' computers with several backup sites, all equally secure. These computers captured the scientific results from the experiments as well as the operations of the facility. As part of the site's contingency plans – all data would be sent continuously to these ultra-secure backup locations.

"Sir, all data transmission from the facility ended at roughly zero six-thirty this morning. There's been nothing since."

"Does Hook at DoD know?"

"The Secretary was the one who reported the information to me. He told me the facility is just…gone."

"Why the hell didn't he call me? Never mind." Morrison knew the personality of the Secretary of Defense and that he would rely on Thompson to deliver the bad news.

"Do we need a cover story?"

"Not at this time, Sir."

"Have you heard from anyone stationed at the facility?"

"No, sir." Thompson paused. "Mr. Vice President, you need to know that the two men we are interested in, responsible for LA and Las Vegas, were there, Livingston and Harris. We had them there for surveillance and isolation."

"Shit!" Morrison exclaimed, tempted to throw the phone to the floor.

Morrison saw his aide approaching from the direction of the Oval Office.

"Mr. Vice President, the President is ready for your meeting now," Morrison's aide said through the arch to the hallway.

Morrison acknowledged the message with a quick nod, pissed at the interruption to his conversation with the CIA Director.

"Mike, this is too much of a coincidence with those inmates on the loose. Get me the Supervisor."

Morrison thought a moment, "Screw that. She's been jerking us around getting the information we wanted, and now Site 35. The Supervisor must be responsible for this. For God's sake, these were her inmates! She must know something about this. Get me someone on her team. We need to have a conversation with them."

Thompson was perfectly clear the VP's instructions were to grab one of the Supervisor's team. He had reservations. "Do you think…"

Morrison was out of patience. He spoke quietly and succinctly, annunciating each word. "Thompson, do your job. Identify someone on her team that would have the info on Site 35 and the Exit Protocols we want. Have them available in the next 48 hours. I have some questions. Call me with the location." Click.

It was Thompson's turn to express his feelings, "Shit." That about said it all. Grabbing someone from the Supervisor's staff was not a good move. Yes, these were her inmates, but this went over the line of decorum in Washington. A request for inquiry between executives of agencies was standard procedure to prevent it from turning into something more ugly. If they grabbed someone, then his explicative would describe the mess he would need to clean up. This situation was not good, but he could always say it was the VP's call.

# CHAPTER 11

Lincoln Harris and Sarah Anderson walked through a pine and scrub oak forest, looking for a concealed place to change. Harris had surveilled his surroundings and determined the woods were not isolated from civilization. There were numerous indicators of hikers and hunters using the area. The path they were walking on was worn down by more than deer, probably by weekend dirt bikers. He and Sarah were still walking in their jumpsuits. He suspected it was close or slightly past 7:00 a.m., the early hour perhaps the reason for not seeing anyone yet. Harris knew it would not be long before bumping into another person, and while the military uniforms might be hard to explain, the orange jumpsuits yelled prison break.

The two had walked nearly a mile and not spoken a word. Harris had avoided eavesdropping on Sarah's thoughts. With all that they'd just experienced, he believed total silence would be their best therapy in the short term. Harris felt his questions inside him, crying out for forthcoming answers. Harris knew that, eventually, he would need to seek comfort in the wisdom of others, most likely professionals. He needed to try to focus on getting them back to civilization. Back to where? With no money or identification, that would be hard to do, even if he could use his gifts to hotwire a car or have the locks open the door for him.

He broke the silence. "We need to get out of these jumpsuits."

"I was thinking the same thing, or did you already know that?"

"I've not pried where I'm not welcome."

"Smart move Harris. You would not have liked what you were hearing."

"Look," he said, pointing to a tall undergrowth of spindly

vines, undergrowth, and aspiring trees, "how bout you change there? It will give you some privacy."

"Thanks, Harris. I didn't know you had a soft side." Sarah walked in the direction of the undergrowth.

"What the hell did I do to piss her off?" he mumbled.

He unzipped his jumpsuit, pulled it halfway down, and heard his stomach grumble. They were going to need to find water and a snack machine soon. He pulled the suit down his legs, kicked it off, and began to put on the soldier's trousers. As he pulled them up, he realized his waist was much smaller than the last occupant's. He cinched the belt tightly to keep them on and rolled the bottom of the legs into cuffs to sit on top of his tennis shoes. The outer blouse had a rank insignia, sleeve patches, and a name tag attached with Velcro that he ripped off and planned to discard. He wanted no more memories of the soldier that wore his current wardrobe.

Sarah stepped around her wooded blind and walked towards him. The two of them, now wearing the Army Combat Uniforms with their green and brown camouflage pattern, could pass as true outdoors people in the woods.

"What do we do with these?" Sarah asked, holding up her jumpsuit. "And these?" She, too, had pulled the patches and rank off her soldier's blouse.

"Bury them back where you just were. The ground looks soft enough," Harris said, stomping down with his foot. "The fewer people can find of anything that shows we were here, the better."

Sarah agreed. "Okay, for now, you're in charge."

"Really?" Harris said skeptically.

"Just for the digging part." Sarah looked at Harris with a look that puzzled him.

*"What was she thinking?"*

They both found sticks suitable to dig and set to work. Harris could have sworn he saw her smile and used that as an opening.

"What do you think we should do next?" he asked.

"You making small talk, or was that a serious question?"

"Serious question."

Sarah continued to break the ground away as she talked without looking up. "I think we finish here and keep walking the trail. It's going to lead to a small town eventually. Once we get into town, you can use your skills to get us food and transportation. Then we head to Virginia."

Harris nodded, then asked, "Why Virginia?"

Sarah struggled with a small root making her sound exasperated when she answered, "It's where I live. Damn these things!"

Harris cut her off, "Do you really think you can go home? That's the first place they will look for you."

"No kidding. Let me finish."

"Sorry," Harris said. "Forgot my manners. Please continue."

"Virginia is where the answers are. For me, it's where all this started. I was working with a guy who works at the CIA and is very connected to the White House."

"Is that how you ended up in the facility?"

"No, I ended up there because of you and Livingston."

Harris was dumbfounded. "How, we didn't know you. That makes no sense."

Sarah looked down at the hole and looked up at Harris. "I think it's deep enough."

The two stuffed their jumpsuits into the ground and placed the patches reverently on top. Both dropped to their knees and began scooping the dirt into the hole. Harris dug outside, pushing any remaining dirt in, and tried to make it look like the surrounding landscape.

"How about grabbing some of these vines and junk, and let's cover it up."

Sarah just shook her head. "Okay, if you think that will help," she said sarcastically and raised her hands into the air.

Harris remained silent. What a curious woman she was. He did not understand her non-verbal message. They both snapped low-hanging growth and placed it over their hole.

They stepped back and observed their work. It was evident to Harris that someone had dug a hole and tried to conceal it.

"Are you going to leave it that way?" Sarah asked.

The question surprised Harris. "What do you mean?"

Sarah looked at him, sighed loudly, then proceeded, "Can't you just, you know, make it look good? Like it's not there?" She placed her hands in front of her with palms down and waved them as though she was fanning the earth.

Harris looked at her, searching for what she was trying to say.

"For God's sake, we are trying to survive here! Let's use what you got to raise our chances. Could you not have used your superpowers to prevent the whole exercise in hole-digging? I broke a fricking nail!"

Harris felt embarrassed. He had honestly not considered using his skills for this work.

He closed his eyes for a moment, and when he opened them, the ground was seamless with its surroundings.

"Much better," she said. "Where did you send them?"

"What? Where did I send what?"

"The stuff we just buried. Didn't you send it somewhere?"

"I don't think about it like that. I think about it going away, and it does. It's like it those things we buried never existed."

Sarah shook her head, walked over to the hole, and stepped down. The ground was solid. There was no indicator that anyone had disturbed the ground moments before.

Harris wanted to return to their conversation. He began, "How am I responsible for you being in that place?"

"I guess if I don't tell you, you'll just read my mind and get your answer."

Again, Harris was shocked. *"Did she feel he would use his skills and take advantage of her?"* That's not how he worked. He was confused that she would feel this way. Had Harris been in the SOUP too long? What was he missing? He looked into her eyes and tried to let her know that was not his personality.

Sarah continued, not waiting for his answer.

"The job I had in DC. I was supposed to get the videos made of you, Livingston, and some other guy in LA escaping from the feds. I hacked the CIA and DoD computers using some creative thinking. Before I turned the videos over to my boss, I watched them several times."

"So that's how you knew who Livingston and I were! Wait, I didn't even know there were videos."

"You can bet there are. It takes real effort not to be in one just walking across the street. The CIA transport vans and military operations are creating video and sending it to fusion centers everywhere non-stop during operations," She paused, then continued more soulfully. "Well, those videos got me a late-night visit, and next thing I know, I'm at the facility getting job offers."

"So, you saw videos of Liv and me? You've seen what we've done." It was a statement filled with regret and guilt.

"I saw them all right. I have so many questions for you, but first, we need to get to a place that gives us time to talk."

"Job offers?" Harris asked.

"Discussion for another time."

Harris did not believe her. He entered her thoughts and quickly withdrew. *"She's afraid of me. Worried that I would do the same thing to her. She wants to know how I will control myself and wants to get away from me as soon as the opportunity presents itself."*

Harris felt alone and worried that he always would be. *"How will you live the rest of your life?"* The question had a new meaning.

"Let's get walking." Sarah walked past him and stood on the pathway, still standing and not moving. "Well?"

Harris joined her and decided it was his turn to ask questions. "Who are you?"

"You mean you haven't read my mind yet?"

"I'm not like that," Harris snapped. "Just because I have these gifts doesn't mean I don't respect the person. I use them to protect myself and the people I care about. They are not some toy or magic trick. Hell, I don't understand how I even got these gifts, so lay off this bullshit of me always reading your mind or you thinking that you will be the next jello pool that I leave behind!"

"Touched a nerve, did I?" Sarah stopped, grabbed Lincoln's hands, and pulled him to face her. "Okay, stop. Now, look at me."

Harris did as she asked. The two locked eyes, and he saw her studying him intently. It felt like a child's staring contest to decide who would blink first; then, she broke contact.

Sarah started walking again. "I believe you."

Harris took two long strides and caught up. "Why?"

"Because if you were reading my mind just then, we would have a different conversation now."

Harris nodded his head, cleared of her accusations. "So, does this mean you will answer some questions for me now?"

Without answering the question, Sarah began, "My name is Sarah Anderson, and I live in Northern Virginia. I am a computer hacker by profession and damn good too."

"No doubt," Harris said.

"I started working with a Colonel named Ed Baxter. He is the White House liaison to the CIA and works for the National Security Advisor. He asked for a meeting and told me there was a video of you, Livingston, and...."

"His name was Hoffman."

"Good to know since COL Baxter didn't know his name."

"He's gone now. Dead."

"No kidding," Sarah was more surprised than Harris expected. "I didn't think you guys could, you know, cash it in. Superman was my first thought when I saw one of you guys throw a helicopter."

"Even Superman had kryptonite," Harris added.

"Ah, don't tell me. You're a closet nerd." Sarah blushed. It was obvious to both that their discussion was warming up.

"Hey, I read comic books when I was little." Harris smiled back. Sarah saw his expression, stopped to pause, and then continued. "So how do you guys, you know, die?"

"You were telling me about you. Let's keep the conversation there for a while."

Harris would not have thought it possible 48 hours ago that he would be walking through the woods, talking openly about his situation with a stranger. Yet here he was, unoffended by her coarse manner or sarcastic wit.

Sarah nodded and continued, "Anyway, Baxter needed these videos. He didn't explain why; frankly, I didn't want to know. So, I did the job, passed off the files, and went home to celebrate. This job meant early retirement for me. Someone wanted these videos badly and would pay big bucks to get them."

"Then what happened?"

"First of all, I hadn't gotten paid for the second half, which is strange for these arrangements. Usually, I get half up front and the rest when I pass off the work. The funds never showed up. I work at night, so it's about two or so...."

"In the morning? When does a pretty girl like you find time to sleep?" Harris flashed his smile again. *What the hell are you doing, Lincoln? Quit the chit-chat already. Stay focused!*"

Sarah responded to Harris' overt attempt to flirt. "What, don't you like night owls, or are you just afraid of the dark?" Sarah laughed, deciding to engage in some teasing herself.

The comment, well-intentioned as it was, hit close to home. Harris was immediately drawn back to his childhood and abusive parents, whose lives he eventually ended, landing him in the SOUP.

Sarah observed his facial expression. "Hey, you, okay? I didn't mean to say anything that would change the mood of our conversation."

"My fault. Some old memories that I'm still dealing

with."

"I'm sorry. I won't…"

Harris quickly put his finger to his lips. Both stood still, unmoving on the trail. Harris pointed to a mound of rocks that would provide cover, and the two quickly moved behind them.

"I thought the idea was to meet someone and figure out where we are," Sarah whispered.

"We need to wait on this one. I am getting a lot of information. He's looking for us."

"Where is he? Is he alone?"

"About 300 yards or so down the trail. And it appears it's only him."

Both peered over the boulders, unaware of the silhouettes their heads made contrasting against the sky behind them. Harris squinted hard and saw a lone individual walking up the trail, moving in their direction. The man sported comfortable hiking clothes and a vest jacket.

"There he is!"

"I see him!"

Both ducked down. As quickly as the information flowed from the man's mind, it stopped as if someone pulled the plug on the power. The man continued to walk towards them and was now close enough to hear. His footsteps made soft, crunching noises as he snapped small branches littering the trail, and his breathing was steady, unlabored. He was only twenty feet from their hiding place. Should Harris reveal his position and, if necessary, use his gifts to defend Sarah?

The man stopped. Harris put his finger to his lips again, hoping Sarah's anxiety would not reveal them. She looked at Harris with a calm expression and nodded. She was not afraid of the man or unnerved by their situation. Harris imagined the man listening to his surroundings for the slightest hint that he was not alone.

Harris heard the man start walking down the trail again. Sarah slid around the backside of the boulder to observe the man. Before Harris could prevent her, she stood up and said,

"Dr. Apoe?"

The man turned quickly, startled by her voice. "Hello, Sarah. I've been looking for you."

Sarah walked over to Dr. Apoe. Apoe asked her, "Is it just you?"

Sarah turned to see Harris emerging from behind the boulder and pointed her thumb in his direction. "Harris is with me."

"Is it just the two of you? Where is Livingston?"

"He didn't come with us. He chose to stay," Harris said, walking towards the two.

Apoe nodded his head. "Yes, this is all starting to make sense," he said.

Harris was unsure about trusting Dr. Apoe. It was Dr. Apoe that ordered the drugging to stop, which allowed him and Livingston the ability to sense reality again. Dr. Apoe told Livingston they were going to get out, and he was going to help facilitate their escape. But why couldn't Harris read his thoughts now? And why did his ability to do so stop when he walked closer to them on the trail? What was he hiding?

"Don't take this the wrong way, Dr. Apoe," Harris began, "But how in the world did you find us?"

"That's a good question, Dr. Apoe. In all the places in...," Sarah began.

"Virginia," Apoe filled in the remainder of the statement. "You are in Virginia, in the Southeast portion of the state near the Chesapeake Bay."

Harris nodded. That explained the two smelling the salt water. "Okay, let's get back to how you found us," Harris stated.

"Yes, Apoe. How did you find us?" Sarah pressed.

"Simple. Every Friday, Sarah, you received a newly cleaned jumpsuit with a location device sewn into a pocket seam. It was there so that you could not detect the small bump it made. I'm sure you can agree that it makes sense for us to be able to track where our guests are, in the facility or out."

"You tracked our jumpsuits?"

"Anywhere up to 25 miles from the site. You need this device here." Apoe said, removing a small item resembling a smartphone and showing it to Sarah.

She looked at it, unimpressed, and he placed it back into his vest pocket.

"I had locked on to yours until about 30 minutes ago. Then the signal abruptly stopped. So, I just started walking to the last location. I guess luck has its place in circumstances like this."

"Speaking of luck, how did you get out of the facility? And what happened to it?" Sarah questioned.

"Where to start?" Apoe said, staring at the ground. "Have you ever woken up and hated your life?" It was a rhetorical question. Apoe continued, "Let's just say I didn't want a career that harmed or killed innocent people. I started as a young officer, knowing National Security demanded sacrifice, but when sacrifices have no positive impact, the sacrifice no longer seems noble, just wrong. The research at the facility was immoral, and I realized I needed to change not just my career but my life. I was no longer helping people as a doctor but using my medical knowledge for 'other purposes.' Shortly after I unlocked your doors in the facility, I took an alternate exit out. I had an idea of what might happen once the three of you started your escape."

This explanation made sense to Harris. So much of his own experience and his discussions with Liv were about this very subject. *"How will you live the rest of your life?"*

"And the Facility?" Sarah asked.

Apoe thought for a moment, organizing his explanation before answering her question. It would be hard for them to comprehend.

"It's gone," Apoe said. A simple statement, Harris thought. But one that filled Apoe with both regret and relief.

"What do you mean it's gone?" She made quotes in the air when repeating Apoe's answer. "You got nothing more than that? What did you expect to happen, Apoe?" Sarah pressed.

"He knew Livingston, or I would destroy it," Harris commented.

Sarah turned and looked at Harris. The murderer had returned.

"What the hell? Why would you kill all those people?" she screamed, stepping close to his face as she unleashed her verbal wrath.

"Don't blame him," Apoe argued, his voice raised. "Back away!"

Sarah stepped away from both men shaking her head. "What the hell is the matter with you two?"

"There are things here that you don't understand," Apoe began.

Harris realized Dr. Apoe understood more about his and Liv's experience than Harris could have imagined. "*What does he know about us and what we've experienced?*"

"Okay, Apoe, start talking then. Enlighten me as to why killing those people makes sense! Jesus, how can you justify turning people into mush piles of flesh and broken bones?"

"Do you want to talk about this now, Sarah?" Apoe asked.

"Why, you expecting company? It's just us here in the woods. No one around for miles, right?"

Harris could sense the time was short before people started showing up to figure out what had happened to the facility. He did not think they would be looking for the three of them, well maybe Apoe, but finding the source of the site's destruction would be the government's top priority. Maybe Apoe underlined to explain a little to Sarah. It would help to gain her trust and confidence and reveal to Harris, Apoe's purpose for siding with him just now.

"Maybe you should, Dr. Apoe," Harris said.

Apoe looked at Harris. "Okay, Sarah, here goes. The facility you were in is named Site 35. It belongs to the Department of Defense. It is one of several underwater sites the government has. It would be impossible to build a facility like Site 35 above ground and with the population from the major cities around us." Apoe looked at Sarah. Her facial expression registered the shock at what he was explaining.

"Yes, you lived under the Chesapeake Bay. The nature of the experiments at the site made underwater a better physical medium. That's why you had to walk a long distance to exit. You walked several miles to the mainland and ended up near this sparsely populated portion of the Virginia coast."

"You built an underwater city?" Sarah asked.

"Easy to do in this area when you upgrade or build new traffic tunnels. No one asks why all the equipment and activity occurs when the state has a major construction project."

"What kind of experiments, Dr. Apoe?"

"The kind you do when you have people like Livingston and Harris. They are not the only two with gifts like theirs, but their skills are the most developed I've encountered in a while."

Sarah sat down on the trail, pulling her knees to her chest and locking her arms around them. To Harris, she looked like she was having difficulty processing the information.

"There are others like Harris?" she asked.

"Yes, I've made a career by finding and studying them or their impacts."

"How many others were like me?" Harris asked.

Apoe looked at Harris. "I've had two other experiences with individuals with power like you have, and more than I can count that have some skills in telekinesis."

"When you say the facility is gone, Dr. Apoe. What do you mean? Is it cluttering up the ocean bottom somewhere?" Sarah asked.

"No, Sarah, it's gone. We don't know where, but it's like Site 35 never existed."

"But the people? Gone too? Never existed?" Sarah asked.

Apoe did not have an answer.

"The car is only about 350 yards that way," Apoe said, pointing down the trail from where he came. "We can talk more in the car, but we should get going. I have clothes and food for you."

"Wait! How do we know that you will not just turn us back over to the DoD, CIA, or whoever?" Harris asked.

"After all I did helping you get out. After all the destruction, you still have questions about whose side I'm on?"

"Yup," Sarah said, still sitting. "We do."

"Like, why can't I read your thoughts now, Apoe? What are you hiding?"

Apoe removed a second device from his vest. "I doubt you recognize this, Harris, but we had them all through the facility. I had one in our first meeting. They prevent you from reading minds by blocking the lower frequencies associated with telepathy. We call them blockers. I still can't get used to people being able to enter my head. It's a personal quirk. Let me turn it off." Apoe pressed the off switch so Sarah and Harris could see him deactivate the device. Sarah looked at Harris for confirmation.

Harris's mind filled with Apoe's thoughts. He was telling the truth. *"They were heading to Alexandria, VA. Another facility and project. The SOUP! Supervisor, a past colleague working with Apoe. Old friends...oh, oh, and more. The program can help."*

Harris took a deep breath. "Okay, Sarah, we can trust him."

"Do you mind if I turn this back on?" Apoe asked, holding up the device.

"You don't need to worry about me reading your thoughts. But if it makes you feel safer, no offense taken," Harris replied.

Apoe's finger worked to activate the device, and he stopped. "Trust works both ways. I'll leave it off. Let's get moving."

Harris reached down and offered his hand to Sarah to help her up. To his surprise, she accepted his offer. As Sarah rose, she whispered to him, "He didn't explain why killing the people at the site was necessary."

Harris put his mouth close to her ear and replied, "Death is not the end, just a door to walk through."

She pulled her head back and looked at him, offering a faint smile, "Bullshit," she said but held tight to Lincoln's hand. *"A very strange woman indeed."*

# CHAPTER 12

Mr. UT, Chief Medical Officer for the SOUP, looked out his small townhouse window in an ordinary, white-bread neighborhood in Arlington, Virginia. A Virginia-registered Chrysler minivan pulled up every morning at approximately 6:30.

Nobody thought anything about the vehicle since UT had told his neighbors that he car-pooled every morning into the Pentagon. He was just one of many government civilians working in resource management. Once he told his neighbors he worked at the Pentagon and could not talk about his job, they all would say, 'I get it,' and they really did. Nobody asked questions. Working classified employment in Northern Virginia was common and helped him blend into his surroundings. Dressed in his coat and tie, UT walked down to the vehicle every morning and opened the sliding door. The driver always asked, "Had your coffee yet?" UT answered one of two ways, "Yes," which meant take me to the SOUP facility, or "No," which meant "take me to the administrative building. The admin building served as the management offices, training university, and laboratory complex for the program now known across America as the Virtual Life Incarceration Program. Still, UT liked the old name, Secure Operational Unfenced Prison or SOUP. Program names change, but the public always knew what the SOUP was.

The second reason for asking the coffee question was for UT's personal security. He worked with a masked identity. Only Dr. O'Neil knew his real name, buried in one of her program databases. UT also did not know his driver either. Each day, they, too, were switched out for security, but each morning, this phrase identified the driver as a trusted member of the program. For the driver, authenticating UT was not as important, but UT always wore a blue or red tie. If the passenger did not fit this profile, the drivers pulled away and denied entry to the vehicle. It was easy. UT found great calmness in the simplicity of his made-up life.

This morning as he walked out to his ride and opened the sliding door, no one asked if he wanted his coffee. The driver was pressed against the steering wheel, his eyes were wide, and his hands appeared to UT as shaking slightly in his lap. As he walked up to the vehicle, a man was hunched down in the front passenger seat, unseen by UT. In the next row of seats, another man sat behind the driver. Both men were dressed in suits. The one in the back had a pistol pointed at UT. The one in the front, now revealing himself in his seat, pointed his weapon at the driver.

"You can get in, Mr. UT, or we can make a scene. Your call."

"Good morning, Gentleman," UT responded. "A conversation is always preferable to bullets." He thought for a moment to run, but the driver would have suffered for no reason. As he got into the front seat, he noticed two more men on both sides of the townhome unit. The outcome of running would result in him still sitting in the vehicle's chair, just bruised and probably battered.

"Drive," one of the men commanded. "We'll give you directions."

The van left the neighborhood, and the driver was instructed to turn into a small, unoccupied children's park. The suited man in the front seat ordered the driver to stop. The driver complied. The man in the front seat exited the car, walked to the driver's side, and ordered the morning chauffeur to get out. The driver opened his door, exited, and was quickly frisked outside the vehicle. His cell phone and wallet were taken, and the armed person climbed into the driver's seat with the items. The man in the back produced a pair of slip ties and a hood. He bound UT's hands behind him and placed the hood over his head.

The driver pointed his pistol out of the window at the

man in the street and said, "Move on. No one is getting hurt." The agent pulled away and back onto the residential road.

UT could hear the traffic sounds associated with a morning commute but could see nothing. He took this opportunity to think through who might want to take him. As he analyzed each organization of logical suspects, he came up empty.

*"So much for simplicity."*

# CHAPTER 13

Mr. UT was shuffled out of the minivan and moved to the center of a large room. UT could smell damp concrete and felt the humidity that reminded him of the Washington, D.C. summers. His restraints were cut and removed from his wrist. It felt good to bring his arms back to the front of his body. The relief did not last long. UT was turned around, his jacket removed by four hands, and forced into a chair.

Each of his arms was pulled to the front, placed upon the chair's armrest, and zipped with new ties. The hands rolled up his shirt sleeve and positioned his arm upward to expose his forearm underside. UT knew immediately his captors were preparing him for an IV or injection. His hood was ripped unceremoniously from his head.

UT found himself in complete darkness for only a second before a bright light was shined into his face, temporarily blinding him. He forgot how sudden and intense light could cause his eyes to react, and they began secreting tears as protection. He instinctively turned his head away from the light.

"I must be in Hollywood," UT said, using his self-deprecating humor to help defuse the growing feeling that he was only beginning his ordeal.

"Not quite, Mr. UT."

"You seem to know me, but I admit, I've forgotten your name, or we've never been formally introduced."

"I doubt we run in the same social circles, Doctor," came a voice from the darkness.

UT could see nothing of his surroundings. The light was preventing any form of his natural night vision from developing. He surmised there were several people in the room, and he could fix their locations by their footsteps, but that was the limit of his awareness.

A figure created a ghostly outline of a shadow in the light. The specter bent over UT, and as he watched the silhouetted figure, a hand immerged from the darkness and rubbed alcohol onto his upper arm. An injection followed the rubbing. UT sat transfixed as a syringe with a disembodied hand inside a rubber glove pressed the plunger, emptying its contents into his arm. The figure, done with its task, disappeared back into the darkness. Several other hands placed electrodes of various types on his arms and forehead. UT sat in his chair doused in light, surrounded by a swirl of activity that looked as though the attending hands were popping in and out of existence.

UT heard another voice say, "He's ready, and we are recording."

"Says you, I'm not even dressed to go out." UT continued to use humor, knowing he was only moments away from losing his grip on reality from the injected drugs.

"Mr. UT, you've been injected with a harmless substance designed to ensure we can have an open and candid conversation."

UT was surprised to hear a female voice speaking to him. "I want to say from the beginning our intention is not to harm you, only to gather some information, after which you will be released back to your colleagues. You might have a small headache and...."

"I'm a Doctor, Ms. Whoever, so no explanations are required." UT began to feel at ease from the injection, a mellowing out that caused him to set aside his predicament and feel very relaxed. *"Focus. Focus on the questions. You can answer truthfully but still not provide all the information they want. Answer only the question with yes or no if possible. Focus,"* the instructions filled the rapid void filling UT's mind.

"Very well, let's begin," the woman said.

"Your name, please."

"Mr. UT – that's pronounced U-T and not ut."

*"Simple questions first to test the injection. Good. Talk*

*yourself through the events. Focus on the details of what is happening to you. Analyze everything said to keep your mind engaged.*" UT coached himself on the known routine and numerous experiences when he was on the other side of the syringe.

"Where do you work?"

"I work with the Virtual Life Incarceration Program, known as the SOUP."

"Very good. What do you do there?"

"I protect society from the worst criminals and conduct research for inmate reform."

"Are you a medical doctor?"

"That's how I do what I do," UT said, surprising himself. He was beginning to feel giddy and lightheaded. "*Focus, damn it!*"

"I think we all know what the SOUP does to keep criminals off the street, but how do you reform them?" a voice in the darkness asked.

"My dear, it's called epigenetics. That's the beauty of what we do and where the SOUP program moves beyond mere incarceration. Epigenetics allows us real hope of reforming our worst citizens. It is mind over matter, or better yet, mind creating matter."

UT heard a voice whisper, "Pursue this line of questioning. Treatment techniques may provide key information critical to understanding how Exit is accomplished."

UT's mind sharpened for only a moment at hearing the word Exit before returning him to a relaxing haze. "*These bastards want to know how we brought the three inmates out of the SOUP alive. This interview could get very difficult. Focus, and play along. You may be able to get through this yet.*"

"Explain for us the role of epigenetics in your treatments." This time it was a man's voice asking the question.

"Am I speaking with medical professionals or just the

normal help?"

"Answer the question, please. We will let you know if we need clarification."

"Very well. Epigenetics is the study of factors that can cause or limit the expression of genes within your DNA. Think of your DNA as being, let's say, computer hardware. All computers are built the same way. However, consider external factors like your emotions and decisions as the software that runs on your hardware. Each computer's hardware could be the same, but the software drastically alters how the computer is used. After all, for example, Dell makes the computer, but the software it runs depends upon the desired function, the user's nationality for language, a wide variety of variables, etcetera."

"We understand, Doctor. Please continue," the female said.

"I hope, madame, you do not accuse me of mansplaining. Just how technical would you like me to be?" There was silence.

UT continued, "I'm sure you've all seen the standard rat tests that validate nurture over nature. Yes, your emotions and environment can result in what genes are expressed in your body. Grow up in a bad home, and you could become a serial killer. Growing up in a good loving home environment, the person could be a medal of honor winner and a hometown hero. Both persons are capable of violence, but they enact it differently. Society stresses and reinforces their behavior as positive for one person, while for the other, society neglects and leaves them to their struggles. It is society, its environment, and its norms that determine, in this case, which genes are expressed, and which are not. One other item of interest is how the environment and each person's thoughts influence gene expression. Imagine a hypochondriac, over time, actually make their genes express mutations that cause sickness. If you think long enough about yourself, your body manifests the genes for you to become your thoughts. Epigenetics is pretty amazing science! It is with this foundation in science that we begin our treatment. Any questions so far?"

The room was silent. "No, then let me step it up a notch. The real question needing an answer is how do you change someone's life to make them a good person when they've already lived a bad life?" The room remained quiet.

"Does anyone wish to know? After all, aren't you the ones that are supposed to be asking the questions?" Even through the haze of the drug, UT felt he was in charge. *"Typical for these types of professionals. Not a thinking brain cell among them, just questions someone else wants them to ask."*

"Please continue, Doctor," the man's voice said, bodyless in the darkness surrounding him.

"For those not knowing how SOUP entry works in this room, our first inmates began their new virtual lives at the last moment of this reality. Their last memories became what we call the Jump Start – the place where the new virtual reality began and the one we live in disappeared. A while ago, my team and I developed a drug protocol that allowed inmates transferring into the SOUP to clear their minds of the present moment and open it to suggestions – in essence; we replicated the conditions of hypnosis. This open condition of the brain enabled us to walk back the inmate in time to memories before their crimes or happier places in their lives. Once they were in a 'happy place,' we closed the hypnotic condition and made this suggestion their last memory. This method was now the moment they entered the SOUP. This treatment is called Last Memory Reset."

UT was unaware that he had started to roll his head slightly from side to side. Despite this involuntary motion, his voice remained strong and his word diction sharp. *"So far, I have not revealed anything that would help them. Stay focused and in charge."*

"Questions?" UT asked. "No! Are there any scholars among you with the faintest curiosity about this?"

"Please continue, Doctor."

"Why is Last Memory Reset important, you ask – or at least I would," UT chuckled slightly at his humor.

"This condition places our inmates in the SOUP with what we called – with all respect to John Locke – the Tabula Rasa. The Tabula Rasa was our blank slate to write new experiences and create new memories for this moment in time only. We brought them backward in mental time, not time travel, and placed them in a virtual world as though they had a complete future in front of them."

"A new future that you could create, doctor?"

"Exactly. Remember, we only change the inmate's perception of time, not time itself. We were able to accomplish this even while the inmates were drawing new memories from community data – which is the database of inmate memories from which each inmate can create new experiences. Again, I will ask another question for you. If the community database had memories of murderers and other criminals that formed their new reality, how did you positively influence their memories? The answer is we isolated them. We did this through another creation of my team called the Cause-and-Effect Scenario. Because we could see how inmates responded to the community database events, we placed positive scenarios into the database with quantum tags that we knew contained the types of memories the inmates were looking for."

"How was this accomplished, doctor?"

UT smiled. A real question. *"Stay focused."*

"LMR – that's the Last Memory Reset, created a positive place for each entering inmate. We saw that each looked initially for positive experiences and sought out events that returned a positive outcome. The SOUP is just life quantified and explained. If we wish to receive and enjoy affection from, let's say, your mother, we will all find ways to continuously receive that affection. In the SOUP, we can create the inmate's emotional personality from these positive experiences."

"How?" asked a female voice.

"Using Quantum tags on each scenario. Each quantum tag is like an index that can be a pointer to the right type of memory the inmate wants. Like using the card catalog in a library to find a book. Unlike Google, it is a precise search, where you have many results returned, and we select the ones we want. Our test subjects wanted positive memories from their jumpstart points, so we provided positive experiences to each of them, always with successful outcomes. This approach created a desire by the inmate for more positive experiences, which guided them to the next quantum tag and scenario we introduced. We could build new memories and lives for our test subjects through these scenarios. A true maxim of the SOUP is we create experiences that build memories, and memories plus the perception of time equals reality."

"A point of clarification, Doctor."

"Another voice from the dark!" UT exclaimed.

"What specific types of memories did you introduce into the community?"

"We started at the basics, a positive home life with loving parents. If the inmate responded with the results we sought, we added social relationships and personal achievements; each new experience created new entries into the community database for other inmates to use if their desire matched these new quantum tags. Each new experience..." UT paused, "each new experience replacing a life of hate with one of caring. Don't you see reformed citizens whose crimes are washed away by what our program is doing?" UT, despite the drug, was emotional, his voice quivering with heightened pride in their accomplishments.

"Another question, Doctor," the female said. "What happens to the old memories, their real ones."

"They are moved to the hippocampus."

"They become dreams and nightmares?" she declared.

"Ah, a brain among you speaks. Yes, inmate memories become something seen as a fanciful dream or so terrible; our selected inmates choose not to recall them."

"You overwrite their memories," the male voice said.

"Replace them would be more accurate."

UT could hear several discussions emerging from the darkness. Each talking in whispered tones to prevent him from hearing the content. As one conversation would complete, another would begin with a new chorus of voices, their words singing to his soul as they discussed and marveled at his achievements, or so his altered mind believed.

"And how would your inmates start their new lives once they exited the SOUP?" a voice from the darkness asked.

"They would be given new identities, like the Witness Protection Program, and placed in communities where the people would not know them or judge them for their criminal record. To the reformed person, their memories would be their lives, and they would be unaware of their past criminal record. If someone accused them of being a criminal, they would deny the accusation and, in their subconscious, the denial would be the truth."

"This sounds like a great advancement in criminal reform," a different female voice said. "You and your team are to be commended for your accomplishments."

The voice paused, and a man's voice asked, "Do you intend to share your Last Memory Reset and Cause and Effect Scenario technologies with Justice and NIH?"

*"Watch it! They are starting to dig. Lecture time is over."*

"The commercial programs for elder care already have the LMR protocols, but you know that," UT responded.

"And the Cause-and-Effect technology to insert new scenarios into the community database, Mr. UT. What about that?"

"It stays in our control. Elder care has no reason to reform its patients and have them re-enter society."

UT's response caused the darkness to erupt into a series of noises. Each conversation blurred into one enormous buzzing sound that bore no resemblance to structured language. Thankfully, the buzzing stopped as quickly as it began.

"Is the exit solution discovered with the three inmates in California part of the Cause-and-Effect Scenarios."

"Yes and No," UT answered

"Explain your answer, please," a female voice requested.

"The 'yes' part; Scenarios are critical to reforming the inmate, so in this way are necessary to create the optimal conditions for Exit. The 'no' part: while the conditions to exit are needed, they are secondary to the actual Exit process."

"So, the inmate must want to exit before they can?"

"Correct," UT responded. *"Contain yourself, do not provide too much information beyond what is asked. Fight this! Focus."* UT was finding his internal struggle becoming more difficult.

"So, what did allow the three in California to escape, doctor? We've established that there must be a desire to escape. This you just explained. How is that desire placed there?"

*"Do not discuss the Quantum persona technology! Focus on a truthful answer."*

"Each scenario builds upon objectives that eventually lead to a desire to be free. For example, our three inmates were introduced to scenarios that ended with high school graduation. Each was made to experience very successful teenage years and given the idea of escaping from home and entering the world."

"It's hard to see, doctor, how this alone would allow the inmates to Exit. At one time or another, each inmate would free themselves from the SOUP with a thought. This seems impractical. What else is needed to enable the physical exit?"

"The pineal gland," UT said.

UT's mind started to reel with the internal struggle of defending his program's secrets against whoever was seeking them. He could tell he was losing control of his ability to withhold critical information; if UT answered too many questions, he would be broken.

"Excuse me, doctor. What did you say?" one of the

female voices asked. "How does the pineal gland play a role in inmate exit?"

"The pineal gland is exposed to frequencies; it opens the third eye." UT's internal struggle to speak was apparent to the voices and formless bodies in the dark.

"Must use a second frequency to introduce the correct psychic abilities and stabilize the mind's electromagnetic field." As UT struggled, each building phantom knew they were close to the answers they sought.

"What are the procedures, and what are the frequencies, doctor?"

UT struggled. The answers were preparing themselves for disclosure. The administered drug was coaxing, seducing, and pulling the information from him. He had no control to prevent the secret's release except for one.

"*Now is the time,*" UT thought. "*The time to choose. Is it worth living after giving away the power to destroy? Even though he did not understand how telekinesis worked, he knew death would follow for those who used it. Knowing how the power worked was not critical to use it. He would not give that to them.*"

Outside his mind, UT could hear the same question repeatedly asked, as though the repetition of asking would magically allow the drug to answer those that queried him. He felt someone behind him, hand on his shoulder trying to comfort him, to lull him into the security of an understanding touch so that he could empty his mind of all the secrets they contained. So many secrets over so many years. He was so tired. The steady combat continued between his discoveries and those that would use them. And for what? His questioners never told him how they would create a better world using his ideas and genius. They just wanted them. UT decided they could not have them, not today and not from him.

Inside UT's mouth, located in the upper arch in tooth position number 16, was a third molar identified as a wisdom tooth. The irony of the tooth's name was not lost on him. There was never a need to have these teeth removed as a child. In his

110

early adolescence, UT believed by keeping his wisdom teeth, he would remain smarter than his friends who removed theirs.

Today, he would validate that belief by showing the tooth's actual function. He would need his full jaw strength to crack the outer enamel covering the contents inside. It would require an application of extreme pressure at the correct angle that went well beyond everyday chewing habits, a safeguard built to prevent its host from accidentally breaking the top while munching their meals.

The voices asking the questions had stopped, but the questions themselves remained. The drug pulled at UT's memory to dislodge the answer and provide it to his inquisitors.

*"Not today."*

UT positioned his jaw and began a hard and steady bite onto number 16, increasing the pressure. It felt like he was driving his tooth into his jaw. He heard the telltale snap of breaking enamel and could feel the hard outer fragments make their way to his gumline and the back of his throat. UT could taste the almonds and cinnamon mix in a luxurious delicacy as the chemicals released from his tooth. He welcomed his painless departure. His last thoughts were of the program before he joined with the darkness around him.

# CHAPTER 14

The warehouse erupted with activity. The overhead lights turned on to reveal the immenseness of the facility. The questioners sitting at tables outside UT's vision scrambled from their workstations, sending their notes and pens onto the floor. The medical team arrived first at UT's side and checked for signs of life. There were none. A quick examination ruled out a heart attack or other natural causes. Their conclusion, Mr. UT had intended to end his life. No amount of first aid or resuscitation would bring him back.

One of the female voices calmed the room. "Okay, people, settle down. We have work to do!"

The room quieted, and all eyes turned to the woman. "Medical, I want a full autopsy. I want to know the cause of death as soon as you can get it to me. Operations team, clean this place. We were never here. Evaluation team, I want a full report of your assessment of the answers we received from him within two hours. We all know what we need to do. Let's get to it."

The room sprang into action. The woman knew what she needed to do as well. She walked outside the building, lifted her cell phone from her belt, and pushed the item at the top of her memorized numbers list." The woman was unhappy about making this call and knew she would be in administrative jobs for the remainder of her career if lucky.

The number connected and was answered with a simple "yes."

"It's Dr. Seymour." The woman looked at her phone and saw the icon that signified their conversation would be secure and that the voice pattern on the receiving end matched the number she called.

"I hope you have good news for me, doctor."

Seymour took a deep breath, calmed herself as much as

possible in two seconds, and said, "Mr. Thompson, we have a problem."

Seymour heard the silence on the other end. That was her cue to keep the information flowing. "Mr. UT is dead."

"Dead! How? I send you on a routine job and tell you no harm is to come to anyone, and now you are telling me our source is dead! Jesus! Explain!"

"He was sitting in the chair one minute, answering our questions, and in the next moment, he slumped over and was gone. A quick exam shows that he did not die from natural causes or our procedures. Our initial conclusion is he did it to himself. Medical will do an autopsy and have the results as soon as they know; it could be anytime or take several hours."

"Did he tell us anything?"

"Eval will have a preliminary report to me in two hours. I will send it immediately after I receive it."

"I'll ask again. Did UT tell us anything?"

Seymour paused, processing the last 30 minutes of information she'd heard. Explaining this information would be challenging without the context the report would provide. "Yes sir, but without..."

Thompson interrupted. "What the hell did he say? For God's sake, quit being a damn scientist and be an agent."

"*Fine, asshole. Here it comes. Hope you can make something of it without the background.*"

"He spoke about the methods they were using to reform the inmates. My best guess is they stumbled on a combination of variables by accident associated with the inmate's Exit in LA. He mentioned the Cause-and-Effect scenario technology that the SOUP used to create an inmate's new reality. This new life was embedded in their mind and would be the reality of their new life when they Exited. To the inmate, this new reality would be indistinguishable from their real life. Their past would not exist. He discussed quantum tags as the method to implement the scenarios and that each scenario was placed in the community database for access."

"Did you ask if the CE Scenarios played a role in Exit?"

"Yes, Sir. His answer was yes and no. He did indicate that the scenarios built a desire within the inmates to escape their SOUP reality. He stated this was more of an emotional feeling in the inmate's new life experience from the scenarios than a desire to exit the SOUP because they were a prison inmate."

"What else?"

"He talked about Last Memory Reset, which is public information for the Elder Care program."

"When did he die?"

"Sir?"

"What questions were you asking him when he died?"

"He was talking about human pineal glands, opening the third eye ramblings, and multiple frequency sequences."

"Did he reveal the frequencies and sequence?"

"No sir, that's when we lost him."

Silence.

Seymour knew Thompson would not reveal the significance of the information. Her job was to relay what her team had heard and let others put together the big picture. She also sensed the call was over. "I'll send the report as soon as I get it, Sir."

"Make sure that you do." Click.

Thompson leaned back in his chair and considered the information Seymour provided. Unknown to Dr. Seymour, Thompson was a newly appointed member of the 'Committee.' The last Committee meeting was contentious, with the Supervisor unwilling to provide the methods to Exit. She stated for the record, the Exit solution was unknown, and the data was under evaluation. The pineal mumbo jumbo is correct and most likely a part of the Exit process. The Supervisor mentioned the increased growth and health of this gland in the inmates and thought it could be an Exit enabler.

"*It's the frequencies and sequence that hold the key to the SOUP's Exit. The Supervisor played ignorant in our last meeting and would not commit to the scenarios as having any part in the Exit process. It seems now there may be a connection. An emotional desire to leave combined with a frequency sequence for what? That's why he killed himself.*"

He looked at his cell phone, scrolled to the last set of phone numbers on his preset list, and pushed the number. Shit, he hated to have to make this call, but if he wanted <u>any</u> official cooperation from the Supervisor, he would have to show some compassion. She would know it was his agency that caused the death. Despite the apparent conclusion, he would not admit that it was. It's how you did business in Washington, D.C., when you screwed up.

The number rang twice and was answered, "Yes."

"Ms. Supervisor, this is Director Thompson. I'm afraid I have terrible news for you."

# CHAPTER 15

Alec Richardson sat on his bed, unable to sleep. Long after the sunset, he was waiting on his bed in the darkness. Alec was waiting for something his intuition told him would happen, but he could not coax further information from whatever chemical enzymes or electrical impulses were generating his anxiety. Attempting to take his mind off these feelings, he focused on the Supervisor and her situation.

In the short time they were together in the conference room, she was able to provide an assessment of the external threat to the program by Vice President Morrison. He had added the Director of the CIA to the committee, and she assessed that the Secretary of Defense would be next. The Vice President's presence afforded him the clearance to know more about how the SOUP operated than anyone else in the Executive Branch. He was also aware that the escaped inmates possessed psychic gifts caused by, but still unknown why, from their time in the SOUP. Using the knowledge shared by the Supervisor and seeing the video of the power of the three exited inmates, Alec knew deep inside him that the program should not fall under the CIA for national security reasons. The Vice President disagreed. Morrison's rationale was associated with a Remote Viewing event performed by the inmates that resolved the Taiwan Straits and the USS Reagan incident. While the President successfully avoided a war, he only knew that his intelligence service had delivered critical information that provided a strong negotiating position, not the source or methods. In the Supervisor's opinion, the President had no clue what power the Vice President was attempting to control. The President, convinced by the VPs argument, had given it to Morrison under a classified Presidential Directive. Alec had learned that the Supervisor decided his Exit was needed to counter the Vice President's efforts and protect the Program.

His unique capabilities were critical to the Supervisor's team and necessary to preserve the program's success. Alec understood UT's objections to him leaving and O'Neil's desire for information about his capabilities. Still, Alec felt, too, the same desire to sort out his own life on his terms which now spanned two different realities. The Supervisor had acquiesced to his wishes to be alone, so now he needed to figure this out, not just for him but for everyone counting on him.

*"Where to start?"*

"Addie." He spoke aloud, surprising himself with the sound of his voice. "How could you not exist? You represent everything good about your mother and me. Adelle, I know you are still alive. Was Addie our daughter?" Alec felt panic as he struggled with piecing together his broken memory fragments and deciding what was real and what only existed in a Virtual world. His mind began to fill with his memories of Addie, growing from a baby to a young woman. Adelle was in so many of them, so proud of their family. Guilt replaced panic as he thought of leaving them. *"How did O'Neil convince me that you were not real?"* Alec could feel the warmth and wetness of tears on his cheeks as he broke into a sob. *"How could I leave you?"*

Alec was jarred from introspection as the room's overhead light and lamps turned on automatically. He sensed no one in the room with him and expanded his internal filters on his senses to be alerted by an intruder's presence. As he heightened his awareness of nature's frequencies, he expected to hear his neighbor's conversations, but there was only silence.

*"Is this part of what I am supposed to experience? Have I lost my gifts already?*

Wiping the tears from his cheeks and burying his emotions, he closed his eyes and focused on breathing. As his mind slowed down, Alec felt the slow erosion of memories, and he began to feel normal again, erasing the guilt and easing his panic.

"*Control. I need to get myself under control.*"

The word 'control' triggered an idea. Much like the volume control used for telepathy, Alec now visualized a dimmer switch. In his mind, he turned his mental controller down, and the lights in the room responded to his wishes. Alec opened one eye to a dim room. Each lamp was emitting only a fraction of light from the previous moment. "*This is weird!*"

Alec was unsure what to do next but continued to breathe slowly. Soon, he experienced, deep within him, a calm that permeated his consciousness allowing him to relax. He tuned his mind to focus on his steady breathing. He was instantly rewarded. Alec could feel a small spot of warmth begin to form on his forehead, centered above his eyes. He shifted his thoughts to focus on the area and felt its size expand and connect to the base of his spine. The warmth began to climb up his back until reaching the bottom of his skull. Instantly, his mind was filled with multicolored light, exploding between his eyes in a Disneyesque production.

Alec recoiled from the light's brilliance, startled by its sudden appearance, and opened his eyes as a reflex.

Alec found himself back in his room, surrounded by the dim lights.

"*I need to try this again,*" he reasoned and closed his eyes.

He focused on his breathing and felt the warmth on his forehead reappear. He concentrated his thoughts there once more and felt the heat move upward from the base of his spine. When the explosion of light happened this time, Alec was prepared and tuned his mind on the light scattering in front of him, viewing each quanta of energy producing the illumination. Alec detected a figure beginning to take shape from within the scattered light and watched as the form coalesced into a human figure, attracting each of the fragments of brilliance onto its shaping body.

Not knowing why Alec thought, "*I am here.*"

The light swirled, creating a large, slowly spinning

pinwheel of white shades and blue that began to sparkle as though some universal light source illuminated each particle, causing it to glimmer and shine.

"As are we." Alec felt the voice deep in the center of his brain. "We assure you; no harm will come to you."

Alec heard a slight ringing in his ears and, once again, visualized his volume knob and turned the noise down until it was non-existent.

"*Who are you*?" Alec used his mind to ask the question. No response came. Alec continued to hold the shining lights in his mind, trying not to allow stray thoughts to take away his focus. He felt the response.

"We are messengers of the one true message."

Messengers? His only reference to messengers in this context was Angels. He read about them many years ago, preparing for a career in journalism.

"Angels?"

There was no answer to the question. Alec's mind asked another question.

"What is that message?" Alec tensed, trying hard to focus on maintaining the light within his mind.

"Whoever has ears, let him hear. There is light within a man of light,

and he lights up the whole world. If he does not shine, he is darkness," the voice said.

As Alec listened, he felt an overwhelming blanket of peace and warmness wrap around him. Never in his life did he feel this safe and accompanied by such immense love. He felt at ease, despite his continued confusion surrounding the origin of his conversation.

"The light created you. Life and light are the creator. All creation is one. Therefore, both life and light are sacred. It is the law."

"What is the law?" The question emerged from Alec's mind without understanding why he would ask.

"Therefore, the Law: No light shall be destroyed. When

you take life without cause, you obliterate the creation and the light. This causes darkness to deepen, and the light grows dimmer. This is not allowed. Many do not understand the law and do not know that darkness will be defeated. When you defeat darkness, all light grows brighter."

"Can darkness be destroyed by light?"

"No - You cannot destroy darkness, only defeat it. To have light, there must be darkness. It is the way of creation. When darkness is defeated, it will return elsewhere. Darkness must exist so that all may choose to give light. Each man has that choice. He was created with light but must choose to use it."

Alec's mind swirled as he grappled with understanding his communication with who? Was he having this discussion in his own mind? Were the things he was hearing real? While still in his euphoric state of safety and love, he began to grapple with how the questions he asked were formed. Was there a specific dialogue expected? Were the questions coming from his mind or somewhere else to receive the information he heard and to understand later?

The next question jumped from his mind without his forming the thought, "How will I know the difference between light and dark?"

"In the law, there is Maat."

"Maat?"

"It is truth and justice according to the Universal Law. To understand Maat is to know that all men cannot change the darkness in their past, yet all can choose their light to shine for their future. Maat is life. It can be light. Both are given to you at creation. When you make the two one, you will become the sons of man, and when you say, 'Mountain, move away,' it will move away."

"Is this why I have these gifts?"

"All men have your gifts, but keep them hidden from themselves. You are blessed because you see and hear."

Alec considered all he was hearing, trying hard to

remember what he was learning. He looked down at his body and was relieved he had not lost his connection to the light by shifting his focus. On his right wrist, he noticed a mark he'd not seen before. It looked like an Egyptian Ankh.

"What is this?" he placed the symbol in his mind. "What does it mean?"

There was a pause. Alec was unsure he would be told why the symbol appeared on his body. The response came.

"It means you have the gift to communicate with the Netjer, the Shiny Ones."

"The what, the Shiny Ones? How is this possible? I don't understand."

The outline of the human shimmering within the light began to focus on the shining blur. Features formed within the illumination transforming into distinct arms, legs, and recognizable facial characteristics. The light was becoming more real to Alec. The phrase 'More solid' was placed in his mind. *"What the hell does that even mean?"*

Alec was fascinated as the human outline merged into a natural person, each part more detailed than moments before. The figure stepped into the room, the light disappearing behind her as remnants created a glow around her. She stood close to Alec, shimmering in white and gold light.

"Hello darling," it said.

"Adelle! How, why?"

Alec felt the collision of joy and excitement as Adelle appeared before him, causing him to weep openly. He reached out from within his mind and with his physical hands to touch her for just a moment. His hands passed through her image.

"I'm not here, Alec, but they thought you would understand if I answered your questions. I will take their answers and provide the 'human' response instead of hearing from them directly."

"How can this be? I left you. I left you and Addie, my entire world! How can you be here now? I am so confused about what is real and what is not! Oh, Adelle, help me understand what happened to me." Alec's tears resumed, rolling down his cheeks, unable to hold back the emotional dam breaking inside.

The figure continued, unaware of Alec's plea for understanding, "Energy exists in the frequencies supported by your world's construction. It's all energy and frequencies, Alec. Energy is neither created nor destroyed. It just changes form as the creator decides. Right now, without you knowing it, you are using your gifts to vibrate at a higher frequency than normal. If someone were to enter your room, they would never see you or me."

"Why?" he asked, attempting to regain control of his emotions.

"The visible frequencies of light limit their vision. They cannot 'see' where we are."

"So, why am I here?" Alec wiped away the remaining tears, becoming aware that his conversation with Adelle possessed a purpose different from his. He was looking to connect with the woman he loved. She was not real, only here to provide information about his life that he desperately craved.

"Because you are. You have reached out to us."

"But you brought me here. You or they guided me to this place."

"We did to facilitate this interaction based upon your wishes, Alec. You had many questions. It was our purpose to answer as many as you could comprehend."

"Why here?"

"Because it is the highest point closest to your city. In your ancient days, those among you who spoke with us climbed mountain tops as you have today. Your energy to speak with us is stronger when you are away from the Earth that grounds you."

"Adelle, how did all this happen?"

Adelle smiled. "They are impressed with your technology, your desire to improve your world. The SOUP is such an advancement! Your technology has facilitated direct, deliberate contact with us that few others in your human history achieved."

"How, why?"

"Your scientist opened a portal, darling. That portal allows humans to connect directly to us."

"How?"

"Each component of energy makes you," the figure of Adelle stopped to recollect her thoughts, "well, you exist within a physical body that does not vibrate as highly as your light does. You call it solid matter. Each of you at creation was given a way back to the One, the source of all light."

"Source of all light?"

"You would not understand the source." Adelle paused, "the source is beyond your comprehension."

"Much of this is beyond my comprehension!"

"You'll understand everything we talk about today Alec, even if you don't now. The answers are revealed to you throughout your life. Many things you must experience to understand. Open your mind, Alec, to new thoughts. You will find many of the answers there."

Alec began to feel he controlled his questions. He had several about the SOUP. It was apparent that whoever he talked with now knew about the system. Understanding their explanation might be complicated.

"Talk to me about the portal, Adelle. Is that what I call you?"

"If you wish. It is why I am here, to provide the image of love in its basic form."

Alec understood that answer completely. Seeing Adelle involuntarily placed him at ease, allowing him to focus more easily on his questions.

"What did the SOUP do? You mentioned a portal."

"Long ago, your kind experienced life differently in this reality. Humans used your portal to connect with Messengers. The Messengers supplied moral nourishment and direction to guide you on the path of light. The eye of those people always opened to the cosmos, and life co-existed with Maat. Over time the eye became unhealthy and no longer functioned. Less and less of your kind could find the Messengers until, eventually, only a few remained that could.

This condition changed when you built the SOUP – as you call it. Your Supervisor discovered each physical body was experiencing rapid and healthy growth of their pineal gland, which opens the third eye."

"Third eye? What does that mean?"

"It is how you are seeing me now. Your eyes are open. Let those with eyes see," Adelle responded.

"So those that can see do so with their third eye," Alec said.

"It is so."

"So, why didn't everyone leave the SOUP when their eyes opened?"

"Each person must make a conscious decision to leave. This decision is in all creation. Everything is alive, Alec. Everything decides. But without the Messengers, humans decided how to live, but unfortunately, they stopped living by Maat. You all were alone."

"I chose to leave the SOUP," Alec said. "It was my decision."

"It must be your decision, for your future is influenced by your choice. It must be yours to make. Eventually, all futures become the past. The past cannot be changed. Then it may be too late."

Alec thought about the three escaped inmates and how their existence disrupted and ended the lives of those in LA and Las Vegas. Why were not all three dead?

"Did the inmates talk with you?"

"In their own way, yes. Despite their past, each wanted to improve their lives and promised to use their gifts correctly. We underestimated the chances of each remembering their real lives. One chose darkness, and we watched the destruction caused by exercising his free will. He returned to us. We underestimated humans and your quick adoption of using the gifts for darkness. You have lived alone too long."

"Returned where?"

"You cannot know everything today."

Alec understood but had one more question.

"How do I separate my realities in my mind?"

"Understand, darling; only the present is real. The past is a record of experiences your mind organizes for you. You can recall the past, but you can never re-live it. This you know to be true. All experience creates memories from emotion. You can know which are real and which are not by putting each in its right place. Over time, the emotion of your false memories will fade. At present, your emotions are very high, all memories colliding within your mind. Time. Time will change your emotions and your memories. When the emotion fades, so does the memory. They are never gone, but you can discern the difference. Time for you is the only answer. You will need to comprehend this before you can understand us."

"Us – who is us?"

"I love you. I will be with you soon," Adelle said.

"Wait, don't go. Don't go!" Alec fell to the floor, begging Adelle to stay longer with him. He felt the massive hole in his life created when she was taken from him. Without the illusion of a virtual world, his loss was more incredible than Alec felt he could withstand. He would not live without her. Alec committed to finding Adelle and bringing her back to him. He knew where she was, and now he needed to find the right time.

The figure of Adelle slowly changed back to a shadowy figure buried in a kaleidoscope of spinning lights, then disappeared in a mosaic of blue and silver reflecting off specks of dust within his room. Deep in his mind, Alec heard a voice query, "How will you live the rest of your life, Alec?"

# CHAPTER 16

D r. Franklin Apoe was driving West on I64 en route to Washington, D.C., via Richmond, Virginia. Lincoln Harris sat next to him, staring out the window as the tall pines of the Virginia landscape eclipsed his view of the scenery beyond the highway. None of the three said anything since leaving their discovery place near Williamsburg as each was processing their individual experiences of the last 24 hours. Sarah Anderson was in the backseat, napping quietly, apparently worn out from their ordeal. As they approached Richmond, Harris cleared his throat. Apoe welcomed the coming conversation.

"So, what made you decide to help us?" Harris asked.

Apoe processed the question. It was a good one, and even he was unsure if discussing it now was the right place. Apoe decided there may not be a better time and decided to answer the question. Apoe responded with what was closest to the truth for him.

"I got tired of watching people used for experiments and justifying what my facility and I were doing for National Security."

"Ah, National Security. I've not been out long, but I've heard that phrase used by many senior people in Las Vegas. It makes a convenient scapegoat as far as I'm concerned."

Apoe nodded, "It doesn't mean what it used to anymore. I've served my country for over 18 years. National Security is more of a justification to achieve personal leadership objectives at whatever cost rather than a focused objective for the country."

"Maybe it's always been like this, but now you can understand its real meaning. The higher you go, the more you see its true purpose. I've learned we are the ones that change. We start young with a narrow perspective of the world and its truths. As we age and gain experience, we find our truths were only a direction, not a destination." Harris said.

Apoe looked at Harris. "I would never have taken you for a philosopher, Harris."

"It's just proof of what I'm saying. Neither would have I a year ago."

Apoe nodded as he maneuvered the vehicle into the right lane to merge onto I-295, the Richmond by-pass would avoid the city traffic. Harris waited for Apoe to transition and re-enter the traffic flow before asking the next question.

"How did you get into this? You know this business of experiments and psychic gifts."

Apoe chuckled at the question. "I don't think I got into this as much as it pulled me in. I was a senior Captain, a medical doctor in Afghanistan. I'll spare you the history, but I experienced something that took me from practicing medicine to researching the 'human condition.' Remember, Lincoln, people with your gifts are not new to me."

"You mean there are others like me that have Exited from the SOUP?"

"No, as far as I know, you are only one of three that have that experience. But many others have some abilities in telepathy or telekinesis. We study or employ them too. But the level of power you have in your gifts is very rare. How people received their gifts is a mystery to me, which is why I started this career. It began with intellectual curiosity and, somewhere, evolved into a job that allowed me to harm people for the good of science and the country."

"So, what other gifts have you seen? In these other experiences, I mean."

"Most of them, as I said, have minimal but proven abilities. However, the three of you have the most evolved abilities I've seen. There were two other similar events I witnessed that were life-changing. The one in Afghanistan started my new career, and one other in China. Both incidents were tied to holy men, monks that were fanatics of their faith.

Are you religious, Lincoln?"

Apoe noticed Harris' facial features had changed. He looked uncomfortable.

"I'm sorry if I asked a question that ..."

Harris interrupted. "No, that's not it. I would never have described myself as being religious at all. Growing up was a difficult experience for me. I never believed God was present in my house."

"I know your background, Lincoln. It must have been difficult growing up like that," Apoe's voice was sincere. Harris sat silently, and Apoe focused on the driving, aware Harris was even now fighting with his internal demons. He would wait for Harris to continue the conversation.

The two men said nothing as the Virginia landscape and escalating traffic provided welcome distractions. The left turn signal's clicking disrupted the low, steady hum of the car's movement on the pavement as Apoe turned onto the exit for I-95 North.

"Apoe," Harris began.

"Call me Franklin."

"Okay, Franklin. Why do you believe three criminals, the farthest thing from devout holy men, were given these gifts? I mean, if there is anything you do not want to give to criminals, it's what I have."

"I have no clue. That was part of what I was supposed to find out while you were at the facility. My experiences enabled my team to develop countermeasures to 'disable' your gifts. Frankly, you scared the hell out of the senior people. They didn't know what to do with you."

"Were you afraid of Livingston and me?"

"To be honest, yes. I'd seen the videos and knew what you three could do."

"Well, there is only me now. The other two are gone."

Apoe shook his head. "I wondered about that. You mentioned Livingston. Who was the other guy?"

"His name was Hoffman. A serial killer."

"What happened to him?"

"You saw the video of our escape in Los Angeles?"

Apoe nodded again.

"After Hoffman 'played' with those men, he became frail. Liv and I took him to a small, deserted shop not far away from the incident, and he disappeared. Strangest damn thing I'd ever seen."

Apoe could feel the excitement start to rise within him. Could it be possible Harris' experience would duplicate his in Afghanistan and China?

"What happened, Lincoln? Describe what happened," Apoe said while trying to focus on his driving.

Harris was becoming excited; reliving the experience had added an animated and succinct rhythm to his answer. "Before he disappeared, Hoffman looked different. He'd aged about 100 years since we escaped from the van. Hoffman woke up yelling he'd broken some law and had to go. He was scared. Hoffman was a tough guy. I never thought I'd see him afraid of anything."

"What next?"

"Then, out of nowhere, there was wind and all these lights, and then he disappeared."

"Was there anything else?"

Harris' animated description of events turned sober. "Don't think I'm crazy, Franklin, but Liv and I heard a voice, and it asked us a question."

Apoe finished for him. "How will you live the rest of your life?"

Harris stared at Apoe. "How...how would you know that?"

"I've been asked the same question twice. I've had the same experience you just described. Lincoln, this question is the <u>real reason</u> I helped you and Sarah escape the facility. I felt I had to do something different with my life. In some circles, I will be called a traitor, I say to them...well, I won't say what I would say to them."

Harris smiled. He understood and felt the same way about those that would criticize him.

Harris affirmed the conversation, nodding his head rapidly up and down. "That's why Liv and I decided, despite our pasts, we would do something good with our lives too, even if it meant helping our government with Remote Viewing stuff. We just wanted the opportunity to redeem ourselves. We remembered who we were in the SOUP and wanted that life to be real. Liv said he could feel all the "bad" things happening in the facility. It's why he stayed behind. Liv saved Sarah's and my life. We might have disintegrated with the rest of the facility."

"Franklin, I heard the voice ask the question again, and then the facility was gone. Do you think that means Liv is gone for good?"

Apoe thought a moment, "I think so, Lincoln."

Harris stared out the window and remained quiet.

Apoe had found some of the answers he was looking for in his conversation with Harris. His intuition about Harris' motives and how he'd use his gifts was correct. He concluded it was not a coincidence that the three of their lives were intertwined, heading North to the Supervisor's Virginia facility. He just didn't know why.

# CHAPTER 17

The Supervisor sat in her chair in the Arlington Facility and put her head into her hands. "How could it be UT was dead?" She stood up and moved to her office door, shutting it quickly. As the latch clicked closed, she could feel the rage, the one emotion she knew needed to be kept in check.

Rage caused rash decisions. Rage created the need for revenge. Rage ended up destroying careers. But here it was. Rising in her like a lightning strike on a meadow's lone tree bringing instant destruction. *"This can't be real!"* The idea of UT's death bordered on the absurd, and as she rationalized the news as mistaken, she knew in her heart it was true. She sat down in an office chair and cried. She let forth the built-up emotions, a container filled so high the only result was to overflow its top. As the tears began, she reexperienced each challenge and each defeat her team suffered. So quickly did the tears develop that she was unprepared for the uncontrollable sobbing that escaped her otherwise calm demeanor.

The Supervisor was unsure how long she remained distraught but felt calm, returning and reasserting control. She walked into her private office bathroom and turned on the light. Staring back from her mirror was a woman that, to her, was unrecognizable.

"Getting old prematurely is a bitch!" she lamented aloud to the face in the mirror.

She returned to her desk when she completed her recovery and called Dr. O'Neil. Knowing the news would also be hard for Dr. O'Neil; she set a late afternoon meeting to discuss options. Dr. O'Neil confirmed the appointment but said nothing more.

Her next call was to Senator Hurst. His staffer said he was on the Senate floor and would have the senator call as soon as possible. She thanked the young man and hung up.

She pulled out a pad and began to scribble down what she could recall of Thompson's phone call. The bastard started the conversation with UT's death. "UT is confirmed dead," he had told her without exchanging false niceties. *"Straight to business,"* she remembered. When she asked how he'd replied, 'apparent suicide.' He continued by explaining UT was picked up for routine questioning, and Thompson had issued instructions for UT not to be harmed.

She had shouted at him, "Why the questioning? And how do you just pick someone up? This is still America," to which Thompson replied calmly, "You know the rules for probable cause do not apply to intelligence services. The time-sensitive nature of the information is valuable to 'national security.'"

The Supervisor replied irately, "THERE IT IS – National Security bull shit. How and the hell is UT's knowledge applicable to National Security?"

"You run a national asset Ms. Supervisor. You are also aware the new Presidential Directive makes it a matter of National Security. The VP wanted answers about the SOUP Exit procedures. Your answers are way past the deadline he gave you. Ms. Supervisor, you have purposely delayed your official responses. UT knew the answers we wanted, and we picked him up."

Thompson paused, "Ms. Supervisor, his death is on your hands, not anyone else's."

"Screw you, Thompson! Your boys are the ones that killed him. How do I know this is not just your normal BS head games you guys play?"

"We will deliver UT to the Arlington facility tomorrow at your time and choosing. That should be proof enough that this information is real. We did not kill him."

She had said nothing, knowing Thompson was not playing games and the Vice President had upped the stakes for getting the information.

"And Ms. Supervisor, while the cause of death appears to

be suicide, we've also done our exam to determine how. Any further types of questioning like this will require us to provide a dental checkup, if you understand my meaning."

She understood. UT volunteered to be the first to have this 'method' installed. She had agreed to the procedure, knowing he comprehended more about the SOUP's medical applications and how they worked with the technology than she or Dr. O'Neil. This knowledge made him a target for this sort of activity, domestic or foreign.

The Supervisor recalled she abruptly ended the call with Thompson. Remaining on the call longer would have given him insight into how valuable UT was to the program and her personally.

Now, with a clearer head, she scribbled on her pad, "They still don't have the Exit solution."

Her secure office phone rang. *"That must be Hurst."*

The Supervisor picked up the phone and listened for the caller to speak first. "It's Senator Hurst, Ms. Supervisor."

"Hello, Senator. I hope everything is going well with you," she said, using her firmest voice. She could feel the quivering of anger and remorse just below the surface.

"The usual, but no one said keeping a Republic was easy," Hurst said, laughing. "What can I help you with?"

"Bad news Senator." She fought back the emotion rising in her voice and repeated herself, "Bad news. Mr. UT is dead."

"Ms. Supervisor, I am so sorry. I know how close the two of you were as colleagues. He will be missed by many at the facility. He was a medical genius."

"Thank you, Senator. Yes, we do miss him already."

"What happened? I take it this was all without warning." Hurst paused again for a moment before continuing, "Not wanting to sound rude, but is this information confirmed?"

"It is. UT's death was unexpected, which is the reason for the urgency of the meeting." The Supervisor let the statement hang before continuing. "Senator, I would like to meet with you in the admin facility as soon as possible. You will be critical to our discussion. I was also wondering if you could convince Dr. Lucia to join you. This is very important."

"I understand. Our slate cleared in the Senate today. I can move my schedule around tomorrow. I'll see if Dr. Lucia can make it."

"The time tomorrow does not matter. Anything you can do to meet would be appreciated."

"Consider it done, Ms. Supervisor. I'll get back to you with the time."

"Thank you, Senator."

"Ms. Supervisor," Hurst said, "My deepest condolences. I know what it's like to lose a dear friend and colleague."

"Thank you again, Senator. See you tomorrow." She returned the phone to its cradle.

*"Thank God for men like Senator Hurst,"* she thought. He had also lost a dear friend, and as far as he knew, Hurst caused the loss. She felt a bit of guilt as she recalled the program's biggest deception.

"Ms. Supervisor?" It was her office admin opening her door. "I saw the red light turn off and knew your conversation was over. Sorry for the intrusion."

"No problem. What's up?"

"There is an unsecured call for you from a man who says he is Dr. Apoe. He said you would know who he was. Do you wish to take it?"

*"Oh, my God! Franklin Apoe. This is not the time for you to return to my life,"* she thought.

"Yes, I'll take the call in here."

"Yes, ma'am." The admin exited, closing the door behind her.

The Supervisor's phone rang, and she picked it up. "Franklin, this is an unexpected call."

"I know. I'm coming up I-95 now. I'm at Quantico. Send me instructions for your facility entry. I have something you may be interested in."

"Franklin, what is it? I just can't provide you with clearance. I need time to make the security preparations." That was only a half-truth. The real reason, the Supervisor was unsure if she could handle all the emotional baggage he brought with him.

"Look, we don't have time for that. I have one of the people you've been looking for and his traveling companion. There is only one left."

The Supervisor was aware of Dr. Apoe's facility and the research he was overseeing. Their careers had crossed multiple times, and they had collaborated on numerous unexplained events while in the Army. His career left medicine, and he moved to the Army's paranormal activity studies office for his experience in Afghanistan. Earlier, they were more than collaborating professionals. He was one of only a few that would recognize her, all of her, and know her real identity. That part of their life ended several years ago when he chose DoD Research and Development, and she decided to leave the Army. Somehow, they could not sustain their relationship, and she found a home and a new start in the Justice Department.

*"This is a big risk letting him in the facility on so many levels,"* she reminded herself. *"And what about the people with him? Can they be trusted not to destroy this facility?"* Deep down, she knew she could trust him, and her concerns, while legitimate, were unfounded with him.

"Do we need to isolate your companions, or is your access request for them also?"

"Everyone," Apoe replied. "You will want to hear what they have to say."

"Do you have secure email capabilities?"

"SECRET only on my phone."

"That's all you'll need. I'll send the clearance shortly. See you in about 45 minutes."

"Thanks. Much to discuss," Apoe said.

"Yeah, me too."

# CHAPTER 18

The Supervisor was waiting at the Security Access Point inside the SOUP's Arlington Administrative and Support building. She stood back from the security detail busily processing visitors for building access, not to allow her presence as the boss to interfere with the crucial tasks her teams conducted daily. As the team worked in front of her, she continuously scanned the small entryway for signs of Apoe. The windows on the doors were the only light allowed into the building. The architects designed the front entrance for security in case of a threat to the inhabitants, not sightseeing. She understood the reason, but today would've been an excellent day for an expansive view.

She was fidgeting and rubbing her hands together as she always did when she became anxious. *"Why?"* Was it that so much depended upon the upcoming visit with Hurst and her next program decisions, or was it because Apoe was about to re-enter her life? She never answered the question. Dr. Apoe and his party walked through the outer door. She and Apoe made eye contact, and both smiled. She stood back, projecting calmness while her security team performed their routine on her guests, which included checking their access credentials against a central database for all government facilities.

"Ma'am. Dr. Apoe's credentials are flagged? Should I still grant access?" one of the security team asked.

"What kind of flag?" she asked, attempting to determine if the DoD would be her next visitor.

"It shows him as deceased," the guard responded.

"Well, he apparently is not. He's standing in front of you. More than likely a system problem again. I will grant access to these personnel on my authority. Badge them as Escorts Required."

"Yes, ma'am."

The security team completed their checks and allowed the three access to the facility.

Apoe led the group to the Supervisor, who observed the group closely as they approached the lobby next to the elevators.

"Welcome to the facility," she said and offered her hand to Apoe. He bypassed the gesture and gave her a quick, perfunctory hug that would not break the decorum of professionalism.

"I see you two know each other," Anderson said. She turned and gave Harris a quick wink.

"This way, please." The Supervisor pointed with her hand to the elevators on their right. The four entered, and the Supervisor slid her card through the security reader and pushed the desired floor button. The ride to the top floor was silent, each of the four familiarizing themselves with each other and their surroundings. The doors opened, and the Supervisor's admin was waiting for them.

"I have you set up in the main conference room, ma'am. Dr. O'Neil called. She is on her way."

"*Good timing. Sandra's expertise will be helpful.*" She looked at her admin and said, "Please show our guests the restrooms and kitchen before we get started."

The admin nodded her head. Her duties were defined and standard procedure for all guests requiring an escort. Make them comfortable, keep them under watch, and isolated from everyone else.

The Supervisor returned to her office and called her Deputy in charge of Administration. Moments later, he had instructions for the covert arrangements with the Agency for receiving UT's remains in the morning. "Take him directly to the site. Dr. O'Neil and I will be by tomorrow morning around 0900. We'll use the standard disposal protocol."

As the Supervisor walked back to the office, she thought about the irony of bringing one of her own into a funeral home in a casket. While this was standard procedure for all new inmates, she would never believe UT would be a participant in the process he helped to create. She and Dr. O'Neil would say their last words to him, and like several before him, the system would identify his life signs had stopped and execute its programmed instructions. It was the way people with masked identities Exited this reality.

The Supervisor found Dr. O'Neil had joined the three. As the four sat in the conference room's comfortable chairs chatting, the Supervisor overheard Anderson ask the question to Apoe, "So doc. Did you and the Supervisor have a thing? You know..." Dr. O'Neil blushed and was stunned by the question. The Supervisor reacted as though the question was never asked and saved Apoe from a difficult and embarrassing answer. "Let's get started. Dr. Apoe, what's going on, and why are you here? And why are you dead?" she said, taking a chair.

"Much of what we will tell you today," he started, "is well beyond the clearance levels we collectively hold." Apoe paused, then continued, "Others could view it as treason."

"*Treason! Good God, Franklin. What have you done, and why are you bringing it here?*" she thought. The Supervisor continued calmly, observing Apoe and his group more intently.

"I understand your concerns, Dr. Apoe. However, this will be the first of several discussions that exceed our clearances in the coming days. Is there anyone here that wishes to leave understanding a treasonable offense could be involved?" The Supervisor was not surprised but relieved as no one stood up to exit. Each person shook their head 'no.'

"This is Dr. O'Neil. She is the VLIP Chief Scientist." The Supervisor pointed to Dr. O'Neil.

"VLIP?" Anderson asked.

"Virtual Life Incarceration Program, otherwise known as the SOUP," The Supervisor said.

Dr. O'Neil continued, "There are two programs, this one which the government runs and another for the elderly called the Virtual Life Elder Care program or VLEC. Private Industry runs those facilities."

"Get used to the acronyms," Harris whispered to Anderson.

Apoe, grateful again for the save, began with his companion's introductions. The Supervisor and Dr. O'Neil needed no introduction to Lincoln Harris. Both had worked with him during his Remote Viewing session in Los Angeles and recognized Harris from the later videos. The Supervisor was introduced to Sarah Anderson and, through a quick introduction, learned she was responsible for hacking the CIA and DoD sites to bring the videos to the White House. "I didn't work alone. I had support from inside the White House," she said. The Supervisor was unsure if Anderson had made this comment to cover her ass, thinking prosecution was still possible, or wanted to make known she provided the videos to someone who deserved part of the credit. The Supervisor made the connection that the other person was the same Colonel assisting Anderson and was suspiciously killed in an automobile crash. She learned this in her meeting with White House Chief of Staff Aaron McAllister and Senator Hurst shortly after the accident. The Supervisor would hold this information back for the time being, unsure of how the news would impact Anderson's demeanor. She needed to know what these three had experienced and how the grief she was still fighting affected her decision-making.

As Apoe discussed his role at Site 35 and the projects under his control, the Supervisor began to appreciate his accomplishments and personal sacrifices. *That event in Afghanistan really changed his life. I wonder if he knows how far from practicing medicine he is?*

Apoe finished his remarks, and the Supervisor commented, "Well, that explains why the DoD thinks you're dead. I guess the big question is, why did you help them?"

"I think you'll understand when you hear Harris' experience. Okay, Lincoln, you're up."

Harris began. The Supervisor and Dr. O'Neil let him talk without interruption or question. The Supervisor noticed

Anderson looked enthralled by his account. She believed Harris and Anderson had not discussed this in their short time together. Still, it was apparent to the Supervisor that Anderson sympathized deeply with Harris's experiences.

The Supervisor stopped Harris when he began to discuss the incident with Hoffman.

"What happened in the Cigar Shop?" the Supervisor asked.

"Liv, that's Livingston, and I had carried him there. He had no energy, and when we laid him on a cot we found, he started talking about laws he had broken with his new gifts. Hoffman said he needed to be punished for what he did. When Liv and I went to him, we were drinking beer off to the side. He looked like an old man, shriveled up and barely alive. He started talking about Shiny Ones and that they were coming."

The Supervisor looked at Apoe. She knew how this account was going to end.

Harris continued, unaware of the non-verbal communication between the Supervisor and Apoe. "He was terrified, and I got to be honest when the wind started blowing inside the shop, but nothing was moving. I was too."

"What happened next?" It was Dr. O'Neil's question.

"As I said, the whole room in the shop was blowing hard, then the light started coming from everywhere, and the next thing I knew, Hoffman was becoming part of the light, and then he was gone – poof in thin air."

"What do you mean, becoming part of the light?" the Supervisor asked.

"He turned, dissolved, I guess is the best way to say it, into the light."

"But you and Livingston had not left the shop?" Dr. O'Neil pressed.

"No, ma'am. We were right where we were supposed to be."

"Did anything else happen?"

"Yes, ma'am. When he was gone, Liv and I heard

someone ask us...."

"How are you going to live the rest of your life?" The Supervisor finished his sentence.

"Yes, ma'am." Harris looked at Apoe and back to the Supervisor, "How did you know?"

"I just do," she said, looking at Apoe.

Apoe and the Supervisor shared an experience in China, creating a bond between them years ago, and now it was uniting them again. Apoe nodded his head to affirm the Supervisor's gaze.

The Supervisor would not reveal to the group that it was an experience she and Apoe lived together years ago, instigated by a Buddhist holy man. She, Apoe, and a Special Operations team were covertly dropped into China to determine if the monk's gifts were legitimate and convince the man to work with the United States on shared objectives. When the two found him, he was a shriveled prune of a man among hundreds of disfigured corpses.

She witnessed the same events Harris described when the priest killed an entire village of people just because he could. Observing this type of death and being asked by some presence how she would live the rest of her life called her to action. At that moment and in that small village in China, the Supervisor knew more was needed from her. As she surveyed the dead families, brought to this end by no reason she could comprehend, she committed to making life better for all and not via new ways of power discovered by research. That event in China was her catalyst to change careers, and since Apoe made clear he did not want to join her, they separated.

She had the answer to her question. Just as she had sought redemption by changing her life and working for the Department of Justice, Apoe had sought redemption by helping these two escape and return to her.

The Supervisor was aware of all in the conference room looking at her, looking into space. "My apologies. There is a lot to take in here," she said.

"Mr. Harris, we can fill in the blanks from the videos for most of your time between Los Angeles and Las Vegas," Dr. O'Neil continued. "But is there anything you want to tell us about your escape, such as where Mr. Livingston is?"

"Livingston stayed behind. He saved our lives," Anderson said.

"But where is he now?" Dr. O'Neil wanted to know.

"We're unsure," Apoe answered. "But wherever he is, my facility is with him."

"The whole facility is gone, Dr. Apoe?" the Supervisor asked.

"Gone. It's like it was never there."

"How do you know this?"

"Because," Anderson began, "When Lincoln and I were outside, we tried to get back in. The door inside the shack we'd come out of was gone. There was no way to get back inside. We're not talking rubble here, like an explosion. The door didn't exist."

Apoe was nodding his head. "My experience is the same. I came out of one of the service road entrances. As I was driving away, I felt a shove in my back. When I looked in the rear-view mirror, the asphalt changed into green trees and shrubs. The road was gone. I got out and walked to where the road should be connected to a warehouse. The warehouse was there; the access point was not."

The Supervisor nodded and knew Apoe was not fabricating his side of the events. If his account was accurate, the others must also be telling the truth.

"This brings us to you, Ms. Anderson," Dr. O'Neil said.

"My story is pretty simple, Dr. O'Neil. As I said when we sat down, I'm a system hacker, self-taught. I was hired by the White House and worked exclusively with a man named Colonel Baxter. "I did certain jobs for him. He was my contact. One day, he came to me with a unique tasking to find the videos you've mentioned, ma'am, of Mr. Harris and the others."

"You were successful; congratulations. How did you

hack the DoD and CIA?"

"Dr. O'Neil, let's not get into the details, though I am really proud of how I did it and am happy to explain it later."

"We have time now, Ms. Anderson."

"Not really," she replied.

Dr. O'Neil looked at the Supervisor. "Maybe later, Dr. O'Neil. Please continue, Ms. Anderson."

"Not everybody was as impressed with my work, however. I was paid an early morning visit by some guys dressed like ninjas. They knocked me out cold. I guess they ghosted my stuff and hauled me off to Dr. Apoe's place where surprisingly, the lady in charge of a highly specialized hacking team offered me a job."

"Congratulations again," Dr. O'Neil offered.

The Supervisor noticed Dr. O'Neil's accolade was said in earnest but suspected the compliment was not received in the spirit in which it was intended.

Anderson changed her expression. Harris immediately detected the change. Anderson's eyebrows raised, and she created a larger-than-life smile that covered the space between her cheekbones. It reminded Harris of a child failing to restrain their excitement on Christmas morning. He shook his head slightly at her, pleading with his eyes that she would not do whatever she had planned.

"So, what happened?" The Supervisor asked, also observing Anderson's facial change and thinking she might be lighting the fuse for what was to follow.

"I played along with them, you know, cause this girl's no fool, so I acted all serious, and THEN, Dr. Apoe gives me the Times crossword that says he's helping me out and to take Harris and Livingston with me. So, I figure, that's cool. These guys can hang with me; besides, I had recognized the two of them 'cause of the videos I hacked, so I knew they were important. If I got into something, I figured these GUYS GOT SKILLS I could use. Then, BOOM! Out we go using directions I learned snooping my new workplace. Man, you should have seen the boys. I mean, they were throwing SHADE EVERYWHERE! No one could stop us! I mean, bullets bouncing off those two covered in blue stuff, shit flying everywhere being all SHOT UP, but no one shooting at us being killed – just knocked out, I mean, LAYING them OUT. Harris and Liv, the inmate duo, DANCIN' their magic to unlock the doors and turn glass into SANDPAPER. It was crazy cool. Then just as we're gettin' ready to bounce, Liv stays back, putting his hands up like to say 'stay back,' and my man Harris goes to talk him DOWN, know what I'm saying? And while they're bromancin', I can feel the wind Lincoln talked about in his stuff. Liv is yelling at us to 'get out man!' and I'm yellin' at Harris, COME ON, all the while the breeze is jumping and gettin' BIGGER, and Lincoln finally gets to me, and we haul ASS. Then we walk FOREVER, wondering when time is UP, and the whole place is gonna BLOW, but not talking about it, just doing it, ya know, one foot in front of the other – getting things done, ya know, walking OUT."

Anderson noticed Apoe slightly nodding his head in agreement.

Anderson stopped and pointed at Apoe, "See, he gits it!"

Harris buried his head in his hands. "Aw shit!"

Anderson continued, "That's what we were in, Harris, for sure! I guess Liv had to take out, as in kill a couple of the guards topside, because when we reached the exit, things were pretty messed up. I was totally BUMMIN' about this cause the boys were doing great with no killing. Seein' the dead peopled caused a rumbling DEEP DOWN, and I ran out and hurled dinner on the ROSES. Harris was all cool and helped me out. We went back in, grabbed some NEW LOOKs to wear, and headed to the woods to keep out of sight. And wouldn't you know it! Dr. Apoe comes walkin' DOWN the path and finds us. Says he was using the location device in my jumpsuit. I say that's PRETTY DOPE stuff 'cause we buried that mess when we changed clothes. At first, we dug with sticks like troglodytes till it got stupid, and I said, Lincoln, boy, use what God gave you, and Lincoln was all SHY when he used his stuff to hide where we'd dug the hole. Then, we hopped in Dr. Apoe's car, and as they say, here we are." Anderson opened her arms as though welcoming the world. The supervisor would have expected her to bow if she were not sitting.

"Yes, here you are," the Supervisor said, sounding relieved that Anderson's accounting of the events, while expressive, was short and to the point.

Anderson dropped her arms and looked at Dr. O'Neil, "Anything else you want to know, Dr. O'Neil?"

"Naw, we good," Dr. O'Neil said, leaning back in her chair.

The Supervisor wondered how O'Neil had answered with a straight face.

No one said a word, but it was apparent to them all something had just happened. The Supervisor understood. She needed O'Neil's humor and felt it warm the winter in her heart put there by UT's death. Despite knowing that the loss of Apoe's facility and the staff was not humorous, the Supervisor accepted this group's immediate need to use the time to prove their lives were not over. She was mourning the dead, and so were they. The Supervisor acknowledged that while Anderson's account was less than professional, each person mourned in their own way. She hoped they all felt the warmth the humor produced as it had in her. Soon, they would need to move on, and she hoped Anderson's unique telling of events could provide that walk back to humanity.

"Are you both willing to help us defend this facility against the people that had you placed in Site 35?"

Harris nodded his head, "Most definitely."

"I'm helping if he's helping," Anderson stated.

"You are one strange woman," Harris whispered to her.

"Gotta keep'em guessing. I like Dr. O'Neil," she whispered back.

# CHAPTER 19

The Supervisor ended the meeting. "Please stay a moment, Dr. Apoe. Dr. O'Neil, I'll meet you in your office." Apoe remained seated as everyone stood and exited the conference room. The Supervisor's admin appeared at the conference room door and escorted Harris and Anderson to their temporary living quarters.

Apoe thought, "*What now?*"

"So do we need to worry about Anderson or Harris?" the Supervisor asked.

"Getting right to the point, are we?" Apoe looked at the stern look the Supervisor had on her face and thought better of starting a confrontation. Apoe considered her position a moment. Apoe knew the Supervisor had real concerns about her facility security and trusting unknown people.

"If you mean Anderson's response, she is young, early twenties; I suspect and would expect this type of flippant behavior from her personality and skills."

"What do you mean?"

"The reports I received from the facility staff stated she's a genius. It's not uncommon for people with her mental capabilities to be immature. Anderson hacked into the DoD and CIA by masquerading as a classified satellite. That's pretty good." Apoe could not hide the admiration in his comment.

"There is a fine line, Franklin, between genius and insanity."

"Noted. I don't think that's the case here."

"*That's pretty flimsy and only a hunch, but that's all I've got to go on right now.*" Apoe thought.

"Just a hunch, your intuition then, Franklin. You realize I can't trust your intuition when it comes to defending this facility."

"*Damn, how does she do that?*" Apoe nodded his head.

"Yes, I get it. But I believe…"

"More hunches, Franklin?"

Apoe stopped mid-sentence and changed his thought. *"If she wants a professional opinion, I will provide it for her."*

Apoe began, "My assessment is both Anderson and Harris are trustworthy. Both bring the necessary skills to this program and, if <u>properly led and their efforts directed</u>, could turn into high-value contributors to this organization. I assess their risk to this facility as being small but still possible. Both have experienced events in the last several months that may contribute to future mental instability, but there appears to be a rising dynamic that could mitigate this risk."

"What's that?"

"They seem to have established a friendship despite their different backgrounds. Did you see the way the two interacted here? I observed the same supporting behavior in our car ride once Anderson woke up. They care about each other. Their relationship could be the variable that keeps them working with us. It also means they can support each other if problems do start."

The Supervisor nodded. "Yes, I saw them. Kind of cute."

*"Good, she's backing off the 'I'm in charge' BS."*

Apoe continued, "She is a force of nature, something to be reckoned with. He is a passive, caring person that seems to have found his way despite his past. His experiences with Liv and the third guy…."

"His name was Hoffman," she said.

"His experience with Liv and Hoffman and their exposure to other intelligence seem to be a big part of his change. No surprise, given our shared experiences with whatever happens to people with these gifts. Knowing what happens if you abuse those gifts is a real motivator to changing any thoughts of senseless destruction."

"Does she know about his past?"

"That he murdered his parents? Yes. He told her on the trip up despite me being there in the car with them. He accepts what he's done and wants to atone for it."

"How did she respond?"

"She handled it well. She sees Harris as the victim that has paid his debt to society. She reached over the seat and took his hand when he told her. They are both looking for a new start. There's real caring there."

"There is a real risk here," the Supervisor said.

Apoe spoke calmly, attempting to convince the Supervisor of his convictions. "That's our job, to take risks. This program's original supervisor took huge risks to create what you have today. He believed, despite the probabilities, he could build something of value for our nation, and he did. Despite the risks, those two will be assets, not liabilities."

*"There, he'd said it. His ass was now officially hanging in the wind. He had personally vouched for Anderson and Harris. If things went south, he would be the one responsible."*

The Supervisor thought a moment, then looked into Apoe's eyes across the table.

"Okay," she acknowledged. She stood up and walked around the conference room table to Apoe's side. "I have one more problem."

*"Here it comes,"* Apoe thought. *"Our past relationship, personal baggage. Can't stay here."*

"Yes," he said calmly.

"I recently learned a dear friend and the Chief Medical Officer for the program committed suicide."

"Oh, God. How did it happen?"

"He was grabbed by the CIA, Franklin. They took him for questioning. I knew nothing about it. He prepared for an event like this. He ended his life before providing any program secrets to the agency. If you think your 'treason' will be a problem, I suspect they already know you are here, thanks to security checking your credentials downstairs. I don't think they will move on you yet. You are under my protection. But you must know you are getting into something really ugly too. This loss cannot go unanswered."

Apoe grasped what she was saying, stood up, and embraced her. She surprised him and pulled him close. He had always thought she valued her work over human companionship, and those relationships she built were strictly for accomplishing the job. He was wrong. He could sense her pain and admired her for her strength in handling the meeting just moments before under these conditions.

*"My God, she has a full plate right now."*

The closeness between the two caused Apoe's thoughts to drift from supporting the person who opened him to love's existence years ago to who he was, a man in the arms of this beautiful woman. Apoe's mind unlocked long-closed areas, allowing everything he felt for this woman to pour through, fueling the feelings he believed buried years ago. Now his emotions were betraying him, rising like the phoenix from the ashes. He hated the stirring and feelings happening south of his waist and recognized the movement of his growing erection immediately. His physical response was a betrayal of his commitment to never allow love into his life again after her. His physical response mocked his long success of withdrawing from his emotions. He pulled away, embarrassed, and hopefully before she noticed anything.

"I'm sorry," she said, pulling back from the embrace. The Supervisor stood erect and sniffed while wiping away a tiny tear with her fingers.

"That's terrible news."

"Thank you, Franklin," One last sniffle. "Yes, which brings me back to my problem. I need a new Chief Medical Officer. I want you to take the job."

*"What the hell! I was not expecting this?"*

Apoe considered what she was asking. She needed him now more than ever; he would not dispute this. While he would have to learn what his predecessor had done, he had the medical training. He was the only person in the world with three paranormal experiences involving situations like Harris, counting site 35. If he was being honest, this is what he wanted. Apoe chose to come back to her after leaving his facility. He changed his thinking about his career and life, his own redemption, as he called it. This woman was the missing piece of his soul's restoration and connection to the living. He was unsure of their future, but he knew being with her was his first step at reconciling the hole in his heart created when they separated. He never wanted the destruction or whatever the hell had happened to his site; no sane leader would. He knew he would need to deal with those emotions later when he had more facts. But right now, Apoe knew that night in his office where he declared 'no more needless pain of others' that his beliefs now aligned with hers. He wanted this.

"Before you answer, I want you to know I've scheduled a meeting, time to be determined, for tomorrow with Senator Hurst and Dr. Carol Lucia. This meeting is about the situation I explained, and I could use your help. I need someone with your credentials I can trust. I want you to attend."

"That's pretty tall cotton. A powerhouse senator and the National Security Advisor."

*"Play this next part correctly, Apoe."*

"Under one condition. For now, this is a temporary job for me."

The Supervisor fired quickly, "Afraid to commit Franklin?"

*"Ouch, that stung! Keep your cool. Stay calm."*

"Sorry," the Supervisor said. "That was unfair. I would appreciate your help if only temporarily."

"Okay then, count me in. But now I have one question."

The Supervisor cocked her head, smiled slightly, and said slowly, "Yes?"

"How do I address you?"

"Do you understand why my true name is masked?"

"I have an idea why it is," Apoe said, thinking immediately of the meeting with the National Security Advisor the next day.

"Good. Then Ms. Supervisor works." The Supervisor

looked back into his eyes and said sincerely, "Thank you, Franklin, and welcome to the team."

# CHAPTER 20

The Supervisor sat quietly with her thoughts in the conference room. Senator Hurst had called her with a confirmation time for today's meeting the previous evening. For the first time in months, she slept in her temporary living quarters at the facility, not wanting to be away from the building and the strength she needed, created daily by a loyal staff committed to their work.

She awoke early and met Dr. O'Neil in the Washington, D.C. facility, where they witnessed UT's last preparations and farewell in the system's crematorium. She did not wish to say any final words, nor did Dr. O'Neil. No one knew UT as they did and selfishly decided not to share their memories, most of which were classified above the security personnel and small medical staff in attendance. She signed the death certificate as part of her official duties. UT was the official listing for the deceased name. Somewhere in one of Dr. O'Neil's databases, a digital key linked two tables that would unite his title to the real identity of the man that gave so much to his nation. It was heartbreaking that outside the walls of the facility, no one would bow their head and remember the passing of this great man, for to them, he never existed.

She acknowledged the need to think about the future. UT's passing delineated the closing of a project phase and began a transition into a redefined mission and operational improvement. UT created the medical protocols enabling the VLIP program to offer the most significant value to the nation. The medical team under Dr. Apoe would continue to refine and enhance those capabilities. But Dr. Apoe would also bring experience to the program no one could have envisioned at its creation, not even the first Supervisor, Matthew Boyd. His extraordinary vision was to solve the nation's crime problem, find a way to redeem each inmate, and reintroduce them back to society as contributing citizens. A noble pursuit for a great man. But alas, not even the great Boyd could have foreseen the SOUP as the pathway to creating a new type of human capable of altering physical reality with their thoughts. This background made Apoe very valuable in a different way than UT. Apoe was the most experienced professional in the world involving paranormal activities, and only he knew details of the events, their conditions, and outcomes. The facts about who the Shiny Ones were and why they controlled the use of the gifts eluded them. If the SOUP's purpose for the nation were evolving to produce the next generation of super soldiers, she at least would like to understand who was creating them. She understood their genesis, not the reason or purpose, at least the quantifiable one.

However, she could not deny the power of their message and its impact on her. "How will you live the rest of your life?" Was it a warning? She had taken it as a call to action, and now it appeared Apoe had done the same. When did he realize his experimental lab mice had become humans with souls with lives he was taking from them? And for what, the greater good? Did Apoe finally understand he wanted to change how he lived the rest of his life? If she was honest with herself, she was glad he was here. Did he change his life for her? Was there some power that, as UT departed, orchestrated the arrival of Apoe? She stuck a pin in those thoughts for later and focused back on the challenge in front of her.

Was it the fate of all humanity to try and improve and one day rise above the pettiness that separated people, or was our species destined to drive itself to extinction with false intellect and rationalization? She had to admit that even in a program with noble purposes, such as the SOUP, they had abused their power and put 230 innocent people into a virtual world, disrupting their real lives. Who would judge their actions for that move? Was the team meeting today any nobler than those they were opposing? Perhaps that was the answer to the simple question of 'who is right,' she struggled with so often. Maybe using the SOUP to create these 'new warriors' the Vice President wanted was not wrong and could prove to be a great asset for defense, but without further information and facts, the risks were too high to create them now. Maybe it was not an issue of right or wrong but just making big mistakes, each derived from ignorance, disregard for outcomes, power, and hubris, resulting in innocent deaths she opposed so much. Perhaps, the issue wasn't wrong; just the means the Vice President used to bring it about. Future paranormal warfighters: she was still fuzzy on how she felt about those. Ignorance of the risks of controlling that power and the demise of innocents, the Supervisor had no ambiguity about evil as their source and her need to fight them. The VP's way, she was convinced, had already caused multiple needless deaths, including UT's. That was unacceptable.

As her admin appeared in the doorway, the Supervisor knew her guests were arriving and moving through security. She acknowledged her assistant with a nod and finalized her analysis. The SOUP is still an incredible asset for the nation; even creating people with gifts to protect the lives of all might have its place in the mission. She resolved her remaining thoughts and concluded, *"it is the methods and moral compass this administration uses to implement their power that needs to be opposed, not their purpose. The value of their purpose remains to be determined."* Her mind was clear. UT would be the last to die on her watch.

The Supervisor stood up as her guests arrived at the conference room door. She leaned over to her admin and said, "Let Doctors Apoe and O'Neil know our guests are here." The admin excused herself and departed to her office to make the calls.

"Ms. Supervisor, it is good to see you again," Senator Hurst said. "May I introduce you to our National Security Advisor, Dr. Carol Lucia?"

The Supervisor looked closely at Dr. Lucia. She was an attractive professional who had been impressive in her recent fight with the Vice President to block the presidential directive.

"Welcome to the Facility."

"It's a pleasure to be here, Ms. Supervisor. Senator Hurst speaks highly of you,"

"It's the Senator's job to speak highly of everyone," the Supervisor said. Both women laughed as Hurst said, "Guilty as charged."

Dr. O'Neil walked up. Dr. Lucia and Dr. O'Neil exchanged cordial greetings. The Supervisor realized the two must cross paths frequently with Dr. O'Neil's other programs in the Defense Department. "You two know each other, I take it," the Supervisor said, pointing to the chairs.

"Yes, ma'am. Dr. Lucia and I work together occasionally, supporting special projects." The Supervisor was already aware of Senator Hurst's and Dr. O'Neil's relationship that pre-dated the incident with Supervisor Boyd. Each was seated when Dr. Apoe arrived. The Supervisor smiled and said, "Dr. Apoe, please join us."

"Senator Hurst, Dr. Lucia, this is Dr. Franklin Apoe, my new acting Chief Medical Officer." Each acknowledged Apoe with a nod as he moved to his seat.

Hurst and Lucia looked at the Supervisor. "Ms. Supervisor, may I offer my condolences on your recent loss. Senator Hurst has filled me in," Lucia said.

"Thank you, Dr. Lucia. Mr. UT will be missed." The Supervisor paused a moment before saying, "Thank you all for coming. We have a lot to discuss today. I want everyone to discuss what has happened in their areas, so we all share the same information. Much of what we cover will be at the various security levels, but it's my opinion our decisions today will set in motion the defense of this program. I ask we suspend all restrictions on information sharing. I believe each of us understands the significance of having the meeting. Is this agreeable?"

Everyone nodded their heads in agreement.

Senator Hurst, will you lead off, please."

"Sure. Let's start with the program's governance board, called the Committee. Vice President Morrison placed the committee under the Central Intelligence Agency and used that as his authority to take the Chairman position and add the Director of the CIA to the membership. He now controls the direction of the program and its leaning towards Defense and Intelligence."

"To piggyback, the President signed a classified Directive placing this program under the CIA," Lucia added. "He pulled a complete end-around with POTUS using the intelligence to resolve the Taiwan Strait incident to justify the move."

"I'm the new guy," Apoe said. "So, what's the Vice President trying to do?"

"I'll talk to the political motive," Hurst said. "It's the Presidency. Everyone knows POTUS thinks of Morrison as his heir apparent. Morrison might likely win, but he saw how positively the American people responded to the announcement of the SOUP to handle crime. This new approach using the SOUP won the last election for POTUS. Morrison wants to use the SOUP to win by promising decreased crime and future enhancements, as in protection from future wars with the special weapons he will produce. Americans get nervous about nukes, but they like Special Forces groups like the Seals, Delta, Green Berets, etc. He'll announce a new Special Forces group when convenient. While he won't need to explain how they do it, this nation will be light years ahead of anyone with Remote Viewing capabilities for Intel collection and when DoD troops are needed...."

"Super soldiers," Apoe finished.

Both Lucia and Hurst nodded.

"So as the future president, he will use an announcement of the SOUP's success to win the election and then, unknown to the American people, deploy the assets to make our capabilities untouchable by the rest of the world. The American people know the SOUP has fixed crime but have no idea it is producing other capabilities. Morrison shows international as well as domestic success. This move would make him a formidable president, and if the people buy into his promises, it assures the election." Consolidating these programs under the Executive Branch puts him in control of everything. Something of this magnitude must be shared between Congress and the White House." Hurst concluded. "There is too much power for one branch."

"My concern is the National Security Component. Morrison's seen the videos of what the inmates can do," Lucia said. "He has Director Thompson and Secretary Wellsley all fired up to use these inmates to re-create the capabilities and use them on our adversaries. We don't even know what these people can do or how to control these gifts. This risk is just as possible to drive us to war as to prevent it."

The Supervisor nodded. Her thoughts exactly.

"It gets worse," The Supervisor began. "In the last committee meeting, the Vice President ordered the program to provide him with the Exit sequence. I told him we didn't understand how the inmates were released in Los Angeles. He told me to experiment with my existing inmates to find the solution and provide it to him. I think the VP is obsessed with creating these paranormal assets. Up to now, the DoD and CIA have tried different ideas with the paranormal, but these inmates are game changers. Right now, I have our committee members pounding down my door asking when I will share the Exit info so the DoD can begin building their new facilities. I have new states encouraging me to support the Vice President's program. Morrison has promised them funding – about a billion and a half each, for new contracts, which means new hires with their constituents. Every politician knows jobs equal re-election. No offense, Senator."

Hurst smiled at the Supervisor, "None taken, Ma'am. You speak the truth."

Lucia was angry, "That's great! As President of the Senate, he's bought off congress in the new states where DoD and Intel facilities will be built! How many new locations Ms.

Supervisor?"

"Six new states," the Supervisor paused for the information to be absorbed, "each with high electoral counts. All six want some facility in their state, and our existing six want DoD facilities. At 50 billion a year in cost avoidance in lower crime, legacy prison costs reductions, and revenue from the Elder Care Program, and cost of 12 times 1.5 billion - or 18 billion is roughly 36% of the 50 billion. I hate to say it, but the government can actually afford it,"

"That should get him some real political support," Hurst said. "I had no idea he had that many planned."

"And they're all waiting on me," the Supervisor said.

"And they'll be waiting a while longer, too," Dr. O'Neil added.

The Supervisor acknowledged the commitment of Dr. O'Neil. UT was an exceptional colleague and friend to her as well. Dr. O'Neil was ready for a fight.

"Dr. Apoe," the Supervisor said. "Could you bring everyone up to date with your information?"

Apoe cleared his throat. "I was the Facility Director of Site 35."

"The mid-Atlantic paranormal research facility," Lucia commented. "I've been briefed on some of your programs."

"Me as well," Hurst added.

"So, each of you knows what 'happens' at site 35." Both guests nodded. Apoe continued, "Good. Several weeks ago, we received new guests at the facility. The first one, Sarah Anderson, arrived because she'd hacked into the CIA and DoD computers to retrieve video of the escaped inmates."

"She's the person who got me my videos? I had no idea," Lucia said. "Where is she now?"

Apoe looked at the Supervisor for the green light. "Dr. Apoe, feel free to share all information with Senator Hurst and Dr. Lucia."

Apoe continued, "Three floors down."

Lucia's amazement was observable to all.

"The second set of guests were the escaped inmates themselves. The facility anticipated their arrival and, using previous similar experiences, had developed countermeasures to block their gifts. The first is a device that can impede frequency transmission within telepathy's band. We call them blockers. Once we blocked telepathy, we administered a comprehensive regimen of barbiturates that inhibited thought and suppressed receptors to the pineal gland. I hate to admit it, but we kept them drugged to protect the facility."

"Why was Anderson brought to your facility?" Hurst asked.

"The DoD placed a liaison office there to look for hackers with 'unique skills and problem-solving. A hacker with these talents could discover means to access adversary computers. Anderson has these skills and impressed the liaison office chief. Anderson was offered a chance to work with her. At this time, I realized I oversaw programs that destroyed lives and sometimes even subject deaths. Shortly after these three arrived, I decided I'd had enough. So, I made arrangements for Anderson, Livingston, and Harris' escape. For these three, I could control facility security and other infrastructure. Many other programs were locked down and outside of my reach. I took the inmates off their drugs and brought Anderson into my confidence. During the escape, Livingston remained behind. All we know is he and the facility are gone."

"Gone, what do you mean gone?"

"Senator, I mean gone."

"I was briefed it was no longer operational but GONE. That's something different. It was a submerged facility in the Chesapeake Bay," Lucia's amazement became evident as she commented and then asked, "So that was you?"

"Yes, ma'am, that was me."

"So that means by my count, only one inmate is left. Where is he?" Lucia shifted in her chair, unsure she wanted the answer.

"Three floors down," Apoe responded. "I tracked them

using devices we place in each guest's jumpsuits. We re-connected and drove to this facility."

The expressions on Lucia and Hurst's faces told the Supervisor to provide a pause before continuing. The senator performed basic calculations on the paper pad supplied in front of him, and Lucia jotted down a few questions to jog her memory later. Lucia broke the silence and looked at Hurst, "Ready to proceed?" Hurst nodded.

The Supervisor continued. "So now, let's get to the real challenge facing us," the Supervisor began. "Our cooperation with this Administration and defense of the Program's facilities. We've discussed the Vice President's obsession with seeking the information that will allow him to control the Exit of his new warriors. Let's also not forget the VP's desire for this information brought about UT's death. We've also discussed the value of what the Vice President and his team are trying to accomplish. While his proposal may benefit the nation, his methods of gaining this new capability give me great cause to question what he would do with the power once he has it. On this point, I agree with you, Senator Hurst. You have always proposed studying the idea but advocated for the correct checks and balances if we moved forward. Morrison wants this on his schedule, and we've discussed his political motives. These motives have resulted in unnecessary deaths, including the loss of CIA agents during custody of my inmates after the Los Angeles remote viewing session. The botched attempt to apprehend them in Las Vegas all contributed to the body count, and for what reason?

I believe power. Our revolution was fought in this country not because we no longer wanted to be English but because King George and members of his government were taking away our liberties. The idea of not being English and following English law was secondary to how the King exercised his power."

"So, you are not opposed to creating these new assets, just the way the Vice President wants it done?" Hurst said.

"Yes, I want no further deaths because of his political impatience. We don't know the full extent of what we have created. We must proceed with caution or lose control," the Supervisor replied.

"My liaison to the agency died mysteriously after delivering me the videos. While the investigation is closed, dying by automobile accident is not the reason I attribute to COL Baxter's death. I knew his family well, and they agreed with me. The true cause of his death is being covered up," Lucia said.

"This administration is not evil, just these select people within it. We will not change the President's mind. He doesn't know what he is doing with this directive, just that the White House gets the intel as long as the President agrees with Morrison," Dr. O'Neil added.

The Supervisor noticed a red message notification button on the conference room telephone. Her admin knew not to disturb them unless there was an emergency. The Supervisor looked over at Dr. O'Neil, got her attention with her eyes, and used them to look at the blinking indicator and then at the door. Dr. O'Neil understood, stood up, and walked out of the conference room. No one commented on her departure. The conversation progressed.

"Can we begin by agreeing on two major items before looking to develop our response plan?" the Supervisor asked.

Without waiting for a response, she continued, "Number 1. We agree the Exit solution will be protected at all costs, and Number 2. Of the three inmates Exiting the SOUP, only one remains. Harris appears to be working with us. We should no longer feel we must defend ourselves or the facilities from the escaped inmates and their special gifts."

She looked at the other attendees. All nodded their heads in agreement. "Good. I want to proceed with our response options. Dr. Apoe and I have evaluated each one and feel you will conclude as we have. Any questions before we get started?"

Hurst and Lucia shook their heads. "Let's proceed," Hurst said.

Apoe walked through the first option and presented the information for Protecting the Facilities. Each agreed the number of people required to protect the Program facilities was sufficient with existing security now that the threat of paranormal attacks by the inmates was off the table.

The second option Apoe presented involved destroying the Program's incarceration facilities. The result, he stated, was to prevent the Administration from seizing one or more of these facilities and using them as laboratories to perfect their Exit protocols. It was dismissed outright by Hurst and Lucia as causing each inmate to die and the nation losing its asset to house the worst criminals. Lucia raised the moral issue that equated the program with the administration in terms of destroying innocent lives. Hurst opposed the political fallout from losing the SOUP capabilities, which was overwhelmingly popular with the public.

Option 3 involved leaking all the known information they possessed to the press. None of the attendees could show a positive outcome of the story.

"So that brings us to option 4," Apoe started. "While this has the highest risk for the program and us personally, it also has the best results and outcomes."

"Always saving the best for last," Hurst said, smiling.

"Let's hear it," Lucia said.

"Our problem is not with POTUS and his administration," Apoe began, "but with only three men. The Vice President, Director of the CIA, and the Secretary of Defense."

"That's your information so far," Lucia commented. "There may be others."

"We believe these three are the only senior leaders aware of all the details we have. Of course, we have the Committee members from congress, and there may be others with knowledge of recent events, like the president's Chief of Staff, but these three are setting the agenda to take the program."

"Our analysis of the Las Vegas incident proves the violence was initiated when the CIA arrived. The DoD had the situation under control, and Livingston and Harris surrendered to the Special Ops team after the CIA assets were taken out. Both men had agreed to surrender peacefully to the DoD. Harris confirmed this for us recently," the Supervisor added.

Lucia affirmed the statement, "Our analysis showed us the same thing. So, are you saying the DoD may not be as involved as the other two?"

"We don't know," the Supervisor answered. "But we can't assume Wellsley is any less a threat. While the CIA would benefit from Remote Viewers, the number of individuals Thompson needs is small compared to Wellesley's soldiers with telekinesis capabilities. Wellesley's role may be developing. Of the three, we have the least information on his activities and support to the VP."

"Ok, call me impatient, but what's your option?" Lucia inquired.

"Take these three off the chessboard," Apoe answered. "Remove the key leaders and remove the threat to the Program."

No one spoke, each person contemplating the impact of the presented option.

Hurst broke the silence. "Are you talking about assassinating three of the President's most powerful heads of government?" His question was void of emotion.

"No, Senator," the Supervisor responded. "We've already discussed the moral implications of taking another life for our gain. That solution is unacceptable, and everything else that goes with an assassination."

"Well, it can't be kidnapping. That's ludicrous. The security details for each of these men make that impossible. Plus, kidnapping is a temporary solution. You can't hold them forever as a prisoner for an unproven crime," Lucia said.

"Unless you plan to kidnap each somehow and place them in the SOUP," Lucia thought out loud. "But that is equally undoable since you can't explain where three key leaders disappeared to the public."

"All good points, but that's not the option," Apoe said.

"So, just what are you proposing?" Hurst asked, his tone becoming very serious.

The question hung in the air, unanswered by the Supervisor or Apoe. The very ramifications of the answer had given the Supervisor deep feelings of disgust when she discussed the option with Apoe when preparing for this very moment. While filling her with disdain, she knew it was the only answer that made sense.

"Ms. Supervisor?"

"*Here goes*," she thought. "A series of accidents."

"Accidents?" Lucia asked.

"A series of accidents that will not raise the public's attention," Apoe said.

"You mean like COL Baxter's accident. Everything was thoroughly investigated and wrapped up nicely into a bulletproof police report. I'm not listening to this." Lucia stood up.

"Please sit down, Dr. Lucia and listen to the approach before making your final decision," Apoe offered.

Senator Hurst remained seated and stared at a fixed point on the wall in front of him.

Lucia looked at Senator Hurst. "Senator, do you hear what's being considered?"

"I hear it, Dr. Lucia. I must say, I would like to hear more before making my decision."

Dr. Lucia looked at Senator Hurst, then at the Supervisor. She sat back down, sighing as she did. "This is crazy."

"Our plan is simple. We will find each of the three men when they are most vulnerable and, without causing death, inhibit them from being able to continue with their objectives for our program."

"Tell me how you justify inhibiting them if death is not the outcome," Hurst said. "You intend to physically and mentally cripple or damage them?"

"No, Senator, we do not. The solution lies in an idea that Dr. O'Neil and UT were working on when we discovered the inmates from Los Angeles had re-discovered their old memories and realized they were criminals. We were looking to use this as an additional safeguard as we released inmates back into society. The two began prototyping something called the VITP or the Violence Inhibitor Treatment Protocol."

"What does it do?" Hurst asked.

"It came to us that of all the places to study brain wave patterns representing violent acts; the SOUP was at the top of the list. Every day, our inmates carry out murders, rapes, and other forms of crime in the SOUP, and we record every one of them. Fortunately, we have the data patterns and brain wave signatures from the community database. Our Washington, D.C. facility provided the baseline, and the other facilities confirmed the signatures. We have cataloged hundreds of signature brainwaves associated with their violence."

"So, how do you use these patterns," Lucia asked.

"Our brainwave signatures are not unlike the signatures associated with computer viruses.

The VITP involves implanting nanoscopic, undetectable devices to monitor brain wave activity. The body would accept these devices and eventually fold them into the brain tissue. Each nanodevice would analyze the men's thought patterns and compare them with an internal library of brainwave patterns associated with war, killing, or other destructive thoughts. If it detects a close enough match, the device will transmit electrical signals that overload the brain's synaptic connections and neural transmitters. It will use specific random frequency waves that cancel the violent thoughts and cause confusion. This 'brain fog' will disrupt problem-solving and inhibit the body's physical response. When the brain waves change frequency and return to normal thoughts, the confusion will stop, and the body's motor functions will return. It creates the conditions like walking into a room and forgetting why you entered. It's very passive, very non-evasive."

"You mean you can temporarily paralyze brain activity and prevent physical action based on the brain's thought patterns? Do you have this type of capability?"

"We are working on it, Senator. UTs death has put us behind schedule, but Dr. Apoe is familiar enough with the technology to assist Dr. O'Neil."

"That's amazing!" Lucia smiled broadly as her mind raced with applications for the technology.

"Brain waves are forms of electrical energy sent between the neurons, Dr. Lucia. Negating or confusing the wave signal is not a difficult task. We are closer than you might believe," Apoe said.

"This is an amazing idea, Ms. Supervisor!" Hurst exclaimed.

"The hard part of this technology is matching the existing transmission of electrical energy to specific wave patterns indicating violence. Programming the nanodevices will not be difficult, and Dr. O'Neil assures me the devices, because of their size, will not be detectable with X-rays or other scanning tools," the Supervisor concluded.

"How would you implant the device?"

"Injection would be the preferred technique," Apoe replied.

"As to the justification. Removing these three from their positions and using this type of passive solution would save countless lives and keep the incarceration program free from National Security involvement. We each know their commitment to do anything, including harm to others, so that they can build their new breed of soldier. We could return to our previous mission while working with the Agency and DoD to study the outcomes of producing the types of warriors they want. Right now, they are only looking at the positive results of these gifts regardless of the deaths they have caused, not considering the high potential for negative consequences to the warriors themselves. As I said earlier, it is not the idea of producing their warriors we should oppose, but the methods and schedule they are imposing, which has already cost lives."

"Okay, let's say you can develop and perfect this miracle solution. Finding the schedules and most vulnerable times will be difficult. Other than the Vice President's calendar, the rest are classified and protected on the Agency systems."

"Ms. Anderson, Dr. Lucia," Apoe replied. "If Ms. Anderson can hack the DoD's and CIA's most sensitive systems, finding the schedules of these men should be fairly easy."

"I like this idea Ms. Supervisor. I have one other question. How do you intend to get close enough to make the injection? All three have agency or Secret Service teams that will not let you get within at least a hundred yards unless you are cleared."

"Dr. Lucia, we intend to use Mr. Harris. He has already told us he would be willing to help us. Using his gifts, he could immobilize or put to sleep the security detail when they are at their lowest number and not surrounded by the public. Access problem solved."

Senator Hurst and Dr. Lucia looked at each other. "This is a sound plan, Ms. Supervisor. You and your team have thought this through very well."

"When will you have the device ready, Ms. Supervisor?"

"I need three more months for a working prototype. Now that Dr. Apoe is here, we may be able to shorten the schedule."

Dr. Lucia nodded. "You will let us know when you are ready to begin? I will not support our actions without the device you explained."

"Of course, Dr. Lucia, Senator Hurst. We will keep you informed."

"You know, Ms. Supervisor, with this technology, you may be able to replace your facilities in the future with just a shot," Hurst said.

"Senator, in theory, yes, which is why we are evaluating the facilities for National Security application. If the VITP works, we could be out of a job without the National Security mission. However, we have years of testing and social impact evaluations to conduct before shutting things down. We will always, unfortunately, have criminals."

Hurst nodded his head in agreement. "Quite right, Ms. Supervisor."

"One last thing Ms. Supervisor. If Sarah Anderson decides she no longer wants to support our efforts, please tell her Colonel Baxter was killed by the people we are trying to stop."

"I understand, Dr. Lucia. I hope it won't come to that. Thank you. Any objections with the current course of action to protect our facilities?"

"What do we do until you take action?" Hurst asked

"I would like you to run interference in Congress and the Whitehouse. Deflect attention away from the program when possible and broker the meetings that will be inevitable to settle this matter if we're successful. Lastly, remain detached from what we do, but any intelligence information you can provide will be greatly appreciated."

"I like it. Support but retain deniability," Lucia said. "More cloak and dagger stuff."

"Exactly." The Supervisor said. "It's time for us to take the fight to them."

# CHAPTER 21

Lincoln Harris and Sarah Anderson were locked in their temporary quarters. The admin offered a chance to stay in one room or two. Sarah chose one. The admin assured privacy in the room and informed them permanent jobs would be assigned shortly. A program job would give them greater freedom within the facility, as the job offer confirmed the Supervisor's trust.

They understood why the restrictions were needed and agreed. The admin showed them to their room, and she explained Dr. Apoe would pick them up for additional interviews with Dr. O'Neil and tour the facilities. The admin explained Apoe was currently in a meeting and would be by as soon as possible, estimated 45 minutes. Lincoln and Sarah still felt uncomfortable when they heard the door lock but believed this time was not permanent.

They surveyed the room, which was decorated and furnished much like site 35. Harris sat down on a chair, and Anderson sat cross-legged on the bed.

"I assume there is a reason why you chose one room before dinner as opposed to our separate rooms," Harris began

"There is Lincoln. While the Supervisor and Dr. Apoe are doing whatever, I wanted to take this time to talk."

"About what?"

"About you. You know, where you come from, why you killed your parents, you know, simple stuff."

"It doesn't sound so simple to me."

"Let's give it a try." Sarah bounced on the bed, changing from cross-legged to lying on her stomach. She created a cradle with her hands for her chin and intertwined her legs, causing the feet to face airborne. Anderson's position and mannerisms reminded Harris of a high school girl sharing at a slumber party.

"Sarah, maybe we shouldn't discuss this now."

Anderson moved to the second chair in the room and sat down, creating a balanced distance between the two. This simple gesture made Harris feel he could talk with her as an adult, and she would take his comments seriously.

"You know," she started. "If we are going to work together, it would be helpful to understand some of your experiences. I might even be able to help resolve some of your internal conflicts."

"What conflicts?"

"Well, to start with, how do you separate your memories before the SOUP with those you built while..."

"In the SOUP," Harris finished.

"Yes."

Harris thought for a moment. *This was a pretty good question. I'm not sure I understand the answer myself.*

"Well, I think it comes down to understanding the stark difference between the two types of memories. When I Exited the SOUP, my life consisted of positive memories; high school football athlete heading to a university on a scholarship, decent grades, partying, girls, all the basic stuff for having a great life at that age."

"What changed?"

"Everything. Our gifts were used to do something called remote viewing. We were told we needed to help fix a crisis in the Taiwan Straits, so we did. But afterward, I felt drained, like I could sleep for a week."

"Did you, you know, sleep a long time?"

"Yep. All three of us did, and when we woke up, our memories changed. The stuff that used to be my nightmares was now my real life. By using that part of our brain, Liv and I think we tapped into our old memories and realized they were our real lives or something like that."

"So, how do you deal with having two different sets of memories?"

"This may sound strange, but I look at them as my real

life and what it could be. The SOUP memories are what could be. They are distinct, and all are good memories. It's almost like the movie 'It's A Wonderful Life.' George Bailey was shown his life if he died jumping off the bridge. He could see the good he accomplished by staying alive. We'll for me, I can see the bad. I want to change."

"That's a good example. That helps me to understand better."

"Here's the weird part. All three of us, staying with the Wonderful Life example, were visited by an angel, or so we think."

"What did they say?"

"It asked a simple question."

"What did it ask?"

"How will you live the rest of your life? That question forced us to evaluate both sets of memories. Liv and I discussed this as often as Liv would agree to talk about it. Both sets of memories became a choice for us. We knew the bad, and we knew the good. We just had to choose. We knew we could not change the past but were shown a new future. Once we understood this, the memories became nothing more than examples of right and wrong, like watching a movie that has a big impact on you. The movie becomes part of your memories. After you evaluate the movie as good or bad, you can choose what parts you want to believe. That belief can change your life."

Harris paused and looked at the ceiling. "Without realizing it and talking this through, I guess I always knew why the conflict was never a problem for us."

"Do you feel normal?"

"Yes, there are no conflicts with my memories. Just two movies, and I get to choose parts of each that will influence my future actions. Did you ever have a movie change your life?"

Sarah smiled. "Yes, there were a couple."

"Okay, you tell me yours."

"Ever heard of a movie called 'War Games'?"

"Nope."

"Short version for you. Of course, two young kids, a boy, and a girl, at the beginning of home computers and the internet. The boy learns how to hack different systems, changing grades is one example, but his big hack is a defense system. He hacks NORAD thinking it's a new game. He almost starts World War III."

"What happens?"

"Typical adventure movie. Boy and girl prevent the war using logic with a computer that thinks the US is under attack. The logic used is Tick-Tac-Toe. Anyway, it gets successfully rolled up in about an hour and a half, and no World War III. However, the movie showed me what I could do with computers. I did not want to start the next big war but prevent it. That movie motivated me to learn computers and get really good at understanding them. Next thing I know, I have customers asking for my help and paying big bucks. One day Colonel Baxter reaches out to me. I like him. He's one of the good guys trying to keep the lid from blowing off the can with all we are involved in. I don't know how he found me; probably a referral. I did about four jobs for him before he asked me to get the videos of you guys, and the rest, they say, is history."

"Were you serious with the Supervisor when you said you would help her?"

Harris could see the wheels turning in Anderson's head as she sought the answer. "I'm not sure, Lincoln. Most of me says 'yes,' but another part says to be careful of the Supervisor. I believe we are not seeing the whole picture. Who uses a cover name, runs a program like this, and doesn't have skeletons in the closet and an agenda of her own? I ask you."

"Dr. Apoe then?"

"Good guy. He helped us get out of Site 35 or whatever it's called. I can trust him, for now."

"How about you? Haven't you, you know, looked into their minds to get the answers?"

"I'm trying to be respectful and not eavesdrop on

everyone. Besides, I don't look INTO people's minds. I hear what they think, like a radio turning to a broadcasting station."

"That's cool. I can see that. So, let's get back to the memories with girls. What types of girls did you hang with in the SOUP? I would guess as a football jock, you hung with whores and sluts."

"Sarah," Harris said, sounding disappointed. "Sometimes you are just too direct."

"What, whores and sluts? These are just terms of endearment where I come from."

Harris shook his head, then stood up and walked towards her chair. He dropped to one knee when he reached her and took her hand. Anderson did not pull hers away. Harris looked up and found her eyes, two twinkling gems captivating him with their sparkle. Harris leaned forward and gently kissed her lips. She responded more passionately, parting his lips with her tongue and pulling his head closer, gently but firmly, while still holding his other hand. Harris did not doubt her response to his kiss, which was evolving into an expression of emotional turbulence that lit up Harris' senses. After the kiss concluded, Harris pulled back and asked, "Have you ever been in love, Sarah?"

Sarah slowly pulled her hand away and broke eye contact. "I think we're done talking now," she said demurely.

Harris had promised himself he would respect individual boundaries but wanted to know the answer to the question, but more importantly, what did she want him to do now? He slowly turned up his internal volume control to detect her thoughts, filling the space around him with her passionate energy that resonated to his toes. Harris heard nothing. He increased his energy to hear more of his surroundings and only silence.

"Something's wrong," he said, breaking the developing sexual mood. He repeated himself, this time more frantically, "Something is definitely wrong!"

"I thought the kiss was pretty good, personally

speaking."

"That was very nice," he offered. "Sarah, I can't hear anyone. I can't hear you, the people outside this room. Nothing, only silence."

"Were you just listening to my head?"

"Look, don't be angry. That was incredibly nice. Yes, I wanted to know what you wanted to do next. So, I tried to hear what you were thinking."

"You son of a..."

"Look, Sarah. Think about me here. It's not always you. You are one of the first girls that ever paid attention to me. I really like you. I do not want to mess this up."

"We'll come back to that comment later! For now, calm down. Tell me what's happening."

"I can't hear anyone anymore."

"You told me in the car Apoe's team had these blockers; you called them. They kept you from hearing people around you. Do you think they've turned one on here as well?"

"It's possible, I guess. Let me try something else. The only way they could block our telekinetic gifts was to keep us drugged so we couldn't focus on using them. Let me try something."

Harris closed his eyes and moved his arms in a swooping motion. Nothing in the room moved.

"What the hell does that do, Lincoln?"

"Let me try something else." Harris focused his thoughts on dimming the lights.

"Something's happening. The lights are dimming," Sarah reported. "Okay, now they're off."

"*Good. Still got it.*" Harris felt relieved. He focused his thoughts on turning the lights back on.

"Nothing happening. Still in the dark here."

Harris tried to focus harder on turning the lights back on. From inside, he could feel the familiar warmth in the center of his forehead but could not visualize the lights returning to their previous brightness. Harris opened his eyes to a pitch-black room, unable to see any expression on Sarah's face. He heard her movements but could not determine her direction. Harris was experiencing a smaller version of vertigo, having difficulty processing his surroundings, when the overhead lights illuminated their space again with fluorescence. Harris's vertigo stabilized as he made out the features in the room. Sarah had turned on the overhead lights.

"You okay, Lincoln?"

"I'm not sure. I want to try one more thing." Harris closed his eyes again and visualized the table lamp levitating into midair.

"Nothing's happening," he heard.

Harris opened his eyes. Nothing had moved.

"What does this mean, Lincoln?"

"I don't know, but I don't think it's good."

Both turned suddenly at the sound of the door lock buzzing. It was pushed open by Dr. Apoe, who calmly said, "You both ready for round 2? The team has a lot of questions for you."

Harris looked at Apoe. "Dr. Apoe, are you using any blocking technology that would inhibit my telepathy?"

"No, why. Is there something wrong, Lincoln?"

"I seem to have lost my gifts."

# CHAPTER 22

The Supervisor escorted Senator Hurst and Dr. Lucia down to security and watched their vehicle depart the VIP parking area to the front of the building. As she walked towards the elevator to return to her office, she met Dr. O'Neil.

"Sandra, what was the emergency?"

"Ms. Supervisor, one of my other Programs called. I'm needed at a remote site. This location is a special project we are developing for a classified entity, much like this program, ma'am. I need to leave immediately."

The Supervisor hated sharing Dr. O'Neil with other programs, but she was the face of Artificial Intelligence within the government. Her involvement in multiple programs that shared her technology, her role while interfacing with industry as a technology expert, frequent congressional testimony, and technical journal publications had all determined her identity would remain public. Fortunately, most of her work was delegated to subordinates, allowing most of her time to be dedicated to the Supervisor. *"This must be a high-priority need for her to leave."*

"Return as quickly as you can, Sandra. I need you here now more than ever to finish the VITP."

"Yes, ma'am. I will." Dr. O'Neil passed through security and was gone.

The Supervisor entered the elevator and returned to her office, contemplating the schedule and the remaining technology problems for the promised solution.

The Supervisor exited the elevator and headed for the admin's office. Her admin was already standing behind her desk, anticipating her boss' return.

"What was the emergency?"

"We received a call from Alec Richardson, Ma'am. He's

A TIME TO STAND

coming back."

"Did he say where he was calling from?" the Supervisor asked.

"Yes, ma'am. He called from Front Royal about an hour ago."

She looked at the office clock hanging on the wall. "Alec should be here any time. Did you tell this to Dr. O'Neil?"

"Yes, Ma'am."

*"Why didn't O'Neil mention this?"*

"Thank you. Instruct security to let Mr. Richardson through. Escort him up to my office. Please call Dr. Apoe and tell him about these developments. Dr. O'Neil has departed to handle 'something' with another program. I'll be in my office." The Supervisor entered her office and shut the door.

*"This is an interesting turn of events,"* she thought. *"Did Dr. O'Neil have a real emergency, or is she trying to avoid Alec? Why would she do that?"*

The Supervisor began to think through Dr. O'Neil's other programs. Most were with the DoD and Intelligence Community, the two organizations with which her program had just declared hostilities. After the last couple of years, had she misplaced her trust in Dr. O'Neil? No. She did not believe so. UT and she worked closely together on maintaining the system and integrating its capabilities with UTs medical applications. The results spoke for themselves. Both their efforts on the new VITP project showed outstanding results. If she had provided the Exit Protocols to the VP, Director, or Secretary, what would be their motivation for grabbing UT and creating the conditions of his death?

The Supervisor organized her reasoning, thinking through the relevant chronology and actions. *"If Dr. O'Neil is not loyal to the program, then consider this scenario:*

*Dr. O'Neil has already provided the VP with the Exit methods.*

*Having this information, Morrison convinced the President to sign the new Directive placing the SOUP under the CIA. The VP could make his promises to POTUS for the types of Intelligence he wanted, assured he would control the development of the remote viewers.*

*The Directive would lead to the turnover of the facilities to the CIA. Did Dr. O'Neil also leak to Morrison the efforts to build the VITP? If so, sharing this information means Dr. Lucia might be involved with the Vice President. She played ignorant today, like she had not heard of the VITP, and will now report on our efforts. I let the fox into the hen house!*

*They grabbed UT and killed him to delay the efforts to finish the VITP until after their operations were running because they <u>knew</u> if VITP was used on them, they could never complete the takeover of the SOUP. Without fear of the Violence Inhibitor, nothing could prevent the CIA/DoD from operationalizing the facilities to create their new assets.*

*VITP could become, as Dr. Lucia stated, the new Crime solution, but the DoD would control the development.*

*It all made sense and added up. But it might not be true."* She concluded.

"It is, though, very compelling," she said aloud. "What proof points do I need to validate this scenario is correct, and what evidence will be presented by people I trust to show me it is wrong."

She had no questions about Senator Hurst's loyalty. Information from him was to be trusted. Was Apoe on board with her? She <u>had</u> to believe he was. Their history and his sincerity had convinced her when he arrived. She decided to provide no new information to Dr. O'Neil or Dr. Lucia until the facility was safe and in her control.

The risk for her program, both functionally and politically, was in the balance and held severe repercussions for the American people if she failed. From this point forward, she would manage this very closely. She was committed to defeating anyone that threatened her program. She was not going to lose this fight.

# CHAPTER 23

Alec Richardson was greeted warmly by the Supervisor when he entered her office. "Alec, I'm so glad you are back! Please sit down. There is so much to bring you up to speed on," the Supervisor gushed.

Alec found her behavior slightly off from the calm and reserved Supervisor he'd met a few days before. *"What had happened, that would change her personality to reflect outward so differently?"* He felt the Supervisor was between giddy and depressed, two emotions he never expected to see displayed by the program's senior executive.

"I have much to talk with you about as well, Ms. Supervisor. Some of it I find hard to believe and would like your assessment."

"Are you reading my thoughts now, Alec?"

Alec had decided to "tune out" the world around him by filtering out the noise and voices that constantly bombarded his mind and using his gift only when needed or requested.

"No, ma'am, I'm not. But with your permission, I would be happy to share your thoughts."

The Supervisor nodded her head. "Let me know when you are ready."

Alec slightly turned his mental tuning illusion up until he could detect her thoughts. "Okay," he said and closed his eyes. Alec was unprepared for the barrage of information that he received.

*"Dr. O'Neil might be a mole. Here are the reasons why...Met with Senator Hurst and Dr. Lucia, the National Security Advisor. Not sure about Dr. Lucia. Be on guard. We will strike back at the Vice President using technology Dr. O'Neil and Mr. UT were developing. It's the only way to protect the program... Senator Hurst thinks you're dead – here is why..., Dr. Apoe is here with Sarah Anderson and Lincoln Harris. Lincoln is one of the escaped*

*inmates from the SOUP in Los Angeles...Dr. Apoe and I were very close, as in lovers, several years ago...Both of us have had experience with the Shiny Ones. Here is the information...Here is the Exit Solution worked out by UT and Dr. O'Neil...My Chief Medical Officer, you knew him as Mr. UT, was killed by the CIA shortly after you left."*

While Richardson was impressed with the chronological order of the Supervisor's news, some of the information had loose ends, requiring further questioning to tie the concepts together. It was the news about UT that jerked him back to reality. UT was the first to contact Richardson. Through UT, Alec was invited to tour the first facility and write a series of articles explaining to the public what the SOUP was and how it would benefit America. He had many other memories of UT but was still unsure which memories were true or created by the SOUP. It was irrelevant if the memories were Real or created. Both generated the profound loss he felt for his comrade.

Alec opened his eyes and sensed a tear on his cheek and a hollow feeling in his stomach. The death of UT was emotional, but he had to focus his thoughts on the future. He could not change the news about UT's death, but he could influence his own present.

His first thought was about what he had heard concerning the Supervisor and her emotional condition. How much of this was her response to UT? He could not understand why Dr. O'Neil could no longer be trusted by her, despite the Supervisor's rationale for suspecting. Had he sensed paranoia? Richardson decided not to challenge her beliefs outright but to work with the team to provide the information she wanted to disprove her perception.

"You were right," Alec began. "A lot <u>has</u> happened." He looked at the Supervisor. She moved across the room and sat in one of the several visitor chairs that comprised an intimate space for conversations in her office.

"Dr. Apoe will be joining us shortly. He had a last-minute

item he needed to attend to before coming up. I had originally planned to have dinner with Dr. O'Neil, but with her departure, the facts you now know, I called Dr. Apoe up to the office. We might have a late dinner. Are you hungry now?"

"No, Ms. Supervisor, I will be fine for a while."

There was a knock on the closed office door.

"Yes?" the Supervisor said aloud.

The door opened, and the Supervisor's admin appeared. "Ma'am, Dr. Apoe just called and is on his way. Will there be anything else this evening?"

"No, I don't think so. See you in the morning."

"Thank you, Ma'am. Good night." The admin left the office door open and departed the outer office. Shortly afterward, Richardson heard the buzz of the exterior security lock, and Dr. Apoe entered the outer office, then came to the meeting inside.

"You seem to be using your new credentials well, Franklin."

"Yes, thank you for approving them. While I liked your admin staff, I was getting short on small talk as they escorted me around the building."

The Supervisor smiled and stood up. "Dr. Franklin Apoe, may I present Mr. Alec Richardson? Alec, Dr. Apoe is our new Chief Medical Officer. Alec is our first successful non-criminal inmate to be Exited from the SOUP."

"It's a pleasure to meet you, Dr. Apoe." Alec rose also and shook Apoe's hand.

"Are you the same Alec Ricardson who wrote the SOUP article? A Pulitzer Prize winner if I recall correctly."

"One and the same, Dr. Apoe."

"You look very well for a man declared missing and presumed dead while researching war refugees in the middle east."

"*He is just now piecing together the false narrative on my death,*" Alec thought. "*That must have hit a nerve. He's put his guard up.*"

"And if you are still alive, then I assume your traveling partner, Adelle Hall..."

"Still in the SOUP. Dr. O'Neil and UT exited Alec as our first steps to defend the program." The Supervisor provided the missing information while pointing to a chair for Dr. Apoe. Each sat down.

"Do you have the same gifts as the others, Alec?"

"I have gifts, as to whether they are the same...."

"Telepathy and Telekinesis," Apoe said.

"Yes. I have them both."

"Are you using them now?"

"No, I haven't figured out how to filter all the noise from multiple conversations and thoughts unless it's one person. I find it easier to communicate the old-fashioned way." Alec smiled, hoping to put Apoe at ease.

"Dr. Apoe, I thought tonight would be more social. What were you working on that was so urgent?"

"Ms. Supervisor, I believe we have a problem."

"Okay, Franklin, what's going on?"

"Tonight, I was with Harris and Anderson. I was picking them up and getting ready to join you for dinner. When Harris opened the door, he looked distraught and asked if we had implemented 'countermeasures' in the building."

"I don't understand," the Supervisor said.

"Ma'am, Harris has lost his powers."

The Supervisor remained silent and stared at Apoe while she processed her thoughts from this new information. It was apparent to both men; the Supervisor was disturbed by the news. She shifted in her chair and asked, "How do we know this?"

"I tested him, Ms. Supervisor. His telepathy is gone, and his brain wave energy associated with telekinesis is hardly registering. He tried moving different objects and was unsuccessful."

"Why do you believe this happened?" Alec asked the question while observing the Supervisor shift in her chair as if looking for the perfect spot on the cushion to support her body. Both men noticed she was visibly agitated.

"Alec, UT discovered something strange with each inmate, which is a critical part of Exiting. Each occupant's pineal gland is becoming healthier and enlarging. There is a direct correlation between the length of time in the SOUP and the gland's health. I tested Harris. His pineal has shrunk by over 30% and is beginning to show signs of calcification."

"And," the Supervisor asked.

"This means he is becoming more normal like the rest of humanity. The size and health of Harris' pineal gland is now the same as yours and mine, Ms. Supervisor."

"And mine?" Alec wanted to know.

"With testing, I expect yours to be much larger and healthier. Size and health may determine the length of time your gifts exist. You've been in the SOUP for over two years. Depending on their use, I would say your gifts may last longer than Harris'. He is a relatively young inmate at around one year."

"This changes everything," the Supervisor spoke, her statement clear and her decisiveness evident.

"How so, Ms. Supervisor."

"Alec, you've received the information. We intended to counter the VP with a passive solution. Dr. Apoe..." she said, looking at him, "will need time to digest UT's part of the Violence Inhibitor. Understanding the concept alone may take three months to accomplish."

"You told the others it might not take that long," Apoe said.

"Salesmanship. I needed their political support to counter the VP. My intent was honest, and I wanted to use the Violence Inhibitor, but now, this information tells me the gifts are finite. Dr. O'Neil's schedule has also changed, which will cause delays. Need I remind you the aggressive action taken against this program will not decrease during the next three months? If the VITP takes longer to develop, we may lose the program and control of its facilities. THEY want our solution, and they killed UT trying to get it."

"What were you going to do while the Inhibitor was being perfected or took longer than three months," Richardson asked.

"You, Alec. You were our defense until we could perfect and use it. Your gifts could counter their efforts and block their attempts to steal our technology. Now, that's not possible. Our only option is you, and your clock is ticking."

"But you did not tell them that!" Apoe yelled. "You forgot I was in the meeting with you."

The Supervisor's response was cold and without emotion. "Dr. Apoe, Senator Hurst believes Alec is dead. Alec understands this and knows Hurst can't know the truth. Because of him, we have congressional support and a strong political ally today. Much of that support is because Senator Hurst believes his best friend, and first supervisor Matthew Boyd, murdered Alec. Senator Hurst decided to put him in the SOUP rather than prosecute him. Hurst can never be told, now for political reasons nor later, for fear he would want his friend removed. The Senator knows we have an Exit solution; he can never know the murder he used to justify Boyd's conviction was a lie we told him, or he will want his friend back."

"Why lie to the Senator?" Apoe asked, regaining his composure.

"That is a complex answer. The simplified version is the Last Memory Reset could do incredible things for this country. It's used today in the Elder Care program to take senior citizens back to their youth while in their Virtual World. More important was Boyd's belief it could bring true inmate reform. Boyd also missed his family, who were murdered during a robbery in their home. He believed if he tested the Last Memory Reset on himself, he could regain his family in a virtual world and help this country to solve major crime problems."

Apoe nodded, acknowledging he was beginning to

understand the big picture.

Alec had memories of revenge against the Supervisor and his program. He believed Adelle died because of the Supervisor's decisions. Alec knew all of this history was not real. He understood now the Supervisor used Cause and Effect scenarios to guide his direction in the SOUP and prove they worked as part of the reform efforts.

His perspective of Boyd's achievements was different now. He respected the man's memory for dealing with the despair of lost loved ones and his desire to serve his nation.

"So, what now?" Apoe asked.

"We only have one solution," the Supervisor began. "We need to Exit others from the SOUP to cover our defense in the event Alec's gifts are lost as suddenly as Harris. Dr. Apoe, you will need to work with Dr. O'Neil on the VITP as our objective solution. We are still on defense but taking necessary steps to take the fight to the administration. Their next move will determine our counter actions."

"Who do we Exit?"

"That's obvious, Dr. Apoe. Adelle and Grant. Neither are criminals and can be trusted to use their gifts correctly," Alec said.

"I agree." The Supervisor concurred with Richardson's suggestion.

"What about Senator Hurst and Dr. Lucia? Don't you believe they should know?"

"Know what, Dr. Apoe? As promised, we are still working on the VITP, and they don't know about Alec. Adding two more Exits with gifts, still unknown to them, does not change the original plan. Do you agree?"

"Your logic, Ms. Supervisor, is sound. I appreciate you sharing more of the details." Apoe's comment was dry and coarse.

"I know it's unfair to have you drinking out of a fire hose, Franklin. There is so much left yet to tell you."

Apoe nodded, "I have no objections to this course of

action, Ms. Supervisor."

# CHAPTER 24

Director of the CIA, Mike Thompson, picked up his secure phone and placed his call to the Vice President. He was reluctant to do so after the Vice President's last decision to apprehend Mr. UT for questioning, but now another piece of information had reached him requiring him to report.

The Vice President was in his office in the Naval Observatory. He'd found two hours of solace where he could think about how he would make his run for President. Morrison already had the party breathing down his neck, wanting him to take meetings and modify the platform to address the issues emerging from the new power players. He understood all too well the donations the new generation of wealth promised, eager to contribute their self-serving dollars to be part of the win.

Morrison only had one problem with the party's prodding. He was an 'old school' politician who disagreed with the platform changes. How could he, in good conscience, promote several of the policies the nouveau money wanted to push on the American people just because it would create markets that would increase their enormous wealth? He knew, in the end, he would stand up and support the changes. Money births a win, and a win equals power. Morrison knew that given a choice between winning to gain power and losing with integrity, he would choose to win. He had a vision for America, and one needed power and position to make it happen. He saw a Nation once again respected in the world. Not for their technology or innovations but for the might they could wield. Nuclear weapons once placed the US at the top of the most powerful nations in the world. Today, they provided a deterrent with limited value because everyone had them. No one, unless a madman, would use them. They evolved to a high-cost item that helped drain budgets and occasionally spun off a useful technology. Morrison reasoned you needed an edge, something different, to gain leverage over your opponents and prevent them from using their leverage on you.

Most of the new contributors and the dreamers with potential wanted more wealth; unfortunately, the Chinese had discovered this flaw in the American Aristocracy. The American people needed to be saved from themselves and their greed. China and every other wealthy adversary would offer money to buy America from within, and unfortunately, American short-sightedness would lead the nation to war. It was his job as the future leader of the free world to prevent war.

Morrison was a student of history and had witnessed the strategy of corruption in action. What hubris, he wondered, produced a country's policy to sell drugs to meet its foreign policy objectives? He laughed slightly as he recalled the British selling Opium to the Chinese more than a century ago, turning their nation into addicts, just to secure foreign markets and make the men of England wealthier. The war fought between the two was a drawn-out, unbalanced affair. The Chinese army and population strung out on opium, had no chance against the world's finest military, and were defeated. Trade deals with the West opened. Was history repeating itself? Within the last three decades, the Chinese had revealed their hand. The free people of Hong Kong should have known the Chinese would use an iron fist once the city's ownership changed. Assimilation back into the fold was never in doubt. And now, he was surrounded by idiots that didn't realize his own country was falling into the same trap, hollowed out by its addictions. The Chinese never forgot England's attack on their country by addicting its population and buying off its politicians. Morrison smiled. The bastards are using a page out of England's playbook.

The SOUP offered the solution. After seeing the videos of their telekinetic power, Morrison acknowledged he was impressed by the remote viewer's produced intelligence. The telepathic and telekinetic power was the new type of leverage needed. These men and women were the first nuclear weapons before everyone else had them. It could be overwhelming power without overwhelming destruction. To understand your enemy's every move better than their chain of command and insert soldiers with this power to re-establish America's dominance was a critical component of his vision. He knew once the American people were aware of these capabilities and he was the one that developed them, he would win his election easily. Just like the nuclear arsenals and their secrets, so too the mystery of these new powers coming from the SOUP would never be made public. Americans would feel secure and leave the classified details to him. He needed to get control of that program.

His secure cell phone buzzed, breaking his chain of thought. It was Thompson.

He accepted the call. "Yes."

"Mr. Vice President, I hate to disturb you at home, but we have a potential problem I thought you'd want to know about."

*"Potential Problem. Shit, can't he handle the potential ones?"*

"What is it?"

"The Supervisor met with the National Security Advisor and Senator Hurst today."

"Go on."

"Our assessment indicates they will act to prevent the transfer of the program to my organization. We know this means they have no intention of providing the Exit protocols. If we want the protocols, we need to be more aggressive."

"What do you suggest?"

"Sir, I did not initially see the wisdom of your decision to pick up their Chief Medical Officer, but I've changed my perspective. We need to question their Chief Technology Officer, Dr. Sandra O'Neil. She has an unmasked identity which presents a risk, but if done correctly, she'll never remember the session."

"Is she in public or living in the facility like the Supervisor?"

"She has other programs she must visit. That's a problem being indispensable and a genius, I guess. There are windows where we can pick her up."

Morrison thought for a moment. Could he trust Thompson not to screw this up? For the most part, he is competent and would need him in his administration. Loyalty and experience like his are not grown overnight.

"Screw this one up, and you're done with me. Are you hearing me, Thompson?"

"I have your concurrence, then, Mr. Vice President."

"Do it."

# CHAPTER 25

Alec Richardson and Dr. Franklin Apoe sat in the conference room. It was an impromptu meeting after the Supervisor provided her directions and concluded their meeting. Both men agreed that further information and perspectives needed to be checked and validated, and they should discuss the Exit protocol before using it. Alec began the conversation. "I am sensing the Supervisor is not herself."

"Rather direct, aren't you, Alec."

"*Damn right, I'm being direct. The Supervisor has her back pinned against the wall, is dealing with losing a personal friend, and could be hyper-paranoid about Dr. O'Neil leaking information and, worse, relying on me to fix things. I'm not sure my head is screwed on correctly.*" Alec wanted to say these things to Apoe. Instead, he said, "We don't have much time if the situation is as serious as she paints it."

"I've known the Supervisor a long time. She is not exaggerating the situation."

"Have you known her ever to be paranoid, Dr. Apoe?"

Apoe looked at Richardson. "Are you reading my thoughts?"

"No."

"Good. You would not have liked what you heard."

"*Well, you would not like what I am thinking either, buddy. We are in over our heads here!*" Alec continued differently, not trying to sound like an alarmist, "Look, she shared a lot of information with me. She has real doubts about Dr. O'Neil's loyalty to the program." Alec said, "and she's not so sure about another person, Dr. Lucia."

"She's the National Security Advisor to the president. As you can see, the stakes are pretty high. There is a real threat to this program," Apoe said.

"She explained that as well. The Presidential Directive,

that's the threat," Alec confirmed.

"As I said, she's juggling a lot of balls right now. Losing UT was very significant to her. She's still grieving. Then I show up in her life. She told you about us, too, I guess."

Alec nodded. He was unsure why she had shared that information with him, but she must place some importance on their relationship as value to the program.

"So, what's your opinion of her mental condition, Dr. Apoe?"

"I don't know, Alec. We need to ensure she doesn't make a major mistake. As long as she confides in us and asks our opinion, we should be able to catch anything outright wrong."

Alec thought about this and realized it was the only way forward. It was up to Apoe and him to make sure the Supervisor did not get overwhelmed and act irrationally.

"I agree with that approach."

You might want to 'check in' on her now and then," Apoe said.

"Without her permission?"

"You're the one bringing this up. You're also the only one who can confirm what she is really thinking. I can't see how that would hurt. Do you?"

Apoe was a good number 2 for her. There was no doubt about his loyalty to the Supervisor, but he also understood she was human and prone to errors of judgment. Apoe just asked Alec to ensure she didn't go off the rails. Apoe knew she was under a great deal of stress.

"Dr. Apoe, to be honest with you, I'm not sure I'm the one to judge her mental condition. That's why I asked you."

Apoe thought about Alec's last comment before proceeding with his question. "Is there something going on, Alec? Some problem with you?"

"*Damn, right there is. I'm not sure what's real and what's not. Each day gets better, but this confusion with my memory affects how I understand reality.*"

"I am having problems with my memories," Alec

confessed.

"I thought you might be?" Apoe said. "I can't imagine how you are keeping everything straight."

"I have a difficult time sorting out what memories are real and what are virtual. My life feels," Alec paused, then continued, 'disconnected.' Richardson leaned forward in his seat, bringing himself closer to Apoe. "You were with Harris a while. Was there ever a problem with his understanding of reality?"

"Not that either he or Livingston reported, but we never evaluated their adjustment to the two sets of memories. I can tell you their Exit was different than yours."

"How so?"

"As inmates, the program was using Cause and Effect scenarios to re-program their pre-crime memories. As far as I know, after Boyd proved the concept using you to test the scenarios, you were done with them. Afterward, your new life memories came from the community database. Dr. O'Neil prevented you from accessing the criminal activity and made system adjustments and entries to the community for you. Nothing was done to change your memories like the inmates."

"Well, that would explain why sometimes I can't tell the difference between virtual and real memories. They both converge as one reality leaving me momentarily confused. I have it under control now, I think. I mention it only to let you know officially as the Chief Medical Officer. Memory problems could be important when we Exit Grant and Adelle."

"How are you controlling it, Alec?"

"I'm not trying to control them. It's more like when memories occur. I try to prove or disprove them with my perspective of reality. The Shiny Ones told me…" Alec stopped and looked at Apoe's face, which had turned from a sincere, caring expression to pure amazement. Alec stopped speaking.

"You've had experience with Shiny Ones? When, what was their message?"

"You know about them?" Alec stood up and began to

pace the conference room.

"I've had a little experience with them. Firsthand in Afghanistan and China and then the information Harris explained. Most of my experience is at the end of the person's life that has the gifts and has misused them."

"Misused them?"

"Most of the evidence points to using the telekinesis gifts not to defend or help but to kill needlessly. Alec, when did you communicate with them? What did they say?"

"Dr. Apoe, are these things real?"

"Very real, Alec." Apoe could not contain his excitement. He stood and started pacing, stopping to hear Alec's details, then walking again as he processed the information.

"I just came back from the Blue Ridge Mountains. They contacted me there." Alec leaned forward onto the conference room table and placed his hands on the glass top.

"The Shining Ones are messengers."

"What do you mean, like Angels?" Apoe was starting to pace.

"They wouldn't answer that question."

"So, what is the message, Alec?"

"There is light in each of us to be used. If it is not used, then darkness takes over. I think they mean evil. Our life needs to be focused on doing what is right for others, and right now, I'm not sure I know right from wrong."

"What is right? Did they say?" Apoe started pacing again, back and forth, shaking his head in disbelief as he covered the same space with his movement.

"They said each of us has the potential for gifts inside us. I believe that's the pineal gland we discussed. They told me something about Maat. They said it was the law."

"Maat! That's amazing. It's Egyptian. It means truth and justice under the law."

"I got the impression the gifts were already available to each of us if we could connect with them, but the Shiny Ones enforce the law as part of the greater message."

"Holy shit! What else?"

"They said evil could never be destroyed," Alec paused and slowed his explanation. "Evil could be defeated but never destroyed. They said evil must exist for light to exist. Some sort of duality or metaphysics stuff."

"Alec, you've had an unexplainable experience, but you've provided many missing pieces in my own experiences."

"I also asked them about this." Alec walked over to Apoe and rolled up his sleeve. "What is it?"

Apoe looked at Richardson's arm and saw the mark immediately. The symbol appeared from under his flesh and pushed upward, unlike a brand or tattoo on the skin's surface.

"It's an Egyptian Ankh."

"They said it was a symbol that marked me as one that could communicate with the Shiny Ones and another name I can't remember."

"The Netjer."

"Yes, that's it. How do you know all this? What does it mean?"

"The Gods." Apoe picked a chair and sat down.

"Come on, Dr. Apoe, this is bordering on some real BS."

"Oh, this is far from BS. Did you ever think you could read minds or do things just by thinking about it? Alec, something is happening in the SOUP, and it's up to us to figure out how it all works. If we can tie together what you just told me to the Exit protocols, we won't have to guess. We'll know exactly what we have and how to control it."

"Let's take a pause here. This is a lot to take in." Alec collapsed into a conference room chair. "Did Harris have this mark?"

"He didn't mention it, but that doesn't mean he didn't."

Alec's mind spun with the new information Apoe provided. Up to now, he could not tell if his memory of the Shiny Ones or the conversation with them was another memory from the SOUP or an actual experience. It seemed so surreal.

"What did they tell you to help readjust to this world?"

"Dr. Apoe, do not think I am crazy with what I'm about to tell you."

"I've heard that statement before, Alec. Nothing you can say will surprise me."

"Adelle was part of the conversation. Not the real Adelle. They used something that looked like her. They wanted me to feel comfortable talking to them," Alec paused, "so they used her to help me understand."

Alec looked at Apoe. His face was expressionless. "What else did they say?" Apoe asked.

"That only the present was real, and once the experience was 'written,' it was unchangeable. The past's value lies only in providing information on which to make future decisions. As I live more in this reality, the emotions used as quantum tags to pull the virtual memories will fade, helping me identify what is real and what is not. In essence, time will take care of my memories. From what the Supervisor transferred to me in her thoughts about the system, the Quantum tags associated with emotions in the SOUP will disappear, and we'll only have the memories of our real life. Those emotions will always remain."

"Where is Dr. O'Neil when you need her?" Apoe said, exasperated with missing the technical side of the system functions. "I need to do more homework on how the SOUP functions."

"I can help. Much of the SOUP's operations the Supervisor provided during our info transfer. Her knowledge of the system function is extensive. Dr. O'Neil knows the technology behind the magic, but the Supervisor knows how it works," Alec said.

"I know this is a lot to take in and process. Whatever authority provided you with your gifts failed to consider the human need to understand why things were happening. How do you feel, Alec? Can you press on?"

"We have to. We're not even sure how long I will have the capabilities I have. We need Adelle and Grant."

"Okay, I agree. Alec, the Supervisor, provided you with the exit protocol. Let's start. What happened first?"

"The Los Angeles facilities were close to the epicenter of a minor earthquake. The team already knew the pineal glands were developing with the inmates. From the quake's duration and magnitude information, they used a strong burst at 7.5 hertz for 20 seconds as step one."

"Excellent; I believe this was required to awaken the pineal gland. Given its health, this may be all that was required. Good, what did they do next?"

"The Team recognized that the frequencies of Theta waves overlapped the piezo-electric ones from the earthquake. What are theta waves?"

"Theta waves are responsible for processing information and making memories," Apoe said.

"I remember UT explaining this to me on my tour of the facility. The Supervisor explained the earthquake frequency acted as an 'amplifier' to the active theta waves in the system, doubling the strength of the theta waves. She said only the inmates, our three guys, were thinking about 'getting out,' starting new lives, etc., from the scenarios, and these thoughts became much stronger during the earthquake."

"That makes sense. The earthquake turns on the pineal gland and amplifies the inmate's desire to Exit. What is the next step?"

"A second frequency used on me. The second frequency opened my third eye to wherever generates the gifts. Does this make sense, Apoe?"

"It does. What frequency did they use?"

"1000 hertz."

"This would be enough energy to open the third eye gateway from this frequency realm to another, much higher one. The higher the frequency, the more enlightened you are supposed to be. 1000 hertz would be more than enough to connect you to wherever and establish the means to receive your gifts. This process explains Harris' condition. When his pineal returned to normal, the gateway to the gifts ended, suddenly without notice."

"Do you believe it's this 'frequency realm' that the Shiny Ones are in?"

"No idea. They could be in another separate one. Certainly, they can see this material world of matter in much lower frequencies." Apoe continued. "I believe your gifts are just energy, and your pineal allows you to access the energy. Once you have access, you use the gifts the way your mind directs you to. Your ego controls your mind. Your mind controls the gifts. If your ego has the wrong values, well, you can see where this goes."

"This makes sense. The last part of the Exit protocol tested involved opinions about my mind using the energy to act upon my amplified feelings to get out. The final step, my gifts set me free," Alec said.

"Now, this is very interesting. Were you thinking about getting out when the second frequency was applied to you?"

"Yes."

"And how did you come to reach this desire to leave?"

"Dr. Apoe, I won't lie. The SOUP is a fantastic place. You are truly at the center of your universe. Everything that happens in the SOUP happens <u>to</u> you just by thinking about it. It's your ego's dream come true. I can say living in the SOUP is...well, it's like taking something like crack that mellows you out and makes the world an awesome place to live. Every thought you have comes true, which is what the system was intended to do; create a utopia for criminals." Richardson could not remember specific memories without confusion but could remember how he felt. Every desire he wanted to happen manifested itself into the SOUP's reality. "To Exit, you really must <u>want</u> to leave."

"So, how did you decide?" Apoe asked.

"It took a lot of convincing. Dr. O'Neil placed herself in my consciousness. She calls her presence in the SOUP her Quantum Persona."

"You mean she convinced you to leave?"

"She convinced me the reality I was living in was not real. She said to get out; I just needed to want to."

"That's it, Alec. The VP is looking for a set of frequencies and sequences of events. But exiting the SOUP comes down to a personal choice to leave. Exercising our free will. His people can look around all day in their labs for the right frequency combination, but without a Quantum persona to convince the person, they will never leave."

"So, who will be the Quantum persona to convince Adelle and Grant to come out? Alec asked.

"I think it has to be you, Alec."

"I am not the guy to program this. We're talking about programming a Cause-and-Effect Scenario. Programming something like this is way beyond my pay grade. We need Dr. O'Neil or one of the facility programmers to do it right."

Apoe nodded.

"You've had experience with other events like this, Dr. Apoe. What do you believe?" Alec asks.

"This is not just a virtual world created as a computer simulation as the SOUP was intended. We have tapped into the solution for opening a gateway into different realities which allow us to express energy in much higher frequencies than we could ever imagine. This information confirms the nature of people with these gifts must be morally straight because their personalities change. These changes lead to abusing this power. These are the results I've witnessed.

Because the Shining Ones are at a higher frequency of existence and understand our condition, they monitor our reality. When they take someone back, they elevate the individual and any witnesses to their reality, possibly through a similar gateway, and then place the witnesses back. This theory supports what Harris and Anderson told me about a strong wind, which didn't move anything in the room, shiny lights, the body's conversion into light and then disappearing."

"What do you think they are?" Apoe asked Richardson.

"I think the Shiny Ones are some intelligence in the higher frequency of existence that enforces the Universal law – maybe Maat. This includes how gifts are used. The law is based upon positive attributes represented by light, or they could be a form of light: love, compassion, and forgiveness. You cannot break the law without penalty.

The Portal opens to the higher frequency realms that turn on the gifts through a healthy pineal gland. Gifts are not given to us by the Shiny Ones. They enforce the law."

Apoe's head was spinning with the information Alec was providing. Apoe responded slowly but with growing confidence in his belief, "You said each of us has the potential to get these gifts. That makes sense. Yes, that's why the Shiny Ones exist – to control how the gifts are used."

Alec could tell from his last response Apoe would need to think about this new information discovered in the previous ten minutes. Both men stopped the discussion. There were more pressing matters at hand.

"Well, we may never know, Alec, if we are right. Let's get the Supervisor to find Dr. O'Neil or get us one of her best programmers. We need to focus on this reality now."

# CHAPTER 26

D r. Sandra O'Neil had kept a low profile after Alec Richardson had Exited the SOUP. She had information that if Alec could read her mind, it might jeopardize the program's future and turn this confrontation with the Administration into a full conflict. Dr. O'Neil knew the Supervisor was passionate about the program and viewed the Vice President's approach to his stated objectives with disdain. She had to admit Morrison was getting heavy-handed with how he chose to get his answers. UT's death solidified that belief for her but did not mean the VP's objectives were wrong. This conflict was a real quandary for her. Even the Supervisor had admitted as much. Both appeared willing to entertain a new mission for the program that included the CIA and DoD missions, but the conflict was in the methods. Rapid implementation is a solution through power at all costs, as opposed to careful study of the risks and proper implementation on the other. A solution had to be achieved with Morrison to keep the peace, and she'd spent two sleepless nights wrestling with her ideas.

Dr. O'Neil was driving from Alexandria, Virginia, home to the US Aberdeen Proving Ground in Maryland. She did not notice the black van pulling behind her when she entered I-95 north from I-495. A second van pulled in front of her and slowed down as she approached the first major exit. Looking in her rear-view mirror, O'Neil saw the second van close and understood immediately. They wanted her to exit. She did so, and the small caravan headed east until reaching a small strip mall containing an auto repair shop. The vehicles pulled into available parking spaces.

"*What happens now?*" she said, unfastening her seatbelt and turning off her engine. Dr. O'Neil opened her car door. A mountain of a man dressed in a professional suit greeted her.

"Dr. O'Neil, this way," he said, pointing to the repair establishment's door.

"What is this, and why are you apprehending me?" Dr. O'Neil felt calm, despite knowing the intent behind the facility. She looked at the agent and guessed he was part of the CIA Director's special security team. He didn't fit her profile for Secret Service and began working through answers the agents might request.

As expected, she received no answer to her question, just the agent's hand pointing at the door to the building. She walked in front of him and opened the door into a waiting area with a service counter and employees. One of the employees started to ask her if she needed assistance until she saw the suited mountain behind her, at which point he sat down and started looking at the daily schedule on the counter's computer.

O'Neil and her escort moved past the counter and walked into a back room which led them to an old car maintenance bay that was empty and looked unused. The agent pointed downward to a car pit used by mechanics to work on items under the car.

"Into the pit, please."

"It's going to be pretty cramped if we both share the space," O'Neil responded.

She walked down into the pit and realized the back wall contained a metal door that could open into an equipment storage area, but she suspected more than maintenance tools were behind the closed barrier. Her suspicions were confirmed when the door opened, and a woman emerged saying, "I have it from here." The mountain remained at the top of the pit in case Dr. O'Neil's calm demeanor eroded, and she decided to try and exit.

The woman was not a security guard. O'Neil could tell by her appearance as well. Behind the door was a brightly lit stairwell descending into a series of platforms and cutbacks until reaching the bottom, approximately 30 feet below her.

"Dr. O'Neil," she started. "I hope you realize you've been afforded certain courtesies to prepare for our session today.

"Such as?"

"No blindfolds, no temporary sleep injections. You know, the normal drill."

*"Ah ha. She's in operations. She's done this before."*

"I thank you for that. I just had my hair done, and your hoods always mess it up."

The woman smiled slightly and handed O'Neil a small, sealed packet with a hard object inside. "Please put this in your mouth, Dr. O'Neil. I assure you it is sterilized and won't hurt."

O'Neil opened the package and found a device she assumed was a mouthguard. She put it in as instructed and tested the device. Her jaws could not clench downward, and her upper teeth could not touch her lower ones.

*"They are not going to make the same mistake twice."*

The woman inspected the device for proper fit, and they started downward. At the bottom of the stairs, a small, clean, and exceptionally equipped space reminded Dr. O'Neil of a hospital emergency room. The centerpiece of the area was an oversized chair that looked borrowed from a nail salon to provide massages to clients receiving pedicures. Two men and another woman organized a mixture of recording equipment and prepared a rolling cart with medical supplies.

"I'm guessing that's my seat," O'Neil mumbled through the mouthguard.

"Yes, ma'am. Please make yourself comfortable. You can take your shoes off and leave them with me."

O'Neil removed her shoes, gave them to the woman, walked to the chair, and sat down.

The three making preparations stopped and took their positions next to their equipment. A tall, attractive man that reminded O'Neil of Brad Pitt walked over to the chair. "Dr. O'Neil. Welcome to our workshop. We have a few questions for you today, but a check-up first."

The man picked up a device, and O'Neil's escort laid a

heavy protective drape across her chest.

"Just an x-ray Dr. O'Neil."

The device beeped, and a picture flashed onto a monitor on his rolling cart showing her teeth. Two more beeps, and the man had a complete picture.

"You have impeccable teeth. A clear sign of good dental hygiene as well as nothing abnormal." He nodded his head to his assistant.

The woman reached near O'Neil's mouth and removed the guard.

"Now, Dr. O'Neil, we will give you something to help us have a worthwhile discussion. The drug will not harm you, and you will be released right after our session."

O'Neil felt the needle pinprick in her arm and felt herself fall into a warm cushion of cotton balls, and her inhibitions disappear.

◆ ◆ ◆

Dr. O'Neil awoke with the same cotton balls in her mouth. She looked around at her surroundings. She was in her car, parked in front of her home. Next to her was a chilled water bottle with a sticky note that said, "Drink me," and a small, opened box of Kleenex.

She picked up the water and emptied the bottle; her first thoughts focused on removing the grunge she felt in her mouth. She remembered her visit to the car repair shop but nothing after going downstairs. Suddenly, she felt nauseous recalling the purpose of her visit. Facts, figures, and explanations danced through her mind, each a likely item disclosed about the program. She opened the car door quickly and leaned out, unable to contain the rising contents of her stomach. Feeling drained and dizzy, she used the steering wheel to pull herself back into the car and wiped her mouth using the Kleenex next to her.

*"Bastards thought of everything."*

Still dazed, she exited the car and walked to the front door of her house. Her analytical mind began working. Her priority was to clear her head of the remaining cloud she found herself in, and secondly, she needed to re-establish contact with the Supervisor and the program. Her best assessment, no matter how she evaluated the facts, was she had told them everything.

# CHAPTER 27

Director of the CIA, Mark Thompson, sat with his technical director, Dr. Paul Forrest, Alison Fletcher, interrogation team lead and several unit members in the main headquarters conference room in Langley, Virginia. It had taken several hours to prepare the Dr. O'Neil interview information for the boss. The information presented was, in many ways, still raw. Despite the missing correlations and substantive conclusions associated with his customary intelligence briefings, Thompson wanted to see the first cut. The Director had handpicked the team that 'interviewed' Dr. O'Neil and was not surprised the questioning session was uneventful.

"Okay, what did we get, Alison?" Thompson asked. He owed an update to the Vice President soon and wanted the maximum amount of time to question the team.

"Sir, I appreciate your confidence in me to get the agency's desired results. My preliminary assessment is the information is reliable." Alison Fletcher, team leader for the effort, began.

"Dr. O'Neil provided her theory for how the initial inmates Exited the SOUP. One of the unexpected benefits of being in the SOUP is each inmate's pineal gland is growing and much healthier than ours."

"Why is this important?"

"The pineal gland is stimulated by the system and plays a role in visualizing the reality for the inmates. This change enables the Exit and accounts for the gifts the inmates possess."

"No kidding. Our pineal gland does all this?" Thompson asked.

"Yes, sir, that's the information provided."

Fletcher walked the Director through the Los Angeles earthquake and the sequence provided by Dr. O'Neil.

"We now have the frequencies in the correct sequence for the Los Angeles Exit."

"This is excellent work, Alison. How long before we can test her information," Thompson asked.

"Sir, we may not have to wait to build our own test environment. Alec Richardson, the writer that revealed the SOUP to the American people, is alive."

"So, what does this mean to me?"

"Sir, Mr. Richardson was declared dead about two and half years ago in the media. He and his fiancé, Adelle Hall, were reported missing and presumed deceased, investigating Syrian refugee camps in Jordon. They're not dead."

"As you just said." Thompson was getting agitated and looked at his watch.

"According to Dr. O'Neil, they were put in the SOUP by the first Supervisor, Matthew Boyd. Alec Richardson successfully Exited about two weeks ago."

"They pulled him out? They've already tested their theory. And Richardson, does he have psychic gifts as well?"

"Yes, Sir. Telepathy and Telekinesis."

"Fantastic!" Thompson exclaimed. He looked around the conference room at the faces of the interrogation team. One team member was staring at the table, unwilling to make eye contact with the Director.

Thompson sensed an adjustment to his exuberance was required. Before he could ask the question, Fletcher pre-empted him.

"There's more, Sir."

"Let's hear it."

"I've asked Dr. Forrest to be here as the next information will require his expertise and comment."

Thompson nodded and rolled his hands to intimate 'continue.'

Dr. Forrest began, "There is a free will component of the sequence that requires a decision by each person to Exit. They must decide they want to."

"Break this down for me, Paul."

Dr. Forrest continued, "As part of the Los Angeles Exit, the inmates underwent a form of therapy designed to make them forget they were criminals. The therapy is implemented through software programs introduced into the inmate's environment with specific 'pointers' called quantum tags that each inmate can find. Ms. Fletcher could only brief me on so much. She must dig deeper into the testimony to fully understand the information."

"Yes, yes. I know this information is pretty raw. Continue," Thompson said, looking at his watch.

"The therapy created the will for those three inmates, their desire to Exit the SOUP. It was an accident, a coincidence of timing with the earthquake that hit when the three inmates were being 'treated.' Dr. O'Neil described the therapy as something called a 'Cause and Effect Scenario.' Alec Richardson was different. They had to build a unique scenario to get Richardson out of the SOUP. In this instance, Dr. O'Neil could program herself into the system and create something called a Quantum Persona."

"You are starting to lose me."

"Put simply, Sir. Dr. O'Neil entered the SOUP and convinced Alec Richardson to make a personal decision to leave in one of these scenarios. I understand this is not easy to accomplish."

"What's not easy? Programming the technology or convincing him to leave?"

"Both, Sir. She described the SOUP as a world in which the inmate's thoughts create every experience they want to live. She described it as being a Virtual Utopia. It was part of the system's initial design to prevent criminals from wanting to leave, though none of the staff conceived of a situation where it would be possible. Matthew Boyd changed all that. He wanted to reform each inmate and have them Exit as newly reformed citizens. That brings us to the technical issues. To accomplish an Exit, we need to understand how to program and create these cause-and-effect scenarios or how to embed a Quantum Persona into the code. This technology is new ground for the Agency."

Thompson exploded. "So, we have the solution, but we don't have the technology or know how to make the technology work! Son of a Bitch! We're back at square one!" His frustration accelerated to his tipping point. Thompson stood up from his chair and began to pace, taking deep, audible breaths. As he breathed deeply, Thompson felt the frustration begin to dissipate. It was not his team's fault. He recalled the Agency's Prep School on the Farm clearly. The first step in intelligence work is to collect facts and disparate pieces of information, database those facts, then build a model correlating the data to create an operational picture of a theory with known risks leading to an actionable decision. Deep breaths, *remember your craft,* he repeated to himself. *"We are still collecting facts. Don't get ahead of what you know works."*

"My apologies, team. I was hoping for more, but I know you've done well with the available time. Keep digging. I want another update in three hours. Paul, I was hoping you could work full-time with Alison on the analysis. Something must be in there we can use."

Dr. Forrest nodded and exited the conference room with the rest of the team. Thompson slumped into his chair. *"Jesus, I have to tell the VP all this. He's not going to understand how we know everything and still can't get started with our own program."* Thompson remained alone in the conference room and thought for several more minutes about what he would recommend if asked. He had reached his conclusion. *"If the VP asks my opinion, I'll tell him; the President's directive gave the CIA the program. We take the program and force their people to build this whatever scenario. Additionally, we might also have to ask Dr. O'Neil a new set of questions."*

# CHAPTER 28

The Supervisor was relieved to hear Dr. O'Neil's voice on the phone. Still, the information O'Neil presented created a pit in the Supervisor's stomach when she relayed her questioning by the agency. More disturbing was the idea that the agency knew the entire Exit sequence. "Had O'Neil been drugged, or did she give up the information willingly? Is this just a ploy to keep her close so she can get information for the VP? I don't know if I can trust her, but I need her." It was a dilemma with no solution other than to isolate Dr. O'Neil from any strategy discussions or defense measures. The Supervisor would curtail Dr. O'Neil's access to the inner circle of decision-making until her trust was restored.

The Supervisor called Apoe and Richardson to her office and provided Dr. O'Neil's new information. All three agreed the VP's next logical move would involve taking over the facility with agency personnel as the president's directive authorized. Each of her facilities nationwide would be under agency control, and she and her staff would be, with or without their support, refocused on the new mission objectives.

The Supervisor was concerned each inmate would become a laboratory experiment, used, and discarded without remorse, the containers the inmates vacated to be filled by members of the agency and the DoD. She envisioned each Exited inmate disappearing into facilities like Site 35 to live the remainder of their existence in a drug-induced prison with no life, virtual or otherwise, until their bodies mercifully expired.

*"This could not be allowed to happen! It goes against everything the program had worked hard to achieve since its inception,"* she thought.

The Supervisor knew implementing the Violence Inhibitor was no longer feasible. This recent development removed any time she had for Apoe and O'Neil to test out a working prototype. No, she needed to modify their course of action to something less passive and more aggressive.

"In light of this new information, we need to accelerate our schedule to remove Hall and Grant from the SOUP," the Supervisor began.

"Where is Dr. O'Neil now?" Apoe asked.

"I've directed her to create the necessary scenarios to visit both in the SOUP. She's on the system as we speak at the D.C. facility."

"I would like to be part of that effort," Alec said.

"That's not possible, Alec. You are present in both their realities, and your persona would confuse Grant and Hall and make the argument more difficult. Dr. O'Neil is a perfect choice. She is an outsider in both of their lives, just like yours when you were in the SOUP."

"How long before she is ready?"

"It should not take long, Franklin. Most of the scenario logic comes from Alec's Exit. We'll tailor the scenario to something in their world that will convince them it's not real. In the meantime, I would like you and Alec to focus on the Exit sequence and be ready to move when Dr. O'Neil gives us the go."

"How will we know she was successful?" Apoe asked.

"The SOUP provides a real-time video of each inmate's experience. It's called a life video and was an early feature of the program, one of Dr. O'Neil's brainchildren. It's a combination of thought waves and community database activity. It's all energy converted into a format we humans can understand. We'll monitor their activity after Dr. O'Neil's Quantum Persona visits each. The scenarios play out in real time, but we'll accelerate their reality timeline after her visits are complete. We should run the first sequence in about two hours."

"How will we know they've decided to Exit?"

"Just like with you, Alec, we'll implement the Exit sequence, but there is no way to confirm the decision until the system responds. We'll know when the system lowers their box to the cell block floor."

"This is a pretty amazing system you have here, Ms. Supervisor," Apoe commented.

"Worth fighting to keep it this way, would you not agree?"

Both men nodded their heads in agreement.

"Is there any danger to Grant or Hall?" Apoe asked.

"None that we can tell. If either decides not to Exit, their virtual life goes on without interruption."

Apoe stood. "If we are going to be ready for this attempt, we should head to the facility and check the equipment."

The Supervisor agreed. "See you at the cell block, gentlemen."

Apoe and Richardson were heading north on I-295 to the funeral home, serving as the cell block for the Washington, D.C. inmates and Richardson's previous home for roughly two and half years. The two men briefly talked about the Exit sequence protocol before the car interior was silent, with only the tires bumping gently on the concrete road to remind them of traveling to their impending task.

Apoe broke the silence with a direct question. "How is your memory conflict? Have you made progress on tying things together?"

Alec answered without contemplation, "Time. Time Dr. Apoe, is the only way my memories will resolve into one contiguous lifeline. I sometimes believe a part of my life is true until I question the event. The experience feels real, but logically I know it's not. The mind is a great machine but can also be a great deceiver. One day, I hope to be able to eliminate the virtual memories and think of my time in the SOUP as being nothing more than a coma. But until that day, I will admit, it's difficult to sort out."

"How do you reconcile them now?"

"I try not to remember anything in the past. My past is no longer..." Alec paused.

"Reliable. I focus on the here and now and what I need to do for my future. My recent memories are organized well enough."

"Do you have any questions for me? My experiences might be able to assist in some way."

Alec thought a moment, then asked, "Why do you think Livingston destroyed your facility? Do you think he confronted some demon in his memories, or do you believe there was another reason?"

"I think it was demons and something else. I talked with Harris about this briefly on our ride up to Arlington. Like Harris, Livingston could <u>feel</u> the things happening at the site. He could sense the lives being ruined or destroyed in our labs with the experiments we were doing. I believe the murder Livingston committed was weighing heavily on him. Being asked how he would live the rest of his life drove home his decision. I think his actions were tied to his need for redemption."

"Destroy an evil place to atone for his crime? Pay his debt to society by destroying your facility?"

"I think that's what it comes down to. How will you live the rest of your life is a powerful question. It speaks directly to redemption. It's a call to action to change your life path and values. It influences your mind's vision of your future. The question also is a call to redeem your past, even though you can't change it. So, I believe that was one reason. But there is also another."

Apoe thought about how he would say his next statement and decided to keep it direct.

"What's that?" Alec asked.

"Don't take this the wrong way, Alec, but the second reason is love. He cared about Harris and was willing to sacrifice his own life so Harris could escape."

"Sounds like Sunday school, Dr. Apoe."

"Call me, Franklin, please. I suspect we will be working together for a while."

"Sounds like Sunday school, Franklin."

Both men laughed.

"Let me ask you something. Given everything we know about the origins of your gifts and the role we think the Shiny Ones have in enforcing, call it a Universal Law of Maat; how far away from love do you think we are? Haven't you ever felt you would sacrifice your own life for someone else?"

Alec had. It was at that moment he became aware of the real world. Dr. O'Neil had transferred him to another box, temporarily removing him from his virtual world. She protected his identity and fabricated the lie Matthew Boyd had killed him. Alec remembered his brush vividly with reality in the SOUP with Adelle and knew he would sacrifice his life to save hers.

"I understand, love. I have difficulty connecting love to the driving force behind everything happening, Franklin?"

"Many scientists believe love is pure light energy Alec, created when the universe was born. In our matter-driven world, light resides in each of us. It reminds us of where we came from and how we should live. Our connection to the creation, if you will."

From his memory, Alec heard a familiar voice in his head, "*Whoever has ears, let him hear. There is light within a man of light, and he lights up the whole world. If he does not shine, he is darkness.*"

Alec repeated the phrase aloud.

"Where did you hear that, Alec?"

"I heard it shortly after Exiting the SOUP. It was during my experience in the mountains. Have you heard it?"

"Yes, and trust me when I say you're not in Sunday school anymore. It comes from a gospel not included in the bible. It's called the Gospel of Thomas. But that's a whole different conversation for another time, but even so, the message is still about love."

"I think I understand how love could be the energy at the center of Livingston's motivation and ours. This verse is pretty black and white; good versus evil based on your life choices."

"It always _is_ about good versus evil, Alec. The hard part is figuring out who is which one."

# CHAPTER 29

The Supervisor stood in the DC facility's Operations/ VLS Creation room and watched Apoe and Richardson walk through the Exit sequence one last time. Dr. O'Neil's Quantum Persona made a persuasive case for leaving the SOUP and returning to reality, and now, Apoe and Richardson evaluated its effectiveness. Apoe studied the wave indicators and the life video created in real-time by Grant and Hall.

"Predominately, beta waves present with accompanying theta waves," Apoe stated.

The Supervisor found it fascinating that while they did not know the exact information the brain wave activity contained, having beta and theta waves confirmed Grant and Adelle were processing information and not sleeping.

"The life video shows both awake and relaxed at home," Alec reported.

Now the team would see if the scenario was successful. Dr. O'Neil asked if she could await the results at the admin building in Arlington. The Supervisor agreed without objection.

Both men looked at the Supervisor. She nodded her head as a signal to proceed. The Supervisor watched as the system sent the 7hz to the Grant and Hall boxes contained in the inmate lattice of storage rows within the cell block. The system replicated the earthquake frequency and duration and then stopped.

"Phase I complete, the pineal gland should be active. I can confirm the earthquake activity amplified the Exit theta wave decision," Apoe said.

"Let's hope the theta wave holds the decision we are looking for," Alec added. "Time to open the portal; send the 1000hz signal." Once again, the system sent focused energy waves to Grant and Hall's containers. A digital counter on the equipment console ticked down the final seconds of the remaining phase and automatically turned off the frequency generator.

"Predominate theta wave activity in Grant, Hall's brainwaves have remained predominately beta." Apoe turned to Richardson. "Are you seeing the same thing, Alec?"

"Yes, I see the waves." Alec was hopeful he would join Grant shortly but could not hide his disappointment at what appeared from the data to be indecision with Adelle.

"Pull up the system maintenance screen, Franklin, and let's see if we have any activity."

Apoe navigated the options on the screen and soon had maintenance data on both containers' information displayed. Suddenly, one of the container images turned green, and the display provided the assembled group with a 'container in motion' message.

"Something's happening!" Apoe exclaimed.

"Who is it that's moving?"

"It's Grant, Ma'am. The system is bringing his box to the ground floor."

"Excellent, we have one. Franklin, you handle medical, and Alec and I will handle recovery. Let's go!"

Apoe moved to the back corner of the room and extracted his readymade medical cart containing equipment and various injection solutions designed for recovery in standard hospital emergency rooms.

The Supervisor and Alec ran towards the cell block, meeting the security team at the door. "Suspend the use of deadly force, Agent Holland, on my authority."

"Yes, Ma'am," the agent replied. Both agents stood at the ready with pistols drawn as the Supervisor entered the code on the combination pad. The door buzzed open, and the two entered the cell block, followed by the security team.

As they entered, the system was building the elevator and support arms to lower the box to the floor. Assembly was near completion. The four walked briskly to the point where the box would be placed on the painted concrete floor and looked up.

"So, this is the place," Alec said, surveying the large open room filled with boxes containing digital displays at the front end of the containers. "I don't really remember the details of my Exit. This place is utterly amazing. I had forgotten my tour with you, Ms. Supervisor, when you were the Warden and just how impressed I was with what our nation had built."

"That seems like an eternity ago." The Supervisor watched the box slide out of its slot and gingerly lowered by the system. She was also constantly amazed by the technology used to operate her facilities. The construction of the elevator system was an engineering marvel.

Apoe had entered the cell block, and his cart of emergency gear rolled silently across the floor. He joined the four waiting for the box to make its last 10 feet to the ground.

Finally, the box touched down. Apoe exhaled heavily, relieved the casket-type container was on the ground. "Now what?" he asked.

"Just wait, Franklin."

All five listened and rewarded with the sound of the electronic opening gears whirling under the cover. The container's top lifted and hissed as the two environments mixed and stabilized. The security team remained fixed at the foot of the container while the other three moved to the top.

"Look," the Supervisor pointed at a small display with successive digits glowing with letters and numbers from left to right. "The crown device is receiving the disconnect code and should break away any second." All three stepped back as the plastic retaining bolts holding the life support jacket in place popped and ricocheted inside the container. Simultaneously the crown separated from the top of the box freeing Grant from all connections to the life support system that sustained him for almost three years. The Supervisor reached into the box, removed the jacket, and placed it on the floor.

Suddenly a voice rose from the box, "I need a beer." Grant sat up in the container and began to look around. Alec moved around to face his old friend.

"How you feeling, Grant?"

"Alec, I'm a little weak right now, or I'd hug you."

"Save that for later. Can you stand up?"

Grant stood up in the box without difficulty and saw the security team with their weapons pointed at him.

"Put the pistols away, boys. I'm a member of the DC Blue."

The Supervisor nodded in agreement with his request. The security team lowered their pistols.

"Grant," Alec began, "this is Dr. Apoe and the Program Supervisor."

"Not the same asshole we were trying to take down, I hope."

The Supervisor smiled warmly, unsure of the animosity's origin. "Welcome back to reality, Mr. Grant. We have other assholes to deal with now."

# CHAPTER 30

Jefferson Grant, a Washington DC metro police officer, spent the first three days of his new life with Alec Richardson. Occasionally, Dr. Apoe would see Grant but only for short visits related to his health.

Dr. Apoe was sitting in his office, reviewing his observations of the past week. He leaned back in his chair and sighed. Apoe had concerns.

Grant's Exit was not as easy as Richardson's, due in part to Grant's physical condition and age when he entered into the SOUP. Because of the medical technology used to sustain the body and its functions combined with the increased energy of receiving his psychic gifts, Apoe expected Grant to be a picture of health; he wasn't. He had early diabetes and other conditions related to many middle-aged adult males. The only explanation Apoe could rationalize for why the gifts had not brought Grant back to a picture of health was Grant was unsure about using them. Richardson confirmed his suspicions with Apoe. Richardson stated his friend knew the consequences of not using his gifts correctly. Unlike Richardson, Grant and his family possessed a solid Christian faith and surmised the DC cop did not want to get on the wrong side of God. It was Richardson's opinion Grant did not want to influence the natural aging within his body. Richardson had told him Jefferson appeared fine with the telepathy, but the power behind the telekinesis frightened him. He had mentioned he did not want to meet the Shiny Ones in the way Richardson had explained them to him. Jefferson's reluctance to use his gifts for fear of running contrary to his religious beliefs was an interesting data point that might re-emerge with future Exited inmates. He would watch this closely.

As a medical doctor, there was substantial data on

Grant and Richardson that would ensure Apoe published in every medical and scientific journal for the next three years. However, the classification of the material would prevent that portion of Apoe's career. Apoe resigned himself to applying this new knowledge to the program, its missions, and the risk associated with Grant and Richardson.

There were risks with these two men. Apoe confirmed Grant's gifts possessed the same energy level as anyone could determine, as Richardson. Grant also had the under-skin brand of the Egyptian ankh.

Apoe had witnessed Grant and Richardson using their telepathic ability to transfer program knowledge and experience. Sometimes the exchange would last for over an hour. To an outsider like him, he saw both men stare at each other, but behind those stares, vast amounts of data and life experiences merged.

Apoe was initially opposed to sharing all information with Grant. Apoe felt if Grant knew everything, he might be reluctant to use his gifts. Richardson quickly pointed out that if Grant was going to help, he needed to know everything that happened with the program. Like Grant's decision to Exit the SOUP, Jefferson also needed compelling information and explanations for why his gifts were required. Only Grant could decide whether he would help by using his gifts, another consideration of Free Will.

The gifts each possessed could be an excellent asset for protecting the program. Still, Apoe also understood Richardson, and now Grant had admitted they recalled experiences from the SOUP they perceived to be true. Apoe noticed these 'false memories' influenced both men and their emotional behavior. When it happened, both men showed signs of confusion with situational awareness and froze as though unable to process their surroundings. A brief period of irrational action followed, driven by anger over their confusion and frustration.

Apoe had not seen Harris and Livingston living outside

of the drug coma he placed them in, but for a short time at Site 35. However, there was nothing he observed in Harris which would indicate he was having problems with memories and confusing realities. When Apoe was not with Grant or Richardson, he studied the problem earnestly and understood all too well what risks this problem could introduce in both men and its negative impact on the program.

Apoe had found a stark contrast between the original inmates that Exited and the two men that will defend the program. The inmates Exited with one set of memories. These memories were created by the scenarios at the LA facility, which also suppressed their natural memories. His theory was the remote viewing incident used their gifts differently, creating a different physiological response by the body. This response caused excessive fatigue, and each fell into a deep sleep. Somehow, the suppressed memories re-emerged from the subconscious, and the inmates simultaneously possessed the programmed and original set of memories. But the inmates did not have the conflict Grant and Richardson were having.

Apoe believed each inmate knew they were criminals and those memories of their lives with crime were real and therefore were positively identified as authentic. The SOUP memories were directly opposite to their actual experiences, portraying a fictitious life each knew they had never lived. Because they recognized these memories of them as 'good people,' it was easy for the inmates to identify these memories as virtual. Internally, each knew their life was not 'good'; why would they be in prison if it was? It was an easy litmus test. How easy would it be to win a card game if all cards were visible to all the players? The inmates had this advantage.

Each man, Apoe reasoned, had both experiences with negative and positive lives and had chosen the positive life. Harris, he felt, was trying to reform his life and might even be getting close to building a positive relationship with Anderson. Livingston sacrificed his life to eliminate the cruel experiments in Site 35. The outlier to his hypothesis was Hoffman. He concluded that he experienced the same events as Harris and Livingston but <u>chose</u> to continue his old life.

*"How will you live the rest of your life?"* Deep reflection on this question had upended Apoe's career and brought him to this place, seeking to rebuild a life he no longer wanted to admit was his. *"The past influences the present, which creates the future."*

Boyd was right about his approach to reform. If criminals could see the positive life they could have, most would choose to do the right thing. Some were incapable of change, like Hoffman. He was a victim of a living environment that manifested the worst genetic expression his mind and body could produce. Being a serial killer was different than death under the influence of alcohol, like Livingston's case, or killing abusive parents in self-defense, like Harris.

He contrasted the situation with Grant and Richardson. Both were good men that did not have conflicting memories; instead, their memories in the SOUP were a continuation of their normal lives. In their case, each virtual memory was 'built upon' the experiences of their real lives. Unfortunately, both men lived in the 'gray space' where all their memories could be real. There were no apparent opposites to measure, no way to quickly isolate one memory as virtual and one as authentic. Therefore, he concluded, their memories were one long, connected, contiguous life providing no frame of reference for their life experiences.

If she chose to Exit, time for these men and Adelle was the only solution. The system implanted unique chemical pointers to each memory experience in their physical brains. Because they were no longer in the SOUP and the quantum tags useless, each man's mind would erase or lose track of the virtual information associated with the memory. When the quantum tag, the signpost to the experience in the SOUP, disappeared, the memory would fade away, not unlike losing real memories to a degraded brain function. How long this would take was unknown, Apoe postulated, just like knowing when someone will experience dementia is different for everyone. Some will encounter this problem early, and some will live their entire lives and never lose a memory.

*"How does this situation create risk for the program?"*

Apoe knew the Supervisor would want to know the program risks associated with using these men. Each had gifts that could defeat easily, the adversaries she'd targeted, but what would be the probability of something going wrong? Wasn't that the point? Wasn't the Supervisor declaring war on this administration because they were unwilling to wait for an optimal solution consisting of decisions made with eyes wide open, knowing the risk and reward for the resources used? Of late, the Supervisor was gambling, using her intuition, and yes, Apoe had to admit, some paranoia to make her decisions. How was that different than the steps taken by the administration? On this point, the Supervisor held the high ground. The administration used its political power to seize the program and place it under the CIA for national security reasons.

*"There was that damned phrase again! Was it the moral reason for exerting and using power, abusing rights to protect those same rights? No irony there!"*

They demanded the Exit solution and directed inmates to be used to perfect the methods. That meant more risk and the chance of taking many lives. They abducted UT, and his death was another emotional weight for the Supervisor. They kidnapped Dr. O'Neil and probably have the Exit information needed to seize the program facilities any day and start implementing their agendas. The Supervisor suspects Dr. O'Neil of sharing the information voluntarily with the agency and made her *persona non grata* at the facility, taking her out of the decision-making loop.

Apoe acknowledged the impact of his and Dr. O'Neil's work on the VITP because of the relationship between the two women. *"We still have more than three months before a prototype is available."* The fracture between the Supervisor and Dr. O'Neil's friendship has to close. There is too much here that Dr. O'Neil makes happen. Apoe would attempt to fix this widening rift.

That brought him to the crux of the problem. Were Grant and Richardson minimal risk assets to use to defend the program under the current conditions? Safety aside, would their activity's results benefit the program?

Apoe closed his eyes and ran his hands through his hair.

It came down to a straightforward fact despite the analysis. Grant and Richardson were the program's only options.

# CHAPTER 31

"Can you really hack the CIA's computer system?" Harris asked. The two were sitting in chairs next to each other, looking at the computer screen. "Yes, but it's going to require using a few tricks. Without my tool kit from home, I will have to rebuild some of my best routines. Shouldn't take long, though. This lab is a pretty sweet setup the Supervisor's team has given us. Starting on a classified network will make things much easier. Hmmm…"

"What's the problem?"

"No problem. Just thinking this through." Anderson proceeded to talk aloud, allowing Harris to share her thoughts.

"The goons that took my stuff probably found my best hacking tools and have put countermeasures in place. I'll need to modify my techniques slightly. These systems are built to repel people like me, but I've worked around their best defenses before. You have to be <u>creative</u>." Harris could sense the pride in Anderson's pronouncement while also hearing her emphasis on the last word.

"The advantage I have is the Director's schedule is not with the <u>deepest</u> secrets the CIA wants to protect." Harris watched the hint of a smile appear on Anderson's face.

She continued, slowly pronouncing each word, "But just because the security will be easier to <u>penetrate</u>…." Anderson moaned aloud and turned to face Harris. She looked deeply into his eyes. "That doesn't mean it's <u>easy</u>," she said in a sultry voice.

Harris heard the words and connected the hidden meaning. He blushed. Wanting to stay on mission and do something, anything, to change the tone of her voice, he offered. "It's a shame I lost my gifts. I could open the system and give you access." Harris rose out of his chair and stood behind Anderson. He leaned over her shoulder to get a better view of the screen and get back to business. Anderson opened a script editor and started composing code. Harris marveled at her fluid hand activity across the keyboard as she prepped her programs for the opening moves.

Returning to Harris' lamenting the loss of his gifts, Anderson said, "We don't know the server's location or the distance, and we're not set up for remote viewing here. I'm not sure your gifts would've worked anyway."

Her activity stopped for a moment. She turned slightly so that her cheek pressed very gently against his, sending a physical and emotional charge through Harris' body. "Besides, you've not lost all your gifts, Lincoln," she said slowly, each whispered word spoken into his ear amplified by the energy it produced. "You still have the power to move things."

Harris' body lit up like Times Square on New Year's Eve, and he pulled back quickly, trying to avoid further innuendo combined with her close physical touching.

*"Damn, how does she do that to me?"*

"Let's focus on getting the schedule information!" he said, his face blushing red a second time.

Anderson's voice returned to normal. "Why don't you sit over there and let me work." She pointed to another desk in the workspace they were using.

Anderson returned to her preparations, her smile indicating she was having fun on the keyboard and off.

*"Vixen! I feel like Ulysses drawn to the Sirens' singing; helpless but wanting more."*

Harris thought her suggestion a good one and sat down in the chair, a safe twenty feet from Anderson.

*"Get a grip on yourself, Lincoln!"* he thought.

Harris was seldom successful with the opposite sex. He had a fling with a woman named Dawn while he and Liv were residing in Las Vegas, but he believed that was more about sharing monthly rent than a romantic attraction. It was his first time with a woman, and he wondered, if not for Liv if he would have pursued finding a female roommate.

Harris had always found books to provide his adventures. Liv was different; he knew how to live! Harris even wondered if Dawn was pleased with his performance in the bedroom or if her profession as a stripper compelled her to give Harris exaggerated encouragement.

This thing, whatever it was with Sarah, was different. He <u>felt</u> something with her. She appealed to him intellectually, matching his book learning IQ point for point. But there was more. Simple gestures like her smile or touching his hand in the car when he revealed the crime that sent him to the SOUP. There was compassion and understanding. Then this last exchange, *"Damn, she was exciting!"* He did not believe he was capable of flirting as she did. There was something about how she used her eyes and dropped her dual-meaning comments to take him places he never thought existed. Harris hoped she was not toying with him, and these were her opening moves off her computer keyboard for something long-term. She was sending all the right signals to him, but did she feel as he did?

Harris heard the steady tapping of her fingers on the keyboard. To him, they sounded rhythmic and soothing. They stopped suddenly.

"Shit! I need to get a soda," Anderson exclaimed. She rose from her chair, pushing it backward in frustration, and walked into the hall, not asking if Harris wanted anything.

Harris remained sitting, trying desperately to turn his thoughts to something else and not wanting to tempt his heart or any other body part, to go with her into the hall. If he did, and she responded favorably, he knew they would lose precious time on personal matters.

She returned with a Mountain Dew from one of the machines available on the floor and sat in her chair. She took a long pull on the drink and placed the plastic bottle next to her below a wall sign that read, "No food or drinks near the computers."

A brief silence followed, then the rhythmic typing started again. Harris resigned himself to continuing his thoughts about Sarah Anderson and the future of their relationship. He realized his respect for her created a large, deep part of his attraction. While hacking was not necessarily an honorable profession, it was like many vocations. Unscrupulous methods were ignored if done for the right reason. It was no different than marketing for a large corporation, he reasoned. Half the claims targeted your emotions, and if truth be told, the content about the product was questionable. Even the pharmaceutical ads required legal mumbo jumbo at the end of each commercial to protect the company from claims of cures that might not be true. But marketing was an honorable pursuit when producing company profits. Using this logic, he had no problems justifying Anderson's hacking. And this didn't even consider the importance of the program's defense. Yes, he concluded. He felt something for her akin to admiration.

"Son of a bitch!" Another unsuccessful attempt. The exclamation produced a brief silence, followed by an immediate, continuous rhythm of key presses by a woman obsessed with success. As the keys pressed into the keyboard, they produced ticking, fast ticking, then slow. Sometimes there was a crashing crescendo of rapid keystrokes followed by slower ones. The pace changed as her mind churned with thoughts involving the correct syntax, logic flow, and attack vector.

Harris moved uncomfortably as his thoughts conjured images of him in intimate positions with her, his motions matching the sounds of the keys. He was feeling warm inside.

The ticking sounds stopped, and a laser printer next to him came to life. Anderson stood up and walked towards him and the printer. She pulled the sheet off the printer top and looked at it. Harris could tell she was pleased.

"Okay," she said. "Let's go show them what we have."

"I'll join you in a moment," Harris said, needing a minute to return his body to normal.

"The Supervisor will not like that. She asked us to stay

together. Don't you think that's better?" Her voice was soft, each word exploding with meaning for him.

Harris smiled. He liked the message he was hearing. "Spoken by a woman who puts her drink under the sign that reads not to put your drinks under the sign." Harris pointed to her soda's plastic bottle. "Since when do you follow instructions?"

"We all follow instructions when they benefit us, Lincoln." Anderson looked at him and smiled. She reached down and took his hand. "Let's go."

# CHAPTER 32

To say the Supervisor was impressed with Sarah Anderson would be an understatement. She made that quite evident in her praise for the young hacker. "Maybe I should hire her full-time on the team," she had said to Apoe.

Dr. Apoe presented the stolen schedule to the Supervisor, and the two quickly identified the best time to implement phase I. The Supervisor circled a date and time and said, "This is the window."

Dr. Apoe suggested once more the Supervisor notify Senator Hurst and Dr. Lucia of the strategy change. Dr. Apoe argued the significant shift from passive nanotechnology to an overt assault on key administration officials with the intent to harm. This was a HUGE change. The Supervisor was curt when replying to Dr. Apoe, "They don't need to know. Hurst and Lucia will have plausible deniability if our attempts go sideways. If our plan works, they may suspect but never know what we did." The conversation ended, and she asked her admin to set up an immediate meeting in the conference room.

Once the plan was put in motion, Apoe expected blowback from the administration. Dr. Apoe had no doubts their plan of attack was treason, but only if the American people learned what happened. Each day citizens lived their lives, never knowing a full-out war was occurring within their government. In the war's secrecy, Apoe found the reasoning he needed to follow the Supervisor down this rabbit hole. If the information about their activity were released to the public, he would ensure all the data was released. The story would make no sense unless put into context with the facts. Once the circumstances were known, let everyone be tried in the court of public opinion. As a minimum, jobs and elections would be lost. This public disclosure would be unacceptable to the Vice President. It might cost him the election.

The Supervisor and Dr. Apoe walked together to the conference room and took their seats. Both remained quiet until joined by Richardson, Grant, Anderson, and Harris. The Supervisor began the meeting, "Because of Ms. Anderson's efforts, we now have the information we need to implement, what I am calling, Phase I. She has identified a place in the calendar where the CIA Director is not in public and with only his security team."

Anderson and Harris understood their role and executed flawlessly. Time to move to her following instructions.

"Alec, you and Jefferson are our next point in the plan." Both men nodded and understood it was time to contribute to the program's defense.

"Let me explain why we are doing this," the Supervisor began. "Our government is directing us to use the SOUP facilities to create people with gifts, like Lincoln, for the CIA and Department of Defense. The Vice President wants this done immediately. Why, might you ask? Well, he has an election in 20 months and wants to build his credentials and win his election – regardless of the cost to human life and abuse of power harming others that would result. Because he said these assets would make this Nation stronger and more secure, the Director of the CIA and the Secretary of Defense support his efforts. Both these men stand to gain in the new administration and control incredibly powerful assets that could be used, and God only knows how against the public. In summary, the desire to control our program is about the power that could lead to tyranny. Our job is to prevent this from happening."

Anderson raised her hand, "I'm a little fuzzy on the God-only-knows part. Could you elaborate for me?"

Apoe answered, "When people like the VP get into office, they are not interested in the people they serve, just the power the position gives them. If the VP has hundreds of assets like our team under his control, he may never give up his position, and no one can force him out. Our republic disappears. We may never have an election again. Are you ready for that, Ms. Anderson?"

"You think that could really happen?" Harris asked.

"Your recent gifts are a perfect example, Lincoln. You were not born with those gifts; the SOUP created them. We had no idea the system could do these things. That same uncertainty exists in our country if many gifted people are released into the public. The Vice President thinks he can control what he creates, but can he?" Apoe said.

"We don't know if the next President will not give up power, but it is a huge temptation not to," the Supervisor added.

Apoe continued the information flow, "There is one thing we know the Vice President and his team don't yet. We just found it out ourselves. Your gifts don't last forever. We don't know how long you have them; we believe it involves how fast your pineal gland returns to normal, which causes them to disappear. But we have no idea when that will happen."

"Which is why we need to move on with our plan now. Recent events confirm the Vice President has secured the Exit sequence, which means we could have agents or soldiers at the facility at any time. If they show up, we've lost. They will direct the staff to run tests on the Exit sequence and, if inmates Exit but are not what they want, they will disappear or kill the unfortunate ones selected for the trial."

The Supervisor looked at the assembled group and paused. She returned the gaze of each person looking at her and said, "Our first Supervisor had a vision for the future. That vision saw our nation's worst criminals humanely paying their debt to society. His vision not only revolutionized incarceration but produced technology that benefited others. That vision laid out a way to reform our prison system so one day, each person could be released back into society as a productive citizen, personally unaware of their crimes and society's incriminations."

Anderson reached over and took Harris' hand.

"IF the Vice President is successful, his administration will destroy all that is good in our system and use it for his purposes, not the people. Now is our time to stand against reckless power seeking to harm or kill needlessly. Now is our time to maintain the integrity of our program. Our program was built to provide hope, not suffering."

The Supervisor paused and looked at the faces looking at her, then continued, "Jefferson, you and Alec discussed all the information about the program and your gifts. Do you understand the consequences of misusing the gifts you have?"

"Alec has explained it all," Grant responded.

The Supervisor nodded her head. "Good. Your person of interest is the Director of the CIA. Approach time will be approximately 9:00 p.m. two days from now."

"Ms. Supervisor," Alec interrupted. "I believe I should take the Director. I've been out longer and have re-adjusted to this world better than Grant."

"I agree with you, Alec, but to be successful, we have a narrow window. While Jefferson is confronting the Director in Virginia, you will be in Utah dealing with the Vice President. He's giving a policy speech at Arches National Park. With the time difference of two hours, your action will be close to Jefferson's. I can't emphasize enough how important it will be not to leave behind anything associated with the program. It won't take them long to know who is responsible, and we'll have big problems. Additionally, we assess the Director and VP are driving the effort to control our program. If the Secretary is the man we must bypass, we believe he will respond less aggressively. Please make no mistake, he will act, but he might delay long enough for one of you to get a chance with him. Understood?"

Both men nodded.

"Have you thought about your target parameters with these men?" Apoe asked.

"Non-lethal incapacitation," Grant and Richardson said

simultaneously.

"Such as," the Supervisor inquired.

"We understand our role is to buy time until the VITP is built and tested. That solution will be the objective one. Timeline is six months max," Alec said.

"AND," Apoe started, "<u>all</u> actions you take against these men are not permanent or lethal. These efforts must look natural and must be <u>self-correcting</u>. Use your gifts to delay action against the program, not to cause damage or death."

"To harm them would equate us with their values. If our values are the same, then we've lost the moral high ground," Alec finished.

"That and the Shiny Ones will visit," Grant said. He was visibly disturbed by his comment.

"Well said." The Supervisor stood up. "Sarah, I would like you and Lincoln to provide six-hour updates on the Director's schedule. If it changes, I want to know about it. Also, the same arrangement with the VP's trip."

"On it," Anderson said.

"Alec, you and Jefferson stay flexible. People this senior are always moving appointments around. We will contact you if we decide to abort."

Apoe passed two large, sealed manila envelopes to the men. "Here are documents with information, maps, and other logistic details. Alec, your travel arrangements are in there. You both have about 36 hours of prep time. I am available for questions until you leave. Final Questions?"

The room was silent. "Good luck."

Alec Richardson was in his room, preparing to pack. He opened his envelope to review his travel information. Inside was a smaller envelope marked travel on the front. Alec ripped one of the short edges and pulled out a sheet of paper, expecting to see airline and rental car reservation confirmations. Instead, there was a single note.

"Stay with Grant. He is not stable. Tell no one, especially Grant." It was signed by Apoe.

# CHAPTER 33

The Virginia night was pitch black as Grant moved into his final position. The new moon would work to his advantage as he slowly crawled to a dense growth of trees surrounded by limestone boulders that littered the landscape. Grant pulled a small night vision monoscopic device from his vest pocket and brought it to his right eye while closing his left. He panned slowly from the left edge of the small woods anchoring his location through the target house to his front. He saw nothing that alarmed him. The house was a large structure nestled inside hardwood trees that rose from the earth into a perfectly manicured lawn, a signature look for the most affluent neighborhoods in McLean. Even the newly fallen leaves looked as though they were placed by hand in the yard by the owner to accent the property's beauty.

Grant replaced his night vision device with binoculars and scanned the home's various lit rooms. In the house, there was motion from the occupants. He expected them to be home. The resident couple was old friends with Director Thompson. They moved to Northern Virginia to be appointees within the President's administration after the last election. The couple moved in the same circles as Thompson and frequently saw him at work events. Both husband and wife were professionals, which meant personal socializing outside work functions was seldom done. After months of haranguing, Thompson had consented to an evening visit. "After all," the wife said during one of her invitations, "Langley is close enough from the house to hit with a rock. Call first, and if we're home, then drop by." Grant had thought those details odd in his briefing packet until he realized the accounts came from someone close to the couple, which was a second source to verify Thompson's scheduled appointment for the evening. The Supervisor's team had put together a really good mission folder. This level of detail proved the Supervisor had resources close to the Director and gave Grant a small boost of confidence.

Grant rolled over on his back and pulled up his jacket collar. He had planned to arrive two hours before the appointment and was right on schedule. Grant wanted to see Thompson arrive and watch the security team move to its position. From his vantage point, he could look down the long driveway curving around a large clumping of trees about a hundred yards in front of the house. With this view, Grant could see the approach cleanly. Now he would wait and listen.

"*Listen,*" Grant thought. There was a word with a new meaning.

Grant reflected on his time spent with Alec over the last 72 hours. Alec shared the visualization techniques of using a volume control to filter out the noise and clutter. Grant had learned people constantly emit their energy thoughts, and the further away from the person, the harder it was to isolate their energy. Grant had no idea there were so many sounds he could never hear before the SOUP. At the admin building, his mind was bombarded by constant noise and random thoughts. Alec had explained to Grant there were times he would shut down that part of his gifts. Without identifying the person's 'voice,' there was no way to associate and tie the conversations and sounds together. Alec advised getting as close to the person or people emitting the thoughts as possible and focusing on their thoughts. The closer, the better. Alec described using telepathy beyond ten feet as talking with your date while standing in front of the speakers at a rock concert. Grant knew immediately what Alec meant.

That applied to his telekinetic gifts as well. Control your thoughts, Alec had told him. Focus on what you are trying to accomplish. Grant felt better knowing his random thoughts did not produce results, but only concentration on a specific idea would activate the energy. Alec had introduced him to Lincoln Harris at the building. Harris shared his experiences using the telekinetic gifts. He told Grant telekinetic energy also had distance limitations. Harris believed up to 50 feet would work. Beyond that, he said, the energy weakened. Harris described the force he used in Las Vegas as 'infinite power,' but as the distance increased, the energy levels fell dramatically. Harris also relayed that with the proper preparation, the gifts could do something called Remote Viewing, but required trained people to activate the right parts of the brain and channel the energy.

*"Harris was one badass,"* Grant thought, recalling Harris' Las Vegas experience. He thought about the power of future soldiers. The Supervisor was right. We need to delay these bastards until we figure out more about the ups and downsides of what we have.

Grant's mind turned to other badasses he knew, and it wasn't long before he remembered Maggie, his eyes on the streets of DC with a heart of gold as he recalled. She was not afraid of anyone or anything and was the source that eventually led him to investigate the SOUP before it was public knowledge. Grant felt angry as he remembered the women and children of incarcerated inmates brought to reside in the SOUP as part of some twisted government program. He suspected when Maggie disappeared, she was in the SOUP, placed there to prevent her from talking. More innocent lives have been turned upside down because of politicians and corruption. He was sick of it.

The quiet was interrupted by a vehicle's headlights bouncing in the trees above Grant. He rolled over and saw the vehicle stop in front of the target house. He brought the binoculars up to his eyes. He observed several men and women exiting a large black vehicle. Their voices carried through the night, and Grant heard, "everyone know their positions? Good, the boss will be here in about 40 minutes. Do your recons and settle in for the next couple of hours. Give me an all-clear, and I will let the boss know it's safe to be here. Any questions? None, then let's get started."

The person talking walked to the front door of the house and knocked. Grant counted eight agents. Five were coming in his direction, and two headed to the other side of the house. Grant lost visibility of those two quickly. The door opened, and the agent invited in, most likely to explain his team's role in the evening social visit.

*"Time to move."*

Grant suspected the agents would set up a barrier between the house and the stream he'd crossed and create an outer ring of protection. Grant crawled backward quietly until far enough away to stand, cross the creek on the county-provided crossing stones, and take up his alternative position.

Grant had just laid down when he could hear the agents creeping through the woods, beginning their sweeps. He looked through his night vision device and could see the five agents as they moved as a wave down to the creek and stopped. He quickly turned off his device. The agents also wore night vision devices and would detect the active infrared light used by his instrument to shine on objects to 'light them up at night.'

*"Use your gifts to see and hear them."*

The agent closest to him was twenty feet from his position. Grant expanded the range of his telepathy skill and eavesdropped on the guard busily scanning his surroundings.

*"Nothing here. All looks safe. Make extra sure. The Threat Level is elevated this evening."*
The agent whispered his report into the microphone on a small communications device worn on his head. "This is position six. All secure."

*"Okay, tighten the perimeter toward the house but keep your sectors in sight."* Grant could not hear a word in the forest but understood the message received by the agent. *"These guys are good,"* Grant thought.

*"Roger."* The Agent responded as he turned around and started walking to the vantage point Grant left earlier.

*"Feel them. Where are they?"* Grant reached out further

with his mind and found all five. Grant's mind was overwhelmed with each independent thought streams from each agent. He listened for a minute and sorted out the random personal conversations as the agents took their positions. Grant detected one common thread shared among the five. They were on a heightened level of alert. One of the agents thought this was not a nightly babysitting job for the Director.

Grant heard one of the agents communicate, *"positions secure."*

*"I'll inform the boss. Inbound and will arrive in approximately 15 minutes."*

*"The Director was early!"* Grant thought. *"Good, let's get this over with."*

Grant remained silent, knowing the Director needed to arrive and go into the house before he could make his move. While he had not observed the man initially approaching the house, he knew from his police experience he was somewhere in the woods. That meant eight in the ring. When the Director arrived, Grant suspected there would be four more agents. Two would remain with the vehicle for a rapid departure. The other two would most likely take up positions near the main road to defend the exit route from the neighborhood. That meant, including the Director, there were 13 people in play, plus the couple in the house. *"Should be easy enough."*

Everyone was in position, and their random thoughts began to creep into the conversations as they waited. Grant felt embarrassed listening to the personal thoughts of the agents as they contemplated their sex lives, desires for money, divorcing their spouse, or personal morning routines. Grant decreased his telepathy range and felt better immediately as the conversations stopped. He looked at his watch. He would grab 5-8 minutes of quiet before using his gifts again.

He needed to move quickly when the time came. Grant had located the five agents in their positions, and the closest was about 80 feet from where he was now. That meant the others would need to clump together in response to him, or he would have to take out each position. Harris had told him how he put the staff asleep escaping Site 35. Grant intended to do the same. The DC cop also knew he would be visible with their night vision devices as soon as he moved. He would close the distance as fast as possible. Harris explained his defense to Grant. He was comfortable knowing that while speed was essential to reach the Director, their weapons would not threaten his personal life. Grant liked the feeling of being immortal, immune to the bullets the agents would fire at him until he was in range to use his gifts.

Grant would respond with *"non-lethal action."*

He watched the second hand click away the minutes. Slowly he increased his telepathy range and began to hear the agents to his front.

*"Roger, sir, the boss is in the house."*

Grant looked up from his hiding place and surveyed the ground. There was a slight rise in the terrain as the woods increased their distance from the stream.

*"Let's move,"* he said to himself and, in one motion, began a quick walk to the crossing stones. Halfway across the creek, the agent confronted him. "Stop! Who are you?"

Grant did not slow and continued to the other side of the water.

"Stop. I am a US agent authorized to use deadly force."

Grant continued headlong into the darkness, up the rise towards the voice.

"One last warning!"

Grant could hear the man issuing verbal commands to other agents in range.

*"Sleep!"*

The man's voice stopped abruptly, as did a second interloper thinking about shooting.

*"Two down, three to go. Protect!"*

Grant felt a warmth immerse his body. While he knew it surrounded him. There was no light from the heat that spilled into the darkness. His defenses were activated.

The familiar pop of a pistol fired with a silencer came from his right. A dull blue glow on his body registered the hit. Two more pops, followed by multiple shots, all silenced in the dark, the bullet impacts creating a blue glow around him. Grant continued to the top of the rise with voices chattering loudly. The agents shared their conversations on the communication devices with the entire security team. The remaining agents and, most likely, the Director knew about his presence. Grant thought, 'Sleep!' once more, and two more voices disappeared into the dark.

As he crested the small ridge, he identified two vehicles parked in front of the house. He needed to get close enough to immobilize them before the Director could escape and sprinted down the hill, taking fire from front and left. As he approached the first vehicle, he flattened the tires and broke the rear axle. The axle created a loud bang when the vehicle's weight pushed down on the cracked steel and flat tires, collapsing as a clump in the driveway.

"*Try using the tranquilizer darts,*" Grant heard, walking to the house.

"*Tranquilizer darts? Why would they have them?*" And then Grant understood. They knew he was coming!

Grant's outer exterior lit the night bright blue, hit by dozens of bullets suddenly fired by automatic weapons to his rear. To his front was a half-height stone wall which he jumped and slouched behind to use as cover, all done by instinct. Each weapon continued to fire volumes of lead, chipping away at the stone wall, their reports silenced by the devices on their barrels. Grant looked at the house. The lights had turned off, but there was no movement to get the Director to the second vehicle. He increased the distance so that he could detect voices but heard nothing, yet bullets continued to shred the top of the wall structure.

"*Blockers, they are using blockers. How many agents are here?*"

As if in response, Grant's exterior turned bright blue

as his body took the hits from a volume of gunfire from his unprotected right side.

"*I need to focus on the Director. Move to the house.*" He started moving quickly towards the building, oblivious to the brightness surrounding him as, round after round, tried to penetrate the defense his gifts provided. As he approached the second van, there were no drivers, and the vehicle was not running, another indicator that no one was leaving.

"*They intend to capture or bring me down! I am not going back into the SOUP!*"

Parked closer to him and next to the government's signature black suburban was the Lexus SUV belonging to the house owners. Grant disabled the second government vehicle using the same method as the first. He was about 20 feet from the house when he commanded, "Sleep." If the Director were inside, he would not be going anywhere now, but he needed to find him fast.

Grant looked to his left and saw numerous figures moving through the darkness toward the house, too far away to incapacitate. Another large group of what he estimated to be 30 or more came up behind him, each shooting at his blue signature, illuminating the darkness. Grant moved and turned to face the group, who provided continuous fire as they advanced, lighting the evening sky with muzzle flashes that made no sound. He heard the noise before he understood what was happening; bullets were ricocheting off him and entering the metal exterior of the couple's car parked next to him. It sounded like rain on a tin roof and then...a brief flash before the explosion's fireball rolled over him. While unphased by the detonation, he felt the soundwave push his head sideways, jarring his cranium. He instinctively dropped and forced himself to the ground, face first. It took him a nanosecond to conclude several errant rounds had found the Lexus gas tank.

Grant heard a steady buzz in his head as he struggled to rise to his feet. He stood, slightly dazed, and looked around him to re-orient himself. The buzzing continued getting louder as a torrent of lead hit him, and then Grant felt a slight pain in his calf. He saw his trousers slit open and a small scratch bleeding slightly. Something had penetrated his defense. The buzz continued to increase and began to build a rhythm of ups and downs dancing in his mind. Grant tried to focus to re-orient himself on the mission, but the loud buzz prevented him from understanding what was happening to him. Each second he stood, dazed by the burning car, numerous blue dots appeared before his eyes as bullets hit his defenses in increasing numbers.

*"Where am I, and why am I here? That's right, I remember. Trying to defeat the bad guys hurting people. Hurting who?"* Grant's mind was on fire as he attempted to organize his thoughts, and then he remembered everything about what he was doing.

*"These are the bastards that put those families in the SOUP! That young boy I saw."* Grant began to recall his purpose, oblivious that he was standing in the front of the house, bullets peppering his exterior. Inside Grant's mind, he began to replay his life's story. His memories rapidly popped in and out of his consciousness, causing him to kneel in pain. Bright flashes of his history and the buzzing sound continued to intensify. Grant yelled out, feeling as if his brain was tearing small strips of itself off in small slices, and still, the groups closed in, continuing their firing and turning him into a blue ball of flame.

Grant felt a hot object penetrate his shoulder, and outside, his blue halo began to dim. Grant looked to his right and saw several agents fall limp to the ground, their automatic weapons ceasing to spew out their silent flame. To his front, a speeding Suburban stopped suddenly and turned sideways, sliding in the Virginia topsoil until meeting strong oak. No one exited the vehicle.

*"What was going on?"* Grant had not focused on those objects. He quickly dismissed the assistance as irrelevant to his mission. Grant was obsessed with finding the Supervisor,

the man responsible for his time in the SOUP. He wanted the people that had made his longtime friend Maggie disappear. Grant wanted the man responsible for taking those innocent lives, taking them from their families. *"I will make him pay."*

Grant's mind placed a secession of images of various people, flashing in his mind for a three-second duration before moving on to the next. Flashed images, light so bright it hurt his eyes, followed quickly by more flashes and continuous pain, all in concert with the buzzing, which grew in intensity, slowly increasing in volume as each face flashed. With each picture, he felt his rage grow stronger, supplanted only by the desire for justice for the innocents, all the while becoming more sensitive to the bullet strikes getting closer to his skin.

Grant sensed the firing had stopped. He no longer felt the pinpricks on his skin and was blinded by the images, which flashed slower on his optic nerve.

*"What happened to Maggie?"*

Instantly his mind recalled her face, the memories coming deep from within his confused psyche. The image remained locked in his mind, and the buzzing stopped. Her features began to move, slowly revealing more of her body tied to a chair in some ethereal place. Its only feature was the wispy smoke that surrounded her. The Supervisor was behind her with two of his team. Grant remembered the assignment, never questioning it's reality - aware only that the emotions were real, driving his actions onward in his present moment. This experience occurred a year ago on an assignment near the funeral home with the SOUP facility. His mind began producing memories of the event, pulling from the Quantum tags that loomed as brightly as a signpost for his demented and confused mind.

There was a major terrorist alert, and he needed to develop his intelligence before striking. Maggie volunteered to do some looking around for Grant and was apprehended. He never saw her after that night. What had happened to her? Maggie looked directly at Grant. Her expression was stern, and she was unafraid. Grant saw her move her lips, never taking her stoic stare away from him. "Make them pay," she said.

The Supervisor stepped forward and pulled Maggie's head backward by her hair, exposing her full neck. He brandished a large knife and crossed her neck with the blade. Moving slowly, he slit her throat, his face registering the pleasure of taking her life, not in one quick slash, but a deliberate slow cut to heighten the pain and deepen the cut. Grant was transfixed by the Supervisor's two agents, laughing as her arteries released the blood pulsing through her body into a red fountain onto the floor in front of him. Maggie tried to scream, but Grant heard small whimpers and gurgling noises as she gasped her last breaths and kicked wildly to free herself from the chair that bound her. The Supervisor pulled back on Maggie's hair roughly and completed his cut, which severed her head. He tossed the severed body part at Grant as her headless torso slumped forward and her remaining life pumped to the ground.

Grant screamed, terrified by the memory his mind recalled and stumbled backward. Alec, seeing the eratic behavior, suspected Grant was on the edge between his real and false memories. Alec watched Grant from his position contemplating how he could help his friend.

Seeing Grant decend further into distress, Alec jumped a half-height stone wall on the other side of the yard and sprinted to his friend. "No!" Alec shouted, running to Grant. "It's not real!" The agents, unsure of what was transpiring, advanced no closer and held their fire.

Grant looked at Alec. The agents kept their distance, unaware that Grant's memories had betrayed him and now his wrath would turn on them. In a quick motion, Grant dropped to one knee, and as it touched the ground, he extended his arms in front of him. Alec heard Grant say, "kill them all."

Alec stopped and said aloud, "defend and protect." Alec hoped his defenses would not falter under Grant's coming release of focused rage.

Grant's body began to emit a bright blue glow, growing in intensity until it looked white. The glow suddenly released itself through the ground, emanating from his place outward in a circle, a thin narrow band of light traveling through the ground at every degree. It touched Alec and passed over the top, sharing its blue glow with him, a minor detour on its way to the more vulnerable. As it touched the agents, they rose quickly as men into the air and fell as a clump of flesh into the dirt; each life extinguished in a second. Grant's energy touched the house, creating no damage as each narrow beam walked up the side of the home, temporarily bending into the window, making a pointed needle of energy inside the room, seeking out any life within, before returning outside the house to continue its climb.

Alec watched as the agents furthest from Grant ran to safety while those close rose and fell, twisting in mid-air as their bones snapped, their fate sealed. Alec saw the beams inching up the side of the house, join at the top, then disappear along with those that traversed the ground. Grant fell forward. As Alec ran to him, Grant's body disappeared.

Alec stopped. He heard the natural sounds of humanity as he regained his senses. The night air carried the noise of barking dogs and neighbors outside talking aloud about an explosion and the small fire burning at the house. Alec could recall hearing nothing during the entire fight except that explosion. The blast seemed out of place when contrasted by the agents' stealth, but Alec saw the change in Grant's demeanor right after the explosion.

Alec could make out cautious movements in the darkness as surviving agents struggled to regain their natural night vision after the blinding blue light and head to the house. Alec quickly moved away from his location and took up a position on the far side of the wall he'd jumped earlier and crouched down behind it. Alec increased the range of his telepathic hearing, and conversations flooded his mind. He filtered out those asking for help with a broken leg or arm and focused his thoughts on the house. He heard the conversation between agents. They were afraid.

"Someone get me a working comm package!"

"Is that the Director?"

"Yes."

"What the hell happened? It looks like every bone in his body is broken!"

"His friends did not fare much better," another agent said. "Holy shit, look at these people. Hey boss, who was that guy? He kicked our ass."

"Shut up! We got to get this place cleaned up. Someone get me some working comms!"

Alec turned down his mental knob and shut out everything around him. He needed to leave. He knew the agents would be looking to contain the area and might, even now, be setting up a perimeter to deny access to neighbors and the press, who might want to snoop into the source of their neighborhood disturbance.

"Jesus, Grant, what did you see that made you do this? You knew what would happen if you used your gifts like this." Alec felt remorse for his friend immediately.

Alec started a slow movement through the woods that blocked the noise of highway 123 from intruding on the neighborhood. He quickened his pace when reaching the highway en route to his car, parked not far away in a church parking. Alec saw the blue lights of the Fairfax County police driving towards him. He stood behind a tree quickly, and the car zoomed by, followed by a firetruck and ambulance racing to their common destination.

As Alec walked to his car, he asked again, "What happened, Grant?" Alec stopped for a moment and asked aloud, "Will the same thing happen to me?"

# CHAPTER 34

This was bad. This was really bad. The Director of the CIA was dead, killed by accident along with approximately 20 of his agents, but dead nonetheless. It didn't matter if it was an accident. Something went wrong, very wrong. The Supervisor and Apoe were sitting in the conference room. The Supervisor was looking for answers.

"*How and the hell could this happen?*" The Supervisor asked herself.

She gave specific instructions for non-lethal force to be used. She covered with them how they would approach their targets. "*God Damn it!*"

The Supervisor slammed her open hand down on the conference room table, creating a slapping sound like the dropping of a large book flatly on the floor. She composed herself, brushing her hair backward with a head flip and sighing loudly, letting the frustration in the room slowly dissipate with her exhaled breath.

"Okay," the Supervisor began. "Let's start with why Alec was not in Utah."

"That was my decision," Apoe said, "I gave him the new mission."

"Why would you do that, and under what authority?"

"Ms. Supervisor, we are opposing this administration because we believe they have no idea how to use the power this system provides and would corrupt it. We are fighting them because they want to use the people in the SOUP to experiment rather than correctly assess the risks in other ways. We don't believe human life is to be discarded."

"Fine, Franklin, what's your point?"

Apoe looked at the Supervisor, pausing to allow the Supervisor to answer her own question.

"Well?"

"My point, Ms. Supervisor, is, so are we. We are doing things to defend this program that is also pushing the boundaries."

"Bull shit!" she yelled.

"It's not!" Apoe yelled back. "Grant's condition, for one. He was not mentally stable. I told you that. He was not ready for this, but you sent him anyway. Jesus, these guys have powers that can kill with a thought, and you feel like you can use them because you believe you are right! Being right does not protect you from things going wrong! We just added 23 new dead people to the headcount. We did! Not them!"

The Supervisor dropped her voice, trying to return civility to the conversation. "We used Grant on your recommendation. We looked at the risks. As you told me, we have no other option. Isn't that what you said, Franklin?"

Apoe also lowered his voice. "It is. That's why I sent Alec to shadow Grant. Alec's mental state is more stable. His memories are sorting themselves out."

The Supervisor stood up and began to pace. "The other three were not like this."

"That's because they Exited differently. They were being 'treated' before Exit, and the frequencies they experienced happened naturally. We've tried duplicating what the earthquake did, but maybe we are missing something."

"Is that your assessment, Doctor?"

Apoe looked at her. "Ms. Supervisor, we are learning more each hour about our Exit sequence and the impacts. Ask me in an hour, and I might have a different answer."

"That does me no good." The Supervisor shot back at Apoe.

"We can't control what happens! What illusion are you under to think you can!"

The Supervisor turned and readied a stern reply but decided that the conversation had no end point or merit, just accusations. She looked down, then over at Apoe, and said, "Shit. What do we do now?"

Apoe lowered his voice again. "If you want to control something, control the fallout of our situation. The Director is dead. That won't be in the news, but even the president will know, and so will a handful in congress. You don't keep something like this hidden. People are going to want answers. Some will want revenge."

The Supervisor nodded.

"Have you heard from Dr. Lucia or Senator Hurst?"

"No, and I don't believe I will, Franklin. They are going to want to stay far away from this. This is my mess. I expect they'll want me to clean it up."

Apoe agreed. "What do you think the VP and SECDEF will do?"

"That's a good question, Franklin. I expect, publicly, there will be no change. I don't expect them to seize the facilities. We've sent a message. A false one, but they don't know that. The Director's death will buy us some time. Maybe a month or more, but not much more."

"What message is that, Ms. Supervisor?"

"Mess with us, and we will kill you. The VP will understand this right away. It gives us a temporary advantage, but if we don't find a way to resolve this correctly, it won't end well for us or the program."

"So, let's find a solution."

The Supervisor looked at Apoe and saw the man she had worked with years ago. The man with whom she had fallen in love. He was here, wanting to bridge the gap in their lives that caused their separation. For this alone, she trusted him to bring in others to help.

"Okay, call them in."

The Supervisor sat down, and Apoe rose, walked to the door, and said, "let's go."

Richardson, Harris, and Anderson walked in, and everyone took their seats.

"Alec, I would like to start with you. I'd like to know what you saw and did," the Supervisor said.

"Okay, Ms. Supervisor. I arrived about an hour before the Director did. I could see that parts of his security team were already in position."

"Did you see, Grant?"

"No, Franklin, I think he made his approach from the South. There were denser woods that would provide concealment."

"What happened next?"

"I saw the car arrive with the Director. I could do a positive ID from the picture you provided me. It was Thompson. Then the commotion started. Grant had made his move. I listened to agents talking, pulling bits and pieces of information from the voices. I heard one agent confirm the Director was here as bait. It was his choice. They knew we were coming."

"How? Sarah, did you cover your exit from their system?"

"Yes, ma'am. The standard SOP for hackers is not to let you know they were there. I used some of my best stuff."

"Any chance," Apoe asked, "That they had developed a profile of your best stuff the last time you went in?"

"It is possible, Dr. Apoe, but I think unlikely." Anderson sounded unsure and less confident of her answer.

"Alec, continue," the Supervisor requested.

"I saw Grant come over the top of a small ravine."

"How did you know it was Grant?"

"Ma'am, the agents began firing. He activated his protection which turns blue when hit by projectiles."

Both the Supervisor and Apoe nodded, familiar with the power of each man in the Las Vegas videos and hearing Harris' accounts of Site 35.

"Go on."

"Something strange happened. All the voices stopped, and then the woods and a small open area behind him erupted. They'd been waiting and were using the blockers Dr. Apoe had used at Site 35 to impede Grant's telepathy. There must have been close to 80 agents, all firing automatic weapons. They all had silencers, so other than the occasional ricochets, there was little noise. Grant was moving towards the house, and I noticed that his protection seemed dimmer."

"You mean like his power was getting weaker?" Apoe asked.

"It was no longer bright blue but was starting to fade. I don't know if Grant's powers were failing or not."

"Continue," the Supervisor directed.

"A new vehicle showed up coming down the road to the house. It was close to my position. I had the truck stop and put the agents to sleep. As more approached my position to try and flank him, I put those agents to sleep too."

The Supervisor nodded.

"Grant was moving steadily towards the house. The agents were putting a lot of fire on him. I saw him disable two government vehicles before a civilian car blew up. I suspect some rounds glanced off Grant and ignited the fuel tank. It was at this point that I could tell something was different. He became more aggressive, and I could hear him yelling. It sounded like he was in pain. That's when he focused his energy on the house and around him. People started dying when he did it."

"What happened to Grant?" Apoe asked.

"I started to run toward him, but before I could reach him, he disappeared right before my eyes."

"They took him." It was a simple statement, but everyone knew Harris' assessment was correct.

"I think so, Lincoln." Alec looked down at the table. It was evident to his friends that Grant's loss would impact Alec significantly.

"I'm sorry for the loss of your friend, Alec," the Supervisor offered. She understood when someone you cared about left your life unexpectantly and tried to share her compassion with Alec.

"Anybody have any questions for Alec?"

Nobody in the room wanted to ask any. They would catch up with him later.

"That's it then. Everybody knows where we stand and what happened. Learn from this team."

Everyone stood up. Alec hung back and waited until it was Apoe and the Supervisor.

"Ms. Supervisor, we need to get Adelle."

"We tried, Alec. She does not want to come out," Apoe said.

"Send me. Ms. Supervisor, you mentioned seeing two of me might cause problems for her. At this point, seeing two of me may convince her that reality is here." Alec pointed to the room's floor.

The Supervisor looked at Apoe. "We still have two targets," she said.

Apoe nodded.

Without waiting for further comments from Apoe, she said, "Dr. O'Neil will alter the scenario and build your Quantum Persona. We'll try again, but this time, I want you to look hard at our protocols and compare our procedures to the actual earthquake results. We may have missed something."

Apoe and Richardson nodded.

"Let's get to it."

# CHAPTER 35

Aaron McAllister, the White House Chief of Staff, sat in the White House situation room deep below the building's main foundation. He was attending an impromptu discussion with an exclusive group of administration officers to discuss the circumstances of Thompson's death. The exclusive group contained the Vice President, National Security Advisor, Director of National Intelligence, and CIA Deputy Director for Operations.

The Vice President began the discussion. "Director Donovan and I agree that Dr. Gregory should temporarily exercise the authority as Director of the Agency."

McAllister was on board with the selection, and confident POTUS would accept the recommendations of his DNI. McAllister knew a second-term president with less than two years remaining wanted to avoid any hint of a scandal. This president would not taint his record with a lengthy public process to select the CIA Director position. Dr. Gregory was a well-respected intelligence community member with an impressive list of accomplishments, none of which the American public had a clue. The president would be pleased with his selection and keeping everything under the radar.

The assembled group provided the briefing to the president less than 15 minutes ago. The president was concerned about Thompson's death but losing the nation's top spy chief was not without precedent. When asked how it happened, the president heard from his DNI, Thomas Donovan, a non-specific narrative tying the incident to his recent presidential directive. Thompson's death, he assured the president, was in the 'performance of duty.' Nothing more be said to keep the president isolated from the political fallout of a public story. The president accepted the explanation and asked about Thompson's replacement. Donovan suggested following the CIA chain of command and recommended one of the agency's deputies. Donovan believed a trusted officer running the organization was best until developing a suitable cover story explaining Thompson's disappearance. Once it was public, the president could send his nomination to the senate. The cover, for now, was Thompson was abroad performing duties related to National Security.

The Vice President approached him shortly after the president's meeting ended. Morrison purposely chose the moment when Dr. Lucia shared her opinions about the matter with McAllister.

"Any problems with Dr. Gregory, Chief?"

"None," McAllister said. "And you, Dr. Lucia?" he asked before the Vice President ignored her and walked away.

"None," Lucia said. "He's an excellent choice."

Hearing support for his selection, the Vice President walked back to the men talking with Gregory.

"You have to talk with him, Aaron. This situation could get way out of control," Lucia said.

"Why don't you talk with the Supervisor again? This situation is obviously her doing, and I'm not so sure I disagree with the Vice President."

"While I have not known her long, I have met her, and she seems reasonable and rational. Senator Hurst speaks highly of her, and I value his assessment of human character."

"I know. I've met her as well. I agree with you, but she is initiating these attacks!" McAllister said, exclaiming while whispering.

"How?" Lucia asked.

"These are her inmates. She needs to find them and put them in the SOUP again or get rid of them."

"I can't get involved with her, Aaron. As soon as I do, this administration gets dragged into it, and I look like I'm on the other side. I can't talk with the VP about this. We're not on the best of terms," she said sarcastically. "But you can. The VP will listen to you."

"You and the Senator have already met with her. You are involved."

"Look, Aaron," she said, giving him a look that provided no doubt about her seriousness and commitment. "We met with her to find out more about COL Baxter's death and to see if we could convince her to work with the Vice President. I won't be meeting with her again, especially after this."

McAllister thought about the request and knew she was right. If he could prevent further violence and work a solution that allowed for the SOUP's assets to be used by the Agency but done so responsibly, that would be a win/win. Right now, he wanted the violence to stop. If these situations escalated and appeared in the media, history would give his boss a black eye.

"Okay, Carol. I'll talk with him."

Dr. Lucia smiled. "Thank you."

"Let's get started with our meeting," Donovan said. "We have some ground to cover."

McAllister took his place at the table and listened as the DNI gave the group the classified incident details. The CIA detected the signature pattern of a previous hacker in their classified, administrative system, and it appeared the hacker was looking for the Director's personal schedule. Thompson accepted the social invitation once the hack was detected and confirmed. He told Gregory he suspected an attack on his life and would be the bait. Gregory's internal deposition said Thompson wanted to be personally involved and wanted the credit if the apprehension was successful. He confided to Gregory that he needed a win with the Vice President. Morrison was unphased by the comment as the DNI shared the known facts.

Gregory was to prepare a large response force and capture the attacker. They were to bring 'the special equipment,' standard munitions, and tranquilizers. Gregory acknowledged the preparation requirements after watching the videos of both Los Angeles and Las Vegas and had full access to the intelligence on the individuals and their gifts. He was the perfect subordinate to oversee the operation. When asked by Morrison whom Gregory thought the assailant could be, he replied, "Lincoln Harris, the remaining SOUP inmate."

Gregory provided the remaining details of the number of dead and his best guess on the cause.

If McAllister had doubts about talking with the VP about finding a truce. After hearing the details of the deceased, he was committed to closing this dispute.

*"Holy crap, how do you break every bone in someone's body?"*

McAllister looked at Lucia. She was also sickened by what she heard.

"That brings us to increased security, Mr. Vice President," Donovan said. "If this was Harris, he could still be at large and, therefore, a threat to you. His body was not found."

"What makes you think I'll be the next target, Tom? Don't forget; the SECDEF could be next."

"Very true, Mr. Vice President. Whatever you decide, we will send a plan to the Secret Service and the SECDEFs protection team."

"I don't want my public appearances to decrease, just the opposite. The election season is starting, and I need to be with the people. They need to see me and hear my position on issues. I still have a primary to win." His last comment drew smiles around the room, except for Lucia.

McAllister knew Morrison was going to be his party's candidate for president. While not endorsed yet by the White House, Morrison continuously received assignments outside the normal vice-presidential job scope to build his resume for just this moment. McAllister had not decided his future yet but considered the ramifications of accepting a cabinet position if offered.

"Understandable. We'll work closely with the Secret Service to alter your transportation methods and increase the personnel on your private detail."

"Thanks, Tom. I leave you and the Secret Service to decide how I get there and security while there. But I will accept nothing that derails the campaign roadmap. Any more questions or are we done with this?"

"That's it for today, Mr. Vice President."

"Thanks, everyone."

The assembled group rose from their chairs. McAllister looked at Lucia, locked eyes, and looked at the door. Lucia understood and left the room along with Gregory.

"May I see you a moment, Mr. Vice President?" McAllister asked.

Morrison was having a quiet conversation with Donovan. "Okay, Tom. I'll look into it."

"Thank you, Mr. Vice President."

"Chief." Donovan acknowledged the president's Chief of Staff when he walked by him. McAllister nodded an acknowledgment.

Morrison engaged first, "What's up, Aaron?"

"Nasty stuff. A terrible way for Thompson to go. I'll be glad when we catch the SOB that murdered those people."

"Yes, horrible stuff. What's your point?" the VP wanted to know.

"And his friends never knew their night would end as it did." McAllister paused. "Mr. Vice President, I can only imagine what I would do if my family members were killed suddenly as part of some collateral damage. I'm not sure I could deal with the outcome."

Morrison looked at McAllister and the Chief of Staff and knew he'd hit a nerve.

"What are you saying, Aaron? Do you think my family could be a target? Worse yet, are you involved in any of this?"

"No, sir." McAllister felt a twinge of resentment. He did not suspect his integrity or loyalty to be questioned during the discussion.

McAllister took a deep breath, "All I'm saying is that the country is not ready for their next president to come to power under a dark cloud. Americans are used to our candidates firing sharp rhetoric and accusations against their opponents, not the loss of family members or even the candidate. Americans want an inauguration unmarred by the memory of a recent funeral caused by the campaign."

"And you think that could happen to me?" Morrison's tone softened.

"It looks like someone is sending a message. We have no idea what could be next."

"Do you think this is because of the Presidential Directive? Could the supervisor direct this to keep me from taking over her program?"

McAllister continued, "I don't know the motive, sir, but I know this country needs a peaceful election and transition of power. I don't need to tell you that we all have people that hate us. But so far, no one has taken a shot at me. The Secret Service will shut them down if they try, but I don't have someone like Harris after me. You know as well as I do the Service is not prepared for someone like him. Until we know more, you and your family are vulnerable, putting this nation in a very delicate place." McAllister stared directly into Morrison's face. *"He needs to hear this!"*

"So, what would you have me do?"

"Take a meeting with the Supervisor or work through intermediaries. Dr. Lucia would represent both sides admirably, or even Senator Hurst. But you have to end this before it gets really serious."

"The hell with the Supervisor, her program, and Dr. Lucia, as far as I'm concerned! I'm not talking with them. This is already really serious! And besides, she may not even be able to control her inmates. Harris might be operating on his own."

"So, what's your next step, Sir? You can't put troops in the facilities. Their locations are classified."

"We have classified locations everywhere. Why are these different?"

"Because, Sir. The public knows these places exist. Once

the locations are known, we'll need a full-time garrison to protect the facilities. We might as well start building brick-and-mortar prisons again.

Secondly, think about the optics with the press. Are you going to march troops into the facility and seize it? I would think you wouldn't unless you want to be the villain on the front of every newspaper. How will that impact your chances for the White House?

Morrison nodded his head. He'd evaluated this part of his next moves and reached the same conclusion.

"The SOUP works, but I don't need to explain to you a major issue in your platform." McAllister felt accomplished making his case. Dr. Lucia was right; the VP was the lynchpin to this problem. Morrison needed to see how his actions would impact the election. That's all that mattered to him.

"Sir, what is this fight going to get you?"

"It's worth a little bad press. Every president has eaten a little crap to get elected. Why should I be any different?"

"Because, Sir, you can avoid it."

"You don't understand, Aaron. Every day that passes, this nation becomes weaker. You see that as well as I do. We are running out of time! Tapping into the SOUP's power will make us the most powerful nation on earth. No one will mess with our country when I have that program working my way. I am tired of dealing with countries that put one hand out for friendship and money while sliding a knife in your back. And why do they knife us, Aaron? Because of détente. We no longer have anything like nukes that once scared the hell out of asshole countries. Now that everyone has them, no one will use them because they are a zero-sum game. The SOUP is the strength and power we need to regain the upper hand. If someone puts a knife in our back, we find out who it was, and they never do it again. When the word gets out we are using this power; the backstabbing will stop."

"Mr. Vice President, I've seen those videos. No one can control people that can do those things. We have to keep them in the SOUP where they belong. If you want to develop these assets, we need to put the right protections in place so that what happened to Thompson does not happen to anyone else. You have a vision for the United States. Make the SOUP part of that vision but do it smartly."

"Thanks for the pep talk, Chief. The president signed that directive giving the CIA authority over the program. I can influence the CIA to take those assets and intend to do so."

"I think that's a very bad decision, sir."

"Noted. Does your boss know you are here, or is this your personal opinion?"

"The president is not aware of this conversation."

"Need I remind you that the president instructed you after the Taiwan Straits incident to keep the intelligence coming, regardless of source? He hit a home run with that information. The Chinese lost some serious face because of insight from those inmates. Imagine our worst criminals saving us from war with China. Thank God that's all classified," Morrison said, smiling.

"No sir, I didn't forget. I was in the room when he directed me to make it happen."

"Good, glad to know your memory is not failing you. Don't piss me off, or I'll let the boss know you are trying to prevent me from keeping that intelligence flowing. I think it best we do not talk about this again." Morrison walked out of the Situation Room and began his trek back to his office.

"Shit!" McAllister exclaimed. He wondered how often that word was used in this room because something went wrong. McAllister left the situation room and headed back upstairs.

# CHAPTER 36

Alec Richardson saw his reality born. The suburban treelined street materialized around him out of coalescing particles and pixels. Kids rode bikes, dogs barked at squirrels, and dads worked the yards to their castles. It was a very typical American neighborhood. All the activity was perfect, complete with smells of fresh-cut grass or hamburgers cooking on charcoal grills. While this world felt real, Richardson knew it was here because of the processing power of computers and the Artificial Intelligence that drove its creation algorithms. To his immediate front was the house he came to visit. The life video observed to choose this exact moment confirmed Adelle was home, and her Alec was not. Alec walked up the driveway and approached a side door to the house, which sprung open in his face. A young girl pushed the door, scampered past Alec, and ran toward the street.

"Hi, Daddy," she said, running past him to meet a group of young girls at the bottom of the driveway.

"Addie! Be home for lunch!"

The appearance of Adelle at the door had no impact on his Quantum Persona. Dr. O'Neil anticipated this meeting between the couple and did not place emotional responses in her code. This persona of Alec needed to convince Adelle to leave, nothing else.

"Hi, honey. What are you doing home? I thought you were working with Johnathan today," Adelle said. She turned and walked back into the kitchen. Alec remained standing outside the door.

"Well, come inside, Alec. I just finished the final details for the network event next week."

Alec opened the door and stepped inside. Adelle cleared the kitchen table, allowing them both to sit down.

"Sorry, you would think we would not generate so much

paper with computers."

"No worries," Alec replied.

Adelle stacked the papers, tapped them on the table, and placed them on an adjacent counter next to a Keurig coffee maker. "Coffee? I'm getting ready for my second cup."

"Sure, that would be great."

Adelle selected a cartridge from her coffee rack, inserted it, and started brewing.

"*I wish I could see myself. I have no idea if I look worried or confident,*" Alec thought. Adelle answered his question for him.

"Honey, you look worried. What's wrong?"

"Nothing's wrong, babe. I just need to talk with you about something."

"Okay," she said slowly. "I hope it's about work."

"Not really," Alec said.

The Keurig finished the first cup, and Adelle brought it to the table and sat in the chair next to him. She looked worried.

"I'm here," she started. "What do we need to discuss?"

Alec paused, thinking about starting the conversation with the woman he loved and telling her she was not living in the real world.

"*Come on, Alec. You can do this. Be honest with her. She'll understand.*"

"Okay," he started. "Did you receive a visit recently from Dr. O'Neil?"

Adelle's face turned white. Alec could see she was formulating her answer. The question, from her expression, was the last question she expected.

"How do you know about that?" she replied slowly. "I haven't told anyone about her."

"Adelle, this is going to be a hard conversation. You are probably not going to believe half of what you hear."

"How did you know?" Adelle emphasized each word as she said it.

Alec looked at her face until he could lock his eyes with

hers. She turned her head away. Alec used his hand to turn her face back to look at him gently. He could feel her slight resistance to look at him, but she surrendered and moved her head to face his.

Alec looked into her eyes. "I need you to hear me and believe me."

She nodded. "I'm listening."

"I work with Dr. O'Neil in a different place. That's how I knew she visited you."

Alec saw tears form in her eyes. "What did she say to you?"

"She said," wiping the tears off her cheeks with a napkin from the table and blotting her eyes, "that this world is not real. She wanted me to consider leaving it. Is it true? How do you know about this?"

Alec decided to try a different approach. He needed to convince her first that he was not real. In doing so, if she accepted that he was not her Alec, then she could accept that the world she lived in was also false.

"I know about these things because your Alec is at work. I am not real. I am a product of software programming and technology. I was put here, at this time, to ask you to leave this place."

"Am I dreaming? That's how I dismissed Dr. O'Neil's conversation. Somehow, I believed I dreamt her."

"She was just like me. A messenger sent to convince you that this world is not the real world."

"She asked me to leave everything! I can't leave Addie or you. I have everything in life I ever wanted."

"Do you ever fight with Alec?"

"What kind of question is that? Of course, we have disagreements. You know that. You are part of them!"

Alec thought a moment, trying to find something unique to convince her. What had Dr. O'Neil used on him? His articles! She had asked him to provide the content of his writings, and he couldn't.

"Adelle, what planning did you just complete for your work event?"

"Here," she said, rising to get her stack of papers. "Let me show you."

"No, please stay seated." She sat back down. "Now, tell me. What's on all that paper?"

Adelle looked at him. She looked confused. "It's all work related to a publicity function next week."

"What's on the paper, Adelle? What did you write about?"

"I can't remember," she said slowly. "Why can't I remember?"

"There is nothing wrong with your memory. You can't recall the details because the papers are props. They provide context and purpose for what you do but don't have the details you believe you worked through. They are like fake fronts to buildings in movies. Did Dr. O'Neil discuss this with you?"

"No." Adelle shook her head slowly.

"What did she say?" Alec reached out and took her hand.

"She said that this world is not real. That to leave it, all I needed to do was believe there was another."

"What else?"

"That I had to decide to leave." Adelle pulled her hand away. "I couldn't do it. There is too much here!"

Alec thought about his personal decision to leave his world in the SOUP. He would still be there without Dr. O'Neil telling him what would happen as a sign of truth.

"Adelle, you, Jefferson Grant, and I were investigating the SOUP and its operations. We found the young children and women in shipping containers heading to Washington through BWI airport."

"I know," she said. "That put our careers on the fast track. We were celebrities for a while. Those were great times, Alec. And if I remember right," she stopped and smiled, "around nine months later, Addie was born."

Alec knew he needed to be careful. Adelle's mind created

a different outcome to their experience and allowed her life to adjust when placed in the SOUP, much like he'd done. To eliminate this world without her permission was to destroy her life. He needed a demonstration that allowed her to reach her conclusion. He could not give her the answer; he would need to show her.

"Adelle, what would it take to convince you that what Dr. O'Neil and I have said is true? Pick something so impractical or improbable that it could not happen."

"What do you mean?"

"What is something unique that would happen to you that you would never expect?"

Adelle thought for a moment. Alec watched her as she considered what he was asking.

"Just to be sure of what you are saying. I pick an event, and if it happens, that is proof of what you are telling me."

Alec nodded, hoping it would be something simple. Dr. O'Neil and her team could influence the reality around each person in the SOUP. If left alone, the system created their existence as they wished. Software programming could alter the system's rendering of their thoughts.

"Yes," Alec said, confirming her understanding.

"Okay, I have one."

"Let's hear it."

"My Alec. Is that correct?"

Alec nodded.

"My Alec will come home from work. He will tell me that he's had an affair, loves someone new, and wants a divorce. Does that work? It will never happen but is that what you are looking for?"

"Yes," Alec replied. "It will happen tonight."

Alec smiled at Adelle. She had chosen an improbable yet very creditable scenario. She has reasoned, he thought, that the likelihood of this scenario happening is zero, but if it does, her emotions will push her to want to leave this life. Adelle will go because she is convinced this world is not authentic or will not want to stay if she is no longer married. Adelle will have made her choice of her own free will. While he could not feel the emotion, he marveled at the pure logic of the code that produced his current awareness, her complete self, and the woman she was. He knew he loved her deeply.

"I'll be right back," she said. "Excuse me." Adelle stood up and walked down the hall and into the bathroom. Alec's world disintegrated around him.

Dr. O'Neil observed the dialog between Adelle and the Washington, D.C., facility. As the couple agreed, she would implement the programming changes required to produce the event. It would take her several hours to code, test, and debug the routine, but O'Neil possessed the luxury of time. She controlled the internal time flow of the SOUP. If she needed more time, she would slow down the reality for the inmates, and as long as experiences were created and lived, the inhabitants would see no difference in the composition of their world.

Dr. O'Neil built this into her system. The body would age without regard to experience; however, the mind was different. As in life, young children waiting for Christmas never thought it would arrive. For the elderly, time sped up. Time was a true universal flow necessary for consciousness for humanity. While she did not understand the physics behind the connection, she knew the two could not be separate. Dr. O'Neil was proud of her work.

She had asked the Supervisor to keep Alec at the Arlington facility while she performed her work. While not understanding, the Supervisor honored her request while trying to regain trust in O'Neil's motives. Hours after O'Neil's announced departure, Apoe, the Supervisor, and Alec arrived at the DC facility.

Dr. O'Neil executed the program, and the three

watched the drama captured in Adelle's life video. Dr. O'Neil did her work well, and thirty minutes later, no one was surprised when the lift system began to move Adelle's container to the concrete floor of the cell block.

# CHAPTER 37

A lec Richardson was lying next to Adelle Hall, sharing his warmth with the woman he loved. Alec listened to the rhythm of her breathing as she slept peacefully. He hoped she was not dreaming.

Her Exit from the SOUP was without incident, and her procedures repeated the same protocol as his and Grants. Her awareness appeared sharp, and she accepted the gray drabness of the cell block without questioning the contrast with the world just left. It was only when Adelle said she remembered her last moments before the SOUP that Apoe and the Supervisor detected something new. They asked her to explain her memories, to which Adelle provided details of her final moments in the warehouse outside of BWI. The Supervisor told Richardson later that neither Grant nor he could recall his last moments in this reality with the same clarity as Adelle. Alec wondered if not recalling his last moments might be the source of his confusion. For him, no clean break existed in his experiences. Adelle could use her last memory at BWI to organize her timeline without confusing virtual memories and this reality.

Remembering her last moments were important, Apoe said. He wanted to note and study every detail of each Exit, especially when there was an anomaly like Adelle's. Apoe used this opportunity to test Adelle's telepathy and provided endless questions during her first two hours after recovery.

Grant's Exit was different. After he recovered, Alec immediately tested his gifts, and the two spent several days exchanging information, with Richardson providing the context.

Alec regretted the time to tell Adelle that Grant was gone and expected that Apoe would want to observe and measure her apparent emotional responses, how they might affect her, and, more importantly, any reaction from her psychic gifts.

As Alec lay there, he replayed what he observed on the life video in his mind. Despite replaying the video several times while in the operations center, there was no mistaking the information. Like him, Adelle had a daughter named Addie in her virtual life. As he replayed the video, not only was Addie in Adelle's world but also in his. In both of their virtual lives, Addie was one of the main reasons for not wanting to leave. Their daughter had anchored both of them in the SOUP.

*"How was this possible?"*

What was the probability that he and Adelle would create a daughter with the same name and physical characteristics in two different worlds?

Alec felt Adelle stir and begin to wake.

"Good morning."

"Mmmmm. Good morning," Adelle replied. "Is it really morning?"

"That's what the clock says, but I'm never sure what time it is anymore."

Adelle pulled away from Alec and turned to look into his eyes. "Are you really here? Am I back, or is this the dream?"

"I'm real, and you're back."

"When did you get so serious in the morning, Alec?" she asked playfully.

Alec thought a moment. Did Adelle not feel like her mind was between two different worlds, generating self-doubt about what was real and where she was?

"Adelle, do you feel like talking about a couple of things before we get poked and prodded today?"

"I was told you, and I would be spending the day together," she smiled.

"That's very true, but there are some things that I have questions about."

That smile. My God. Even in Alec's virtual world, the smile was powerful, but he never felt this response inside. Dr. O'Neil may have synthesized an exceptional virtual world, but she needed improvement in the emotional response part of her creation. He was alive in the real world. That smile just proved it.

Alec continued, "Can you, or will you talk about Addie?"

Alec saw the smile disappear. "Why do you want to bring her up? I know she was just part of my virtual world, but I still have all my feelings for her. She was authentic to me. Losing her is painful, Alec." Adelle moved away from Alec and started to get out of bed.

"Wait, Adelle, I'm sorry. But I need you to help me with something I'm grappling with." She stopped moving and sat down on the edge of the far side of the bed. With her back toward Alec, she said, "I'm listening."

Alec started slowly, "In my virtual world, my daughter's name was Addie too."

Adelle turned around to face him. "A coincidence?"

Alec shook his head, "I don't think so. My Addie and yours look exactly the same."

"What do you think? How could that be?"

"I'm clueless, Adelle. I thought you might have an idea or two."

Alec watched her closely as she thought.

"I don't know," she finally said. "Alec, there is still so much happening in my head. Just the idea that I have some kind of psychic power is unnerving. I am trying to focus on the here and now. Thinking about Addie and why she was in both worlds will take a little time. Before examining my virtual memories, I need to know that this world is real."

When seeing it moments ago, Alec thought of Adelle's smile and heightened feeling of his emotion. Alec rolled over on the bed and pulled Adelle to him.

"I have a theory I would like to try." He whispered closely to her ear. She turned her head slowly and lay back on the bed. Alec moved closer still, his lips touching hers and his hands already exploring the curves of her body. Adelle raised her arms over his head and pulled him closer, connecting their mouths in a passionate kiss igniting hundreds of nerve connections in every part of his body. Alec's heightened sensation rose like a musical crescendo until both became one moving combination of limbs in a blur of heated passion.

Afterward, as both lay on their backs, breathing deeply, feeling sated from their lovemaking experience, Alec asked, "Well?"

In between breaths, Adelle answered, "It was real."

"Yeah, I agree. The SOUP YOU was never this good," Alec panted.

Both of them laughed for the first time together in years.

# CHAPTER 38

The Supervisor entered the conference room and took her seat at the head of the table. The remainder of the team, already seated, ended their conversations and turned their attention to her.

"I've called you here," she began, "to update you on our efforts and what that means in terms of action. Most of you know Dr. Apoe and Dr. O'Neil are working on a prototype for a violence inhibitor designed to be the next generation of the SOUP. While the SOUP is the incarceration and reform facility, the Violence Inhibitor Treatment Protocol is a non-lethal treatment that could eventually prevent crime from occurring when administered to high-risk individuals or, if given to SOUP inmates, prevent it from happening again. Dr. O'Neil and Mr. UT began work on this solution shortly after we returned to Virginia from Los Angeles. The development schedule has slipped right due to Mr. UT's untimely death. This device was to defend the facility from this administration's actions with assistance from Jefferson, Adelle, and Alec. Instead of the VITP's delay, we have no option but to ask Adelle and Alec to use other means to accomplish our mission."

"I thought because the first one was so bad with Grant, we were going to try something different," Anderson said.

"We were Sarah. Our window of time is rapidly closing. I reached out to the National Security Advisor and asked her to float the idea of a working relationship with the administration; a conversation with the VP to find a better solution where both parties win. I just received a message from her. The Vice President is pressing ahead with his plans to make the program part of the CIA."

"How could he do this?" Adelle asked.

"I think his first step is CIA control of one of our facilities. They only need one, and the agency can legally do things that the DoD cannot. This move puts them in a position to conceal all their activity from the public's observation. No one on the outside will know this was done. Once they have a facility, they will start using their Exit solution to recover inmates. We know that nothing will work, and their efforts will become more desperate. Each time they fail, lives are in danger. And each time they succeed, the administration will not allow inmates into the public because of the damage and death already done by them. They will most likely send them to places like Site 35. Therefore, in this facility alone, they can try 1497 times and, if partially successful, destroy or disrupt 1497 lives."

"Why won't their Exit protocols work?"

"It requires the person in the SOUP to want to leave. Do you remember your last thought before you Exited, Lincoln?"

"I do. I was escaping from home and the town of Herndon. I wanted to get into the real world."

"Exactly," the Supervisor said. "It was perfect timing between the earthquake and your place in the scenarios. That's the part of the Exit sequence missing from the Vice President's capability. Without this technology, they will never get a successful Exit unless they take over a facility and force our staff to work the Cause and Effect scenarios," the Supervisor said. "That is the current threat we are facing."

"The Vice President," Apoe said, "is the greatest risk to the program. Our sources indicate that he wants this program under CIA control, regardless of the costs. He is eager to begin and is not interested in talking with the Supervisor about the best approach to sharing the asset. He leads the effort; therefore, he is our next target."

"So how do we get close enough to use our gifts on the VP? His security has undoubtedly increased since the incident with Thompson," Alec asked.

"We can expect more than the normal security, but the one place where he is vulnerable is on the campaign trail. Morrison has to begin his event schedule if he plans to win the nomination and the general election."

"There is no amount of security that can protect him from us," the Supervisor commented. "Alec, you and Adelle will be able to determine if he is a body double very quickly using telepathy. You don't have to read his mind; enough people around you will know the truth. Read theirs.

As to non-lethal actions, once you confirm it's the actual VP on stage, it's a matter of getting close enough. The VP will work the rope lines to shake hands before or after the event. Unless you can get close during the speech, that will be your moment to act."

"What happens if they use blockers," Adelle asked.

The Supervisor was happy to hear Adelle ask the question. Apoe provided the Supervisor daily updates on the exchange of information from Alec and their relationship's strength. There were times that Apoe was invited into the couple's circle to help explain the context of the information. Adelle, like Alec, experienced Grant's death with difficulty, but they relied upon each other. While grieving Grant's loss may take longer, Alec and Adelle relied on each other to stay focused on the mission tasks.

"That's an excellent question, Adelle, and one that Dr. Apoe and I have struggled with. Does anyone have suggestions for backup verification?"

Anderson began, "I expect the Vice President's office took additional countermeasures to hide his official calendar after we hacked Thompson's. Hacking the White House is going to be more difficult now. However, despite their best effort, the GOP's servers should be easy enough for me. They will have more detail about his campaign than the White House anyway, and I think we know that Morrison is going into campaign mode. This exposure is an Achilles heel for him. Morrison will need to stay within many of the state and caucus calendar dates to keep the primary process on schedule. We might not need the White House if we can positively confirm his events and locations from the Party servers. We won't get 100% positive ID if they use blockers but correlating his presence with a confirmed calendar might get us in the ballpark to take a shot."

"I like it," Apoe said, flashing a smile at Anderson. "That's a great suggestion. How soon can you start?"

Anderson put her hands together in front of her and cracked her knuckles. "Lincoln and I will get right on it as soon as we're done here."

"Great, we'll look for our opportunity as soon as you can access the information." The Supervisor looked at the group.

"Let's talk about the non-lethal action. Dr. Apoe and I agree this is a team effort. We would like you to work on the same target together. Alec, Adelle, what are your thoughts?"

The couple looked at each other and smiled. Adelle began, "Ms. Supervisor, Alec and I have discussed our problem, and this is how we think we can accomplish this mission."

# CHAPTER 39

Alec and Adelle sat inside the Congressional Country club in Bethesda, Maryland, watching its patrons finish preparations before enjoying the beautiful late spring weather. It was a beautiful day for golf, but both were content to sit in the lounge area and drink their iced tea, paying close attention to the hustle and bustle of the club. Throughout the building, golfers were connecting foursomes and announcing their arrival through gregarious voices and man-hugs with their partners. Alec noticed most conversations were about game improvement since last playing together, new handicaps and which player brought the best cigars. Adelle focused on the attire and commented to Alec that she figured out who bought all the casual plaid wear advertised in outdoor magazines.

The Vice President had recently traveled to his old rust belt states to verify his grassroots support for his campaign. Morrison's schedule had also taken him and his team to special meetings with Democrat delegations in Pennsylvania, Michigan, Wisconsin, Minnesota, and Arizona. The Supervisor had pointed out that these were five of the six states hoping to receive funding for new SOUP incarceration facilities. The last state hoping for a facility was in his backyard, Maryland. All told, the states accounted for a total of 77 electoral votes, mostly voting blue. Alec suspected he knew at least one carrot the VP used to flip them red in his conversations.

It was 1:45 p.m. This opportunity was an unscheduled visit for both of them and happened quickly when the Supervisor received a message from Senator Hurst. Hurst relayed information from two Democrat Senators and a Congresswoman. They bragged they were playing golf at the Congressional with the VP at 2:00. Hurst was unsure if they were celebrating or just surprised the VP would voluntarily set up an appointment with the opposite party to discuss some matter of importance. Hurst instructed the Supervisor to have Alec and Adelle use his membership, granting access to the bar and facilities. His office would confirm any inquiries from the club. The couple arrived early and walked through the facility, dropping Hurst's name when confronted while becoming familiar with the rooms and routes throughout the club.

Alec and Adelle had also confirmed Morrison's appointment. While no one was verbally speaking, both picked up numerous mental confirmations that the VP was playing the course at 2:00. According to the young lady at guest services, the Secret Service was already in the building after securing the parking lot.

Alec and Adelle stood up and walked to the club's front door. They noticed employees gathering outside to assist with clubs and other items the foursome would need to be carried.

"How about you head to the pro shop Adelle, and I will hang out just on the other side of the driveway. Most likely, he will come your way. You'll know because the Secret Service will ask you to clear out before they take him to where his cart is waiting. I'm unsure if the others in his foursome will be with him. You may get a chance in the pro shop as he passes through. I'll see if I can't close the deal when he gets out of his vehicle."

"Okay," she said, giving him a quick peck on his cheek. "Either way, I'll meet you back at our car."

Alec stared into her sparkling eyes and nodded. "You better," he said.

The phone rang across the driveway, and a steward in charge of valet parking answered. He shook his head twice and hung up. "Ten minutes out," he told the assembled workers. "Be sharp!"

"Off I go," Adelle said and walked away. Alec felt his heart skip a beat as he watched her naturally sway her hips. "*Focus on the mission!*"

Alec walked to his car in the parking lot, opened the trunk, and played around with a pair of shoes. To any passerby, it would look like he was changing them for a round. Alec looked up and saw the small caravan of three black government sedans drive past him and pull up at the front door. He expanded his distance to eavesdrop on the assembled group of employees.

"Welcome to the Congressional," he heard someone say.

"Thanks. This course looks great. We picked a good day to play."

"Yes, Sir. Greens are running a little fast today, Mr. Vice President."

"Good thing, I got a good bit hinging on the outcome. A dollar a hole, wasn't it, Senator."

"Of course, Mr. Vice President."

Alec saw his chance; the vehicles had discharged the foursome and the agents that would escort them through the club and to their carts. The cars began to drive off, exposing the Vice President and his party. Alec walked toward them, pretending not to notice the VIPs standing next to the curb, and headed towards the door. He saw the Secret Service agents watching him. Alec counted down the distance in his head as he approached the club entry, 30, 20, 15 feet. Close enough. Alec closed his eyes and focused his energy on the Vice President, then continued walking into the club and returned to the bar. The Vice President's group had come inside. He heard what he was hoping for from Morrison; a slight cough followed by a clearing throat.

"Are you Okay, Mr. Vice President?"

"Yes, I'm fine. Suddenly, I've got a small tickle in my throat." Morrison looked at the young man carrying his clubs. "Son, would it be too much to ask that you go to the bar and get me a bottle of water?"

"No problem at all, sir." The young man disappeared and returned almost immediately.

Morrison took the bottle and took a large drink. "Much better," he said. "Beautiful weather. Let's go, everyone. We need to get started before something comes along and ruins our day."

Everyone in the group laughed except Morrison. He reached up, felt his neck, and rubbed it slightly.

# CHAPTER 40

The Supervisor was sitting in her office three days later, discussing the Alec's events at the club. Alec reported he felt confident he was successful in their plan to handle the Vice President when her secure smartphone rang. Apoe picked up the device and handed it to the Supervisor. The caller ID showed it was Senator Hurst.

"Good morning, Senator. What a pleasant surprise," she said.

"Are you in your office?" he asked, barely able to contain the urgency in his voice.

"Yes."

"Turn on CNN. They just went to break. Call me when the report finishes." Click.

The Supervisor looked at Apoe, who was already reaching for the remote. He turned the TV on and raised the volume.

The commercials were ending. The TV showed the CNN studio, and sitting behind the desk was the afternoon anchor, an attractive woman about 35. "This just in," she said, her eyes focused on the teleprompter in front of her. "Unnamed but confirmed sources at the White House have just announced that the Vice President is diagnosed with chronic laryngitis and unable to speak." She raised her voice toward the end of the statement, unsure if the sentence was true or a joke.

"Sources knowledgeable of the situation state that Vice President Morrison started feeling ill about three days ago. His voice, according to our source, started getting progressively weaker. Upon further examination, the White House doctor found an inoperable physical malformity that prevented him from speaking. We turn now to our medical expert and CNN frequent contributor, Dr. Elaine Gibson."

The Supervisor's TV showed the anchor and Dr. Gibson

on a split screen. The guest's background read 'American Medical Association' and contained the organization's logo as Dr. Gibson's name and medical credentials scrolled on the bar below her picture.

"Dr. Gibson, this is a bizarre announcement about the Vice President's health."

"It appears, Diane, that this condition was something in the background that doctors missed during a routine medical examination. Something chronic does not usually progress this fast on its own."

"Could you describe for our audience the condition?"

"Sure. Most people experience some form of laryngitis in their life. Larynx inflammation usually occurs within two to three days if we have a cold or exercise our larynx excessively, as many popular singers do. Laryngitis of this type heals quickly with rest and minor medications in about a week. A chronic condition is more serious, unfortunately for the Vice President. Chronic means permanent damage to some part of our 'voice box' preventing us from speaking."

"Is this something that can be treated or repaired?"

"Not likely, Diane. The diagnosis appears to state that there is something wrong with the larynx. It's not a type of growth or something that surgeons remove. His voicebox is just not working."

"Are you saying the Vice President can no longer use his voice?"

"If the diagnosis is correct, it's quite possible he may never speak above a whisper again, if at all."

"Thank you, doctor." The anchor could barely contain her smile.

"You're welcome, Diane."

The screen returned to the image, and a middle-aged, attractive man was sitting next to the anchor.

"For more commentary and the impact on our coming presidential election, John Moray from our political branch joins us. John, thoughts?"

"On the surface, this looks bad. Vice President Morrison prides himself as a communicator. He is someone that can connect with common people through his words. His speeches and communication style have been compared to Ronald Reagan by many. I'm not sure how he will come back from this, Diane. I honestly feel sorry for Vice President Morrison, especially with the New Hampshire primary only four months away. This new development will be an uphill climb for him. The nomination is no longer a sure thing. This will attract others to run that may have decided earlier to sit it out. The field is going to fill quickly, I believe. If I had to call it today, I'm not sure he'll get the Republican nomination."

"Is there a way to use a proxy candidate or technology? Something to overcome this problem?"

"I doubt it, Diane. Political speeches and presidential races are where the candidate needs to make their case for election. They need to convince others of their vision for this country. Many voters rely on how the candidate makes them feel when they hear the candidate talk. If this were a physical problem, like FDR and others in wheelchairs, that would be one thing. When politicians are physically disabled, and people see their condition, they feel the candidate is speaking to them. People interpret that if someone can be successful with their handicap, so can they. Speaking is different. It is the primary way we share our life experiences and create hope for the future. No one wants to have a speech read to them, delivered by someone else, or listen to a metallic voice. The one asset a politician has is his voice. Morrison has lost his."

"Thank you, John." The anchor nodded to show agreement and announce the interview was over. "The rising oil price is next, right after these messages."

"Want to see anymore," Apoe asked.

"No, please turn it off, Franklin." Apoe did so.

"Wow, that's a bombshell. How did it get on the news so fast?"

"I have a feeling that Dr. Lucia had something to do with

providing the information. She would be close to the situation and hear things in the White House."

Apoe nodded, "You might be right. So, can we say this mission was complete? He's going to be very busy with doctors and still trying to figure out how he can run."

"A wounded animal is more dangerous, Franklin. We may have taken his voice away, but he can still communicate. He has not lost his ability to write and wields the power of the office. He is still the Vice President. We need to be very aware of our security."

"I agree. I'll make the arrangements. Want to start planning for the SECDEF?"

"Let me think about that. Now, with the VP 'off the board,' as you say, the SECDEF might be open to a meeting and a little reason. I'll reach out to Dr. Lucia. We can include the VP. If he makes the meeting, he'll know we beat him and should be more open to working together."

"If he shows up, he's going to be very pissed. Working together is not what he'll be thinking," Apoe said.

"Maybe so, but just imagine how he will feel next November after the election when he has a miraculous recovery and can speak again." The Supervisor paused and smiled, "Even the devil has to return to hell now and then. I hope he enjoys his time there."

# CHAPTER 41

The Supervisor and Dr. Apoe arrived at the Pentagon and were taken immediately to a secure office deep within the interior of the building. The Supervisor marveled at the size and complexity of the building. Without the escort of a Marine officer, she doubted whether she and Apoe could have found the room.

True to her word, Dr. Carol Lucia, the president's National Security Advisor, arranged the meeting between Brian Wellsley, Secretary of Defense, and the Supervisor. Their escort inserted his credentialed badge into the security card reader on the door. The device verified his biometrics, and the officer entered the room security code. The door buzzed open, and the Supervisor and Dr. Apoe entered a nicely furnished room that reminded the Supervisor of a lounge more than a conference room. There were four sofas surrounding a small coffee table in the center, with various lamps surrounding the sofas. There were no computer screens or evidence of any IT support for the room. Instead, the walls supported drapes hung over painted landscapes to create the illusion of looking out a window.

"This is different," the Supervisor remarked to Apoe, who also appeared confused by the room's décor. Apoe nodded in agreement.

Their escort said, "Please have a seat. Secretary Wellsley will join you shortly." The officer did an about-face and exited the door leaving the two in silence.

"What now, Franklin?"

"Let's sit down. We discussed this as a meeting tactic. He'll have us wait for about 15 minutes or so. We should expect they are monitoring what we are saying. We might as well get comfortable and talk about the weather."

The Supervisor selected a sofa, and both sat down.

"So, how about those Commanders?" The Supervisor asked, referencing the Washington, D.C., professional football team.

Apoe flashed his smile. "I think there is real potential to get things together. They have a winning history. I'd like to see how things work out for them this season."

The Supervisor could not help but think Apoe's comments contained a hidden meaning concerning their relationship. The closer she listened, the more she resigned herself that Apoe was talking about the Commanders. The two laughed and continued their small talk until the door opened. The Secretary entered first, followed by Dr. Gregory, known by the Supervisor as the Operations Chief for the CIA. The Supervisor and Dr. Apoe stood as the two men entered, and the door closed behind them.

"Everybody know each other?" Wellsley asked, stopping in front of the Supervisor.

"I need introductions," Dr. Gregory announced.

The Secretary of Defense pointed to the Supervisor, "This is the Supervisor of the Virtual Life Incarceration Program." Wellsley turned to look at Apoe. "I feel we've met before, but I can't place you."

*"He knows who you are, Franklin. As soon as we cleared Pentagon security, he received your full profile. Until now, he listed you as dead with the rest of Site 35, but when you entered my building, the security monitoring notified them you were alive and with me,"* the Supervisor thought.

"Dr. Franklin Apoe, Mr. Secretary. I am the Chief Medical Officer for the Program." None of the four shook hands, but all sat on two opposing sofas.

"You asked for the meeting Ms. Supervisor. Why don't you start," Wellsley began.

*"Start bold and watch for reactions,"* she thought.

"Very well, Mr. Secretary. Let's start with the most recent Presidential Directive that places my program under the CIA."

"Ah, Directive 51," Wellsley added.

"Glad to know they finally assigned a number," Apoe said. The Supervisor looked at him sternly and pleaded with her eyes not to inflame the situation with quips like that.

"Yes, Directive 51, Mr. Secretary. We are opposed to the current transfer schedule."

"Ms. Supervisor, I was not aware a schedule was approved yet. My team is still studying the best way forward," Dr. Gregory said.

"*I bet they are. You must be the interim replacement since this directive caused your boss to meet his untimely death.*"

"Yes, I'm sure they are. However, I was under a different assumption given the recent activity on your organization's part, Dr. Gregory."

"Such as?"

"Your organization abducted my previous Chief Medical Officer without provocation. That action resulted in his death. Shortly afterward, your people questioned my Chief Technology Officer against her will. These actions tell me there is a schedule in place. Your organization was directed or acted on its initiative to provoke my program. I really don't care which one it was. These actions were unnecessary and malicious."

Gregory sat unmoving, stoic as the Supervisor made her accusations.

"It was my understanding, Ms. Supervisor, we took these steps because you were withholding information vital to National Security from this administration," Wellsley answered. "PD 51 was signed by the president to ensure alignment between the national security needs and your assets. The fact that your inmates possessed a long-sought-after capability surprised us all. Surely you must understand that the Taiwan Straits incident established your program as crucial to collecting vital intelligence on our adversaries' activities."

"*Be careful here.*"

"I recognize the value of my inmates to National

Security, but the proposed approach offered to use my inmates as test mice and the abduction of my executives all make me question the motives behind how the realignment will occur. Our assessment shows that needless innocent lives would be damaged or destroyed if we continue on our current path."

The Supervisor watched the faces on the opposite sofa. *"These guys were pawns drawn to the VP by loyalty and the hopes a new administration would continue to give them purpose and power. One thing is certain now, without a doubt. The VP was calling the shots until recently. Perhaps one of these two wants to step up now that the VP's election is not quite so certain. With knowledge of the program's operations, either executive would be valuable to the next administration and have their tenure extended."*

"A few lives sacrificed to save many. You've been in this business long enough, Ms. Supervisor, to understand how this all works," Gregory said.

"How do you feel about your organization's sacrifices, Dr. Gregory? It seems your agency is in first place regarding sacrificing personnel."

Unphased by the comment, Gregory continued, "Where are your inmates, Ms. Supervisor?"

*"That's a strange question to ask."*

"Why do you want to know, Dr. Gregory?" Apoe asked.

Apoe looked at the Supervisor. It looked as though he'd made the connection as well. The fog of war lifted for the Supervisor. Neither Wellsley nor Gregory would mention Apoe and Site 35. They knew who Apoe was, but their facility allowed Livingston and Harris to escape again. While they may have many questions for Franklin, they would not ask them today. Neither of the men would know that sitting in front of them was the man that facilitated Site 35's disappearance. Something was off on their side. Their information was incorrect and filled with assumptions.

Gregory looked at the Supervisor, then the SECDEF. Wellsley nodded his head to continue.

"Don't you think they've caused enough destruction? How long before you police them up and return them to the SOUP?"

*"Oh, my God! They think Livingston, Harris, and maybe even Hoffman are causing the attacks. They're pissed at me, not because I am turning my folks on them, but because I have not caught my inmates, and they are holding me responsible."*

"It seems to me, Dr. Gregory, that you had custody of my inmates when I left Los Angeles. Why are you asking me to clean up the Agency's mess? I have no control over their behavior," the Supervisor stated. "It was my understanding that they were no longer my responsibility when taken out of my facility by your agents. I ask you, when are you going to find and police up YOUR inmates."Why am I now being held accountable for men that escaped your custody?

Dr. Gregory ignored the questions and instead responded,

"Which is why we are trying to accelerate the transfer of power to the CIA, Ms. Supervisor. It was evident to our community that we needed to provide countermeasures after seeing the videos of YOUR inmates. We need new assets that we can create to counter the madness your prisoners caused. If I understand the process, it will take a minimum of one year for the pineal gland to mature. The faster we can begin preparing our assets, the lower the risk becomes to this administration. We need to capture and neutralize your inmates. We are running out of time," Gregory said.

*"They are using the attacks by the inmates as the rationale to accelerate their program."*

The Supervisor was unsure if she could trust these two men. The information appeared accurate, but it was not beyond the DoD to exaggerate the threat. She knew where the inmates were, and they posed little or no danger to anyone. So far, her staff controlled the program's facilities, not the CIA or DoD. She resolved to keep it that way.

"What do you propose as the way forward?" the

Supervisor asked.

Wellsley answered, "First, we must find your missing inmates and take care of them."

"By 'take care,' you mean a CIA solution?" Apoe asked.

Wellsley pressed forward without answering. "Second, we need you to designate a facility we can assume control over. Dr. Gregory and I are willing to share the facility, so we only need one. Lastly, your team will provide full cooperation to test and finalize the Exit protocols."

"I thought Dr. O'Neil provided you with that information," the Supervisor offered.

"It's time to quit playing games, Ms. Supervisor. Dr. O'Neil's information was beneficial, but she also alluded to the inmate's desire to leave the SOUP as critical to the Exit. As it stands, only your program has the software to create those conditions. We would like it."

"*There it is. These two still need scenario or Quantum Persona solutions. They are not giving up until they get them. If I give them up, they have no reason for me, and the program becomes theirs. They are only asking for one but will take them all if they control the real keys to Exiting.*"

The Supervisor evaluated their offer and looked over at Apoe. His face was expressionless, revealing no emotion.

"What makes you think we can find the missing inmates?" she asked.

"We understand that the National Security Advisor has offered to assist you. Dr. O'Neil also told us that you've successfully exited another individual and intend to have them help you defend your program. It appears you share the same concern about your escaped inmates as we do, or do you? You're not responsible for the recent violence, are you."

"Of course not, Mr. Secretary. I, too, share your concerns about what the inmates might do next. We should locate them as soon as possible. On this, we agree."

"Good. And the other points," Gregory asked.

"We have some things we would like as well."

Wellsley and Dr. Gregory remained silent.

"First, I would like PD51 revoked until we can determine the risk to your soldiers in the SOUP and how you would control them once they turned loose as your assets. The remote viewers are less of a concern than the telekinetic soldiers you are looking to create, Mr. Secretary. We can both agree on the destructive power our inmates have demonstrated. I would also like this because, despite the needs of the many, Dr. Gregory, I will not use my inmates as lab rats. They are in the SOUP to pay a debt to society, not give their lives for National Defense."

Wellsley nodded. The Supervisor watched Dr. Gregory closely. He was unwilling to show any signs of agreement with her proposals.

"Secondly, in the interim, I would like a new directive that limits the CIA and DoD use to one facility. Again, we agree. I will support a Presidential Directive that is clear on that point. Lastly, the directive will include that we will control the source code and algorithms for creating the Cause-and-Effect Scenarios and the Quantum persona. Both your departments can use the capability, providing objective outcomes and parameters, but the source code, methods, and techniques remain with us."

The room was quiet as Wellsley, and Dr. Gregory analyzed the Supervisor's proposal. If the Supervisor were correct about the Vice President in charge, there would be no answer today. If one of the two men wished to fill the vacuum that the VP would create with an unsuccessful presidential election, she would get an answer before walking out of the room.

"Why is it necessary to negate PD51?" Wellsley asked.

"Because I was never asked before it was signed. My program, still filled with exceedingly high operational risks, was mandated to move to the CIA by the president without understanding those risks. We've discussed them here. Even now, you still believe you can control the men after their release. Those three inmates are the tip of the iceberg, gentleman. We must work this together without the president's order to force the program over to Dr. Gregory."

"Why is it necessary for you to control the software we need?" Gregory remained seated and asked his question without expression.

"I'll say it one last time because neither of us understands what we will set loose. If the program controls the code, we make joint decisions on using it and, at minimum, understand the nightmares resulting from our decision. I am willing to do that."

"If we don't agree on its use?" Wellsley asked.

"We take it to our committee for resolution," she answered.

Wellsley and Dr. Gregory stood up. The Supervisor and Dr. Apoe also stood. The meeting was over. "Dr. Gregory and I would like to discuss your offer. I will call you later with our decision. Knock on the door. Security will escort you out."

Dr. Apoe knocked on the door, and the major appeared, again taking them through the Pentagon maze. At the main visitor exit, he collected their badges. "The metro is that way; parking if you drove that way." The Major pointed to his right. "I apologize for bringing you to the main exit." The major turned and left. Dr. Apoe walked to the visitor's desk and returned after a brief conversation. "The Sergeant says the VIP entrance is out the door and around the building. I gave him the number for our driver."

The Supervisor looked at the desk, and the Sergeant was making a call. He put down his receiver and motioned to Apoe to return. Apoe walked up to the counter. "Your driver will meet you outside the main exit."

"Thanks."

Dr. Apoe walked back to the Supervisor.

"They did this on purpose. Brought us to the visitor exit just to screw with us."

Apoe nodded. "I think this means they don't want to

take your offer."

"Possibly, but I think it's to remind us that we are one program against all this," she said, sweeping her hands through the air and pointing out the size of the Pentagon building filled with numerous professionals bustling back and forth.

"We'll know shortly." The Supervisor paused, then asked, "Franklin, whom do you think is making the decisions?"

"My bet is they must run this by the VP first."

"My thoughts as well. It will be deafening 'no' if that's true. They also know about Alec yet did not tie him to any recent violence."

Apoe nodded, "They played a good game today. They want us to believe it's the inmates doing the damage and nothing you've done. That makes for a good story later if this breaks into the public. But that doesn't mean they think Alec's not involved. His Exit confirmed that we have a solution we can implement, done by us and not an earthquake. That's the solution they want; they have leverage and the president's authority with PD51 to make it happen. That's a lot of power."

"So far, I like your thinking."

"However, as a counterbalance to their authority, they know you're sitting on 1500 inmates in DC alone and could unleash them all, not that you would, of course. That's a big failure because they own the program on paper, and the president would look to them if the inmates got out of control. That makes you the most powerful person in this game, the queen on the chess board, to use our analogy, and that scares the hell out of them."

The Supervisor looked at Apoe and smiled warmly, "Franklin, what a grasp of politics you've acquired."

Franklin softened, looked into her eyes, and replied, "We make a good team."

This time the Supervisor had no doubt he was talking about the two of them.

# CHAPTER 42

T he Supervisor was sitting in her office, trying to focus on the myriad of management actions necessary to run her program, when her secure smartphone rang. "Yes," she said.

"No deal," the voice on the other end said.

*"Crap, now what are they up to?"* she thought.

"What's next then, Mr. Secretary?" She looked up and saw Dr. Apoe standing at the door. He'd been working outside her office at the admin's desk, waiting for the call. She waved him into her office, nodding to affirm it was the message they were expecting. She placed her phone on speaker for Dr. Apoe.

"We intend to move forward with the provisions of PD51. Your cooperation would help immensely with the transition."

"Is this also Dr. Gregory's assessment?"

"He was very insistent we move quickly."

*"This is a threat to take over my facilities. Let me test to see if Apoe was right about the power I have."*

"I am not sure what moving quickly means, Mr. Secretary, but if you intend to use manpower to take my program, I will immediately exit additional inmates to help me defend my facilities. Are you prepared to accept responsibility for what happens?"

There was a long pause. "Mr. Secretary?"

"Dr. Gregory and I discussed that possibility."

"Good, Mr. Secretary. Let me just say this clearly. It would be ill-advised if either agency attempts to seize any of my facilities under PD51 or take my staff for further questioning against their will."

Apoe noticed the Supervisor's primary office line blinking. She was receiving a call on her secure office line. Apoe pointed to the blinking light, and the Supervisor motioned

Apoe to the outer office. Apoe walked out to answer it at the admin's desk.

"I hope we can work this situation out, Ms. Supervisor." Click. The call abruptly ending told her that the next move was hers. But to do what? She had made her offer to Wellsley and Gregory. Was this going to be how they negotiated a solution, a series of phone calls to haggle over details?

"We've got a problem," she heard Apoe say. The Supervisor looked up. Apoe was standing in the doorway, holding the phone in his hand, cupping the mouthpiece at the bottom of the wireless handset.

"What's going on?" she asked, knowing a spectrum of incidents could happen at one of the facilities that required reporting to her.

"That was the Warden from the LA facility. She has a company of Marines outside her facility and two more outside of the Admin and Support building. The officer told her that under the provisions of Presidential Directive 51, the facility and all its support assets, including our staff, are now under the direction of the Central Intelligence Agency, effective immediately. The Warden would receive instructions on mission change from the Director shortly and provide unrestricted access to the Marines to secure the facility. The Marine commander told the Warden to cooperate fully."

"Shit! Are they in the facility or the building?"

"No, they are still outside. The Warden is awaiting instructions from you."

"Authorize immediate access to the admin building and cooperate. Do not answer any questions about the scenarios and their technical composition. Destroy all scenario source code, passcodes, case histories, instructions, and procedures in the facility. Have her send a confirmation when complete. Then grant access and cooperate under the same conditions as the admin building. Under no circumstances will they answer questions or provide technical details about scenario implementation or results. I want situation reports every three hours."

Dr. Apoe removed his hand from the handset and relayed the Supervisor's instructions, nodding his head to confirm the Warden understood.

"What about deadly force?" Apoe asked.

"Deny entry without deadly force unless the Marines try and breach the facility. Have the Warden pass on the Attorney General's rules of deadly force use in prisons. The Marines may not be familiar with them."

The Supervisor knew it would take her team roughly an hour to erase every trace of the scenario code. She hoped she could prevent the LA newspapers and local channels from reporting the Marines storming a local funeral home. After that hour, the immediate crisis would begin to cool, and the Supervisor would still possess the software. She would have to figure out a way to keep the Agency and DoD scientists from beginning their Exit testing, despite having the code. That effort would be the next crisis.

Apoe finished passing the instructions to the Warden and hung up the phone. He walked into the Supervisor's office and flopped onto her sofa.

"We should send policy out to all our facilities with the info you just provided LA."

"I agree. Have your staff send the notice. Then I would like you and your team to begin implementing formal procedures if this happens at another facility."

"I'll need Dr. O'Neil for the details. She is better suited than me to provide instructions." Apoe paused before continuing. "Do you feel Dr. O'Neil is still a risk? We need her here."

The Supervisor nodded her head, "Recall her immediately. They would already have the source code to include the Quantum Persona if she were a risk. They may know how it works, but without the code, they have no solution."

"They do have a facility now. They can begin developing

and testing their Exit sequence."

The Supervisor stared at Apoe. "I guess that was a statement of the obvious," he admitted.

"Okay, Franklin. They've forced our hand. I did not expect them to move so quickly after our meeting. What do you suggest?"

It was Apoe's turn to stare at the Supervisor.

She saw his reaction and knew what he was thinking. "I agree," she said. "Let's get Adelle and Alec ready for their next mission."

# CHAPTER 43

A delle Hall and Alec Richardson observed a man leave the Pentagon and disappear into a dark government sedan from their vantage point less than a quarter of a mile away. Even with night vision devices, it was hard to identify the individual entering the vehicle; despite fitting the profile of the SECDEF. The time was roughly 10:00 p.m. The waxing crescent moon was still small enough to provide near-maximum darkness to accomplish the evening's task.

The SECDEF's caravan of three vehicles departed their pick-up zone and headed towards I-95. Adelle knew they could never follow the procession through the Pentagon's parking lots and small access roads that granted Wellsley special access to the highway, so she and Alec watched and waited outside the pentagon North Parking lot until the vehicles entered the public road. Adelle started the car. She felt Alec's hand touch her arm.

"Look." Alec pointed to a lone car whose headlights had turned on. Adelle saw it. The lone black suburban drove along the access road to exit the lot.

"That's our guy," she said.

Adelle and Alec knew that security protocol for Wellsley's travel would vary each night. It might be redundant vehicles and alternate routes using back roads. Tonight, it looked like an alternate solo car.

"This one's heading north. The others headed south," Adelle noted.

"They will connect somewhere on the route. We need to be prepared for them to show up again. Faster, Adelle, he'll get away." Alec said.

"He's not going anywhere. I've got this."

The car left the parking lot and jumped on one of the chaotic connections of roads around the Potomac River called

Washington Blvd. and continued north. Adelle maintained a steady acceleration and was gaining ground on Wellsley's vehicle and closed to within 300 yards near the Arlington Memorial Bridge. The car continued northeast and connected with the George Washington Memorial Highway.

"Where is he going? This direction is way off his pathway home."

"Maybe he's heading to the CIA. This would be the way to go. Is he meeting with Dr. Gregory?"

"Let's just follow, Adelle. We could wear ourselves out guessing."

"Try picking up his thoughts. Then we won't need to guess, right? We are close enough for you to focus."

Alec looked at Adelle. "You're so smart. That's why I love you."

"That better not be the only reason, mister,"

"It's not. Maybe we need to try reality again a little later."

Adelle smiled. She loved this man deeply, "Focus on the mission. Let's go!"

Alec closed his eyes and began to open his mind. He heard the drivers about 50 yards in front of him and turned his attention to the car they were following. As Alec expanded his distance further, the number of thoughts floating in the air from the motorist around him also multiplied. Adelle could see him struggling to connect.

"Damn!"

"What's the matter, Alec?"

"I think the car is using blockers. I can hear everything around us, but when I focus on our target car, I hear nothing."

"That confirms this could be the SECDEF. No one else has blockers; maybe the CIA."

Alec nodded in agreement. The two remained quiet, focused on the target vehicle, which continued driving along the parkway. They were crossing under the I66 Roosevelt Bridge, the same namesake of the small island beneath the tons of concrete providing a major traffic artery into

Washington, D.C.

Adelle tried to focus on their task. The man they were targeting was the nation's second in command for the world's most powerful armed forces, and the thought of delivering the Supervisor's message to him had her on edge. She was not concerned about her safety, just the idea that they could perpetuate this hidden conflict between the program and administration. She found the whole concept of government in-fighting abhorrent. Still, her experience taught her that life in D.C. was a continuous fight for power and prestige, confirming her belief that the dominant always sought to dominate. Understanding why people fought did nothing to comfort her with the evening task. Alec had explained to her they were on the good side of the fight. She wasn't so sure.

*"I hope the Supervisor knows what the hell she's doing."*

"He's slowing down," Alec said.

The car slowed and made a turn into the parking lot of the Theodore Roosevelt Island Memorial. Adelle quickly closed the distance and turned as well. There would no longer be a need to tail the car. Most likely, the driver was already aware they were being followed. The vehicle drove through the small oblong parking lot and crossed the pedestrian bridge. Despite its name, it was wide enough for maintenance vehicles to traverse, and its supports could handle the heavier trucks and equipment needed to haul the heavy granite blocks during the memorial's initial construction. The car had already reached the other side of the bridge and was disappearing into the island's wooded interior.

Adelle looked at Alec, "Well?"

"You know, once we cross this bridge, we're trapped on the island," he responded.

"Probably a bunch of DoD guys waiting for us on the other side."

"Probably."

Adelle sat behind the wheel, her hand gripping the hard plastic under a leather cover, the car front pointed at the dark forest to her front. "I say we do it. What can happen?"

"Non-lethal force Adelle. I can't lose you now after finding you again."

"You always were a romantic." She gently pushed the accelerator, and the vehicle began to move across the bridge. "Nothing poetic to say?"

Alec responded, "Into the breach, dear friends. Here I go."

"Just kidding, baby," Adelle said, cutting him off. "Stay alert."

Recovering quickly from his poetic shutdown, Alec offered, "Focus on your defense, Adelle, like I showed you. This is usually the time when things get crazy. We are exposed and out in the open."

The car moved slowly across the bridge, each stone of the pebbly surface composition popping or crunching as the tires rolled over them, sounding like small firecrackers in the still night air. Adelle exhaled loudly when the car reached the intersection of hiking paths on the other side. The ominous darkness of the woods surrounded them.

They both saw the trail sign directing hikers to the memorial plaza. Adelle turned the car around on the hiking trail, pointed it back across the bridge if a quick departure was needed, and cut the ignition. Silence joined the ominous darkness. Their world was oblivious to numerous motorists noiselessly traveling on the interstate bridge near them.

Both reached for their Night Optical Devices and exited the car quietly. Once outside the vehicle, both pulled the harness over their head and turned on the NODs. The darkness melted away, and the path through the woods became visible in the eerie green world of amplified light.

Alec motioned for Adelle to follow him. She nodded, and the two began their short trek to the memorial plaza. Adelle opened her mind and began to look for the thoughts of the people they'd followed to the island. She expanded her distance to what she suspected would pull in all transmitted energy within a quarter of a mile. Nothing. They were definitely using blockers.

The trail opened to their front, and Adelle could make out the memorial plaza's structures. Various stone bridges covered the memorial center, and large rectangular slabs formed a loose semicircle around the plaza, pushing their inscribed words skyward. Alec dropped to his knees and motioned for Adelle to close on him and do the same.

"I'm not sure what will happen, but this is where it will. Ideas?"

Adelle thought a moment, then said, "If these gifts are as good as you say they are, then we walk straight in and see what happens."

Alec nodded, "I agree. Did you pick up they were using blockers?"

Adelle looked at Alec and smiled. *"Men, sometimes they state the obvious,"* she thought.

She left the question hanging but knew that even in the romantic green glow of the NODs, Alec would see her smile.

"Okay, Alec, let's find out what these folks have in store for us." Adelle rose to her feet. Alec joined her, and the two walked into the plaza, scanning left and right but seeing nothing. Adelle could begin to detect the memorial's centerpiece and namesake. A tall statue of Theodore Roosevelt, made taller by the extension of his arm into the sky, silhouetted by a stone background. As they were nearing the center of the plaza, they heard a metallic voice saying, "That's far enough."

Adelle and Alec stopped. "We are here to talk with Secretary Wellsley," Alec began. They were blinded instantly by bright lights turned on from concealed locations hidden in the woods. Their Night Optical Devices responded as the equipment registered a large amount of light and tried to reduce its amplification. The devices showed a bright white view and were useless.

Adelle removed her NOD and lifted her arm to screen

her eyes from the light specially focused on blinding them. She noticed Alec had done the same. As quickly as the lights began, they ceased, leaving them both with night blindness. From their left, two lights turned back on, their intensity focused on the couple.

Adelle focused her thoughts, "destroy the lights." The darkness returned with an explosive sound as the light housing assemblies and electrical relay units ricocheted off trees, crashing into the night.

The woods erupted in a cascade of pops as soldiers hidden within the trees began firing their automatic rifles. The silencers muffled each rifle's report as a heavy volume of rounds headed toward the couple from their right flank, each creating a brief blue flash on impact.

"They're firing rubber bullets, Adelle."

"Time to stop this," she said. Adelle focused on each weapon. She envisioned the firing mechanisms fusing with the bolts and carrier housings. Each soldier's location revealed itself quickly as the fusing metal created red glows within the woods that looked like giant fireflies. The firing stopped, and Adelle watched as a succession of small flickering drops of red fell to the ground.

"Now what?" Adelle asked, looking at Alec.

In response to her question, two men emerged from behind the Roosevelt statue and began walking toward them. Three men on each side flanked them. As they approached, Adelle knew that one of the men was Wellsley. She recognized him from the profile info in her mission packet. She opened her mind and searched for any thoughts emanating from them. Nothing. They were still using blockers.

The men closed to within six feet and stopped.

"Before you ask," Wellsley began, clearing his throat in the night air, "tonight was strictly a test. It was a test to evaluate the commitment of your boss and a demonstration of your gifts to my partner, Dr. Gregory."

"What did you find out?" Alec asked, his voice booming

in the night air.

"That this dispute has gone far enough. This difference between our organizations needs to end."

"We could have settled all this over a beer in Georgetown," Adelle quipped. "Why all the driving around."

"I needed to see for myself." Dr. Gregory joined the conversation taking a step forward. "I wanted a first-hand account of the power your boss refers to that needs to be controlled. I've seen the video of the inmates. I wanted to see that the Supervisor was not intent on using you for full destruction."

"Our intent is not to kill or harm anyone. Our boss just wants you the hell out of her program," Alec said.

"You can understand, given the circumstances with Director Thompson, our caution about your intentions."

"I think we've shown that we are not violent nor want to bring harm. If we did, this conversation would already be over."

"Possibly, but you are not the other inmates. They have no problem destroying the property and people around them."

Alec and Adelle remained silent.

"You took a big risk tonight, the both of you being here; why?" Adelle asked.

"It was the best way to demonstrate our commitment. Neither the Secretary nor I want this dispute to continue. I have lost some outstanding agents," Gregory said. Adelle heard the remorse in his voice.

"I have a message from the Supervisor," Adelle began. "It's simple. Get your Marines out of her facilities. You will not find anything you are looking for. We can begin to agree on a way forward if you do this."

"And I thought you two were the message," Wellsley began. "Please let the Supervisor know the Marines stay until we have an agreement. She can bring this to an end by trusting us. We trust you. We hope we showed that tonight."

*"Wellsley is not going to back off. Message delivered. Time to*

*go.*"

Adelle looked at Alec. They had done their job, and no one died.

"By the way, where are the three escaped inmates?" Dr. Gregory asked.

"Why?" Alec responded.

"We would like to know where they are. While they are at large, none of our facilities are secure or safe."

"That situation is under control, and you have nothing to worry about with them," Alec said. "If I were you, I would be more concerned about each other. Are we done here?"

"You two have a good evening. You are free to go," Wellsley added.

Both said nothing walking through the woods back to the car, and they remained quiet, unsure of what awaited them. Adelle started the car and began the drive across the bridge. As they reached the other side, numerous military vehicles occupied several positions in the visitor's lot, each operated by their crews at the ready. Adelle drove through the parking spaces without incident and turned right onto the George Washington Parkway, heading northwest. She knew she would have to leave the parkway to turn around and head back to Arlington.

"Why would they play this cat and mouse game tonight?" It was Adelle that broke the silence.

"I don't know unless it was, as Gregory said, he wanted to see if we would handle this peacefully instead of with force."

"That's too big a risk for two senior administration executives. And in a public place. Roosevelt island is not open now, but it is far from private. If we had started blowing up stuff, how do you explain the loss of a national memorial to the American people?"

"It was a big gamble, Adelle. The only thing I can think

of, and it's not that good of an answer, is that there is a good side to who these guys are. They really did want to show us they were doing what they thought was right. Other than that, I'm stumped."

"Maybe, if they saw us use our gifts with restraint, that confirms that they can grow the soldiers they want and trust them the same way. Wellsley said we were the message tonight, and he and Gregory were concerned about the inmates. It's as though they know the inmates are not controllable, but they know that people with the right values are."

"Maybe, Adelle. They have a lot to learn about people if that's their thinking."

Adelle nodded. Inside she hoped that she and Alec made a difference tonight. The push to control the SOUP and experiment on its humans might be coming to a resolution. She reflected on the number of innocents that had died; Grant was among them. She wondered, *"what drives a person to stop caring about people?"*

She knew she would not find an answer and focused her attention on the road, taking her back to Arlington.

# CHAPTER 44

## *Three Weeks Later*

T he President of the United States sat in the Oval Office with Dr. Lucia, his Chief of Staff Aaron McAllister, Dr. Gregory, Secretary Wellsley, Mr. Mark Langley, a Department of Justice Program Executive Officer, and Senator Hurst. Before the President was a revocation order for his Presidential Directive 51, newly signed which he handed with the folder to McAllister.

"That should close the matter of the vague language of 51," the president said. "This new directive that I've just signed," he said, holding up the document for everyone to see, "provides a special joint task force between the Virtual Life Incarceration Program and the CIA. Each of you provided input, so there should be no surprises. However, I would not be doing my job if I didn't emphasize the key points."

No one in the room disagreed with their Commander and Chief.

"First, losing the intelligence capability we used to resolve the Taiwan Straits incident is not an option. However, given the recent videos provided to me, I want us to exercise caution in pursuing any other activities or capabilities related to the SOUP. Dr. Gregory, your organization's focus will be on enhancing your Remote Viewing capabilities with Agency Assets in the SOUP, nothing else. Is that clearly understood?"

"Yes, Mr. President. Clearly understood."

"Senator Hurst, you are now reappointed Chairman of the Committee overseeing our nation's inmates in the SOUP. Additionally, I have appointed the Secretary of Defense and Agency Director as ex-officio members. We need to keep everyone in the loop. In your capacity as Chairman, the program will provide the information necessary to Exit Dr.

Gregory's assets safely. Further, I leave it to you to determine what laws Congress must pass to codify the lessons we have learned from this affair."

Hurst nodded his head, "Thank you, Mr. President."

The President stood, signaling the meeting was over, and all the attendees rose with him. He began, "We are sitting on top of one of the best technological assets the United States has ever developed." The president continued, "For the time remaining in my administration, we will use this asset as it was intended. We will incarcerate evil, reform our inmates to successfully re-enter and contribute to society, and through our national security efforts, discover additional ways to protect our nation. This is one government. We will work with each other to accomplish these objectives. I know I can count on your support."

"Thank you, Mr. President," each of his executives said. The meeting concluded. The CIA Director and Secretary of Defense headed out of the Oval along with the Justice Executive. Senator Hurst shook hands with the President and departed for Capitol Hill. The National Security Advisor walked towards McAllister's office.

McAllister asked, "Will there be anything else, Mr. President?"

"Done here, for now, Chief. Thanks."

McAllister turned and headed for his office. Dr. Lucia was already seated.

"How soon can I get signed copies, Aaron?"

"Give me a least an hour, Carol. He just signed the thing." McAllister's impatience with her request was evident as he sat down heavily in his chair.

"What has you bothered Aaron?"

"Nothing. I think the documents are well written. There is truly little doubt about who controls what. Wouldn't you agree?"

"Yes, I'm pleased with what he signed. If not the document, Aaron, then what?"

McAllister looked at the wall momentarily, searching for how to answer Dr. Lucia's question. He turned and looked at her.

"What was the final body count needed to sign this agreement today?"

Lucia nodded. She fully understood the price of finally allowing common sense to prevail.

"I see your point. There must be a better way to catch these things before they get out of control," Lucia said. "I don't want to say I told you so, but my voice was the only dissenting one when the Vice President brought 51 in for signature."

"I know, Carol, but you could not produce the videos in time to make your case."

The National Security Advisor stared at McAllister, offended by his comment, despite its truth. He continued, "Regardless, even with these new agreements, there are still so many risks and unknowns associated with this program. Sure, we'll use it only for remote viewing, but anyone exiting the SOUP will have telekinetic powers. What do we do about those? Just ignore them? And do you believe now that the CIA is cleared to produce these assets, they won't use them every way they can?"

"You must have faith in the people doing the job, or fire them, Aaron."

"You're giving me advice now," he said incredulously. "How do you fire the CIA Director?"

"Everyone answers to someone. You and I answer to the president. He answers to the American people. The CIA Director answers to someone. It's when they are no longer required to answer to the people we run into trouble. PD51 was a perfect example of everything done in the dark with no accountability."

McAllister leaned forward and placed his hands on his desk, "Right, as if elected officials will always be accountable. That's not going to happen. We've been turning a blind eye to the law for a very long time now, justifying it all under

National Security or when there was some political advantage. Who are those guys accountable to? Not the American people! No one in DC will want to end their career when they can benefit from someone else's misfortune."

Lucia waited for McAllister to settle back in his chair before responding, "Aaron, over in Virginia, is someone I hope is celebrating tonight because the President revoked PD 51 and signed his new directive. She's the person who makes our elected officials answer to someone."

"The Supervisor, yeah, right! She couldn't find her inmates, and they wreaked havoc on this country. She's as much to blame as anyone."

"Be careful, Aaron. You're starting to believe your own briefings."

"What are you saying, Carol?"

"I'm saying that talk is cheap, and there is lots of it these days. People disagree about everything, making it look like we are ready for something big to split this country, and yes, we have to admit we here, in the White House, are part of it. And then you have the Supervisor. She doesn't say anything to convince anyone to side with her. She listens to what is said, finds her own truth, and picks a side when the time is right or forced into a decision. There is no doubt where she stands. Those people check the CIA, overturn presidential directives, and write new ones that make sense for the country."

"Do you really believe she played a role? Both Gregory and Wellsley approached me and said they wanted more specificity in the directive, and 51 was too vague. They said there was too big a chance of running afoul with congress."

"Right, I'm sure that's exactly what they said to you. Speaking of talking, how is the VP doing these days."

"Ouch, that was kinda low, but I'll give you a pass knowing how well you and he got along together." McAllister smiled. He knew the VP, and Dr. Lucia hated each other.

"So, how's he doing?"

"He still comes to the office, but his productivity and

morale are low. It's amazing how little he gets done when things are put in writing and signed. Sadly, he's watching his dream to be president pass in front of him, and he can't really do or say anything about it."

"How about the boss? What does he think?"

"Morrison fell out of favor when the president realized he was no longer backing a winner. Things are not well between the two. Neither of them talks with me about it, and their rift has stayed out of the press. I have no problems with the recent turn of events."

Lucia nodded, "He's someone else that thought he could take power and use it for his own gain simply because the president backed him. Sorry, Aaron, but I can't feel sorry for the man."

"I don't think he would want any sympathy, especially from you."

Lucia shifted in her chair, a telltale sign to McAllister the conversation was changing.

True to form, Lucia asked, "So, what are your plans when this term is over? Given any thought to what you want to do?"

McAllister leaned forward again. "Carol, I always appreciate our talks, but I've got work to do."

Lucia understood. She stood up. "I'll say one last thing, Aaron. Men like you can make a difference. You're the type of person that can keep things on the rails for this country. You're still too young to take a university position or work in industry. If you really want to know how the SOUP assets will be controlled, be part of its future. You might be pleasantly surprised at what they're working on."

McAllister brushed by her comment. "You said 'one last thing,' Carol, yet you are still here." His exasperation was genuine but softened with humor from his innocent expression.

"So here is the last thing. It's a simple question, one the Supervisor asked me one day recently. How will you live the rest of your life, Aaron?"

McAllister looked at the floor and then at Lucia. "It may be simple, but that's a damn good question."

# CHAPTER 45

The presence of Dr. O'Neil in the Supervisor's office was nothing new, but Apoe could not help but wonder why. It was no secret that Dr. O'Neil was persona non-grata with the Supervisor as of late or that perhaps the Supervisor had lost her trust in Dr. O'Neil as the dispute unraveled over Directive 51. One thing was sure to Apoe. He had missed her counsel as the program grappled with responses to the administration. He also missed her involvement in the lab, helping him to develop the VITP. While communication technology had enhanced the ability to work apart, Apoe had longed to discuss ideas in real time with Dr. O'Neil. It was no surprise that the schedule for the prototype had missed its target date.

Apoe walked into the office just as the Supervisor said, "You have to tell them!" Apoe was unsure what the conversation entailed but could see that the Supervisor was both nervous and elated by the discussion with Dr. O'Neil.

"Franklin, would you please ask Alec and Adelle to come to the office?"

Still unaware of the subject, Apoe did as requested, called the couple from the admin's desk, and relayed the Supervisor's request.

Apoe walked back into the Supervisor's office to find both executives talking as though there was never a disagreement between them.

"They are in the conference room. They'll be right here," Apoe reported.

"Thanks, Franklin," the Supervisor said and turned her attention back to Dr. O'Neil.

"Now that you are comfortable returning to the facility, I know Dr. Apoe will welcome your collaboration on the VITP."

"It will be good to be back, Ms. Supervisor."

The Supervisor turned and looked at Apoe, "Have a

seat, Franklin. Did they say how long it would be before they arrived?"

Alec and Adelle walked through the office door, providing the Supervisor with her answer.

"What's going on, boss?" Adelle asked.

Alec noticed Dr. O'Neil immediately and said, "Welcome back, Sandra. We've missed you here."

"Everyone, please take a seat," the Supervisor directed.

*"What is going on with her? She seems almost euphoric,"* Apoe thought.

Everyone found a place to sit, and the Supervisor began, "As you all have noticed, Dr. O'Neil has worked remotely for the last couple of months. Shortly after Alec Exited, Dr. O'Neil approached me and asked if she could spend more time away from the program. I granted her request without understanding the reasoning. While never out of reach, Dr. O'Neil has continued collaborating remotely with Dr. Apoe. Today, she called and said she needed to tell me why. That reason has brought us together." The Supervisor turned to Dr. O'Neil, "Sandra," she said, pointing to Dr. O'Neil to take over the conversation.

Dr. O'Neil looked nervous to Apoe. He sat back in his chair to observe what was about to be discussed. Being disconnected from the conversation felt good for once.

"Alec," she started. "I was overjoyed when I saw you for the first time in the cell block. Not only because we had watched you in the SOUP interacting with Boyd but because you were also the first successful Exit, UT, and I accomplished. Your Exit was required to defend our program, and the risk was worth the attempt."

"I'm glad you were successful, Sandra. But I am not following where this is going."

"Alec, your Exit also granted you the powers you have today, and it was because of those powers I needed to," O'Neil paused, "Distance myself from the program."

"Why?" Adelle asked.

"Because there was a real need for what you could do for the program. We had to balance your value with what UT and I viewed as a significant liability. You see, UT and I were concerned about your ability to reconcile the memories from both realities. This problem, unfortunately, came true with Grant."

"Dr. O'Neil, get to your point. Were you afraid of me?"

"No, Alec, I was not. As I said, I was more concerned about you being caught between the two worlds, not knowing what was real and what wasn't." O'Neil stopped and stood up. She walked behind the Supervisor's desk.

"I want to tell you about the night you and Adelle entered the SOUP."

Adelle moved closer to Alec on the sofa.

"*What the hell is going on*?" This conversation was not what Apoe expected.

"You both remember BWI and the events leading up to your Entry. So do I. I received a call that night from Supervisor Boyd. A comprehensive health screening is part of all routine checks before entry into the SOUP. When the Supervisor called me, he told me you, Adelle, were about six weeks pregnant."

Alec stood straight upright from the couch. "What the hell are you saying, Dr. O'Neil! Adelle, are you hearing this?" Alec looked down at Adelle, still sitting, looking up at him.

"I knew, Alec," she said softly, "Sit down, please. I knew but had not told you. There was so much going on."

Alec sat back on the couch, dumbfounded by what he was hearing, and confused by Adelle's acceptance.

"Please continue, Sandra," Adelle said.

"The Supervisor asked me to set up an emergency medical procedures team and to be ready to perform a transfer of the embryo."

"To where?"

"To a surrogate mother. We have women prepared to assist with these types of emergency conditions. It was obvious that you could not carry the baby to term in the SOUP, and the Supervisor was not going to sacrifice another life, no matter how young. UT did not perform the transfer, nor was he aware of it. Only I knew besides Boyd and the team, who were not part of the program."

"Is the baby alive now?" Adelle asked.

"Yes, Addie is about three years old." Alec and Adelle looked at each other.

"Addie?" Alec asked.

"Yes, Addie," O'Neil said, nodding her head.

Adelle put her hand to her mouth, "Our little girl." She began to cry and quickly regained control of her emotions, the tears still rolling down her cheeks.

"We thought Addie only existed in the SOUP, part of the reality we created."

"In a way, she was Adelle. I placed the data in the community database about her so you two would find it. Nobody knew how long it would be before we found an Exit protocol. The Supervisor wanted both of you to experience her, to grow up with her, and to love her, if only in your virtual memories."

"That's why we both have memories of her," Alec said slowly. "You gave her to both of us."

"Yes," O'Neil said.

"You stayed away from me. If I read your thoughts and knew Addie was real," Alec started.

"You might take off to find her, sacrificing the mission, or experience God knows what with your memories. Either way, we could not take the risk with the threat to the program," the Supervisor finished.

"Where is she now?" Alec asked.

"She is being raised in a small home in Culpepper, Virginia."

"The birth mother will never give her up," Adelle said sadly. "I never would."

"She already has. The mother gave her up for 'adoption' right after the birth. Addie is in a special home in another of my programs. She is not up for adoption; she is waiting for you two. The parents raising her are more guardians than parents. They are special people." O'Neil finished, "I assure you; she is waiting for her real parents."

"She's ours? We can go get her?" Adelle asked.

"Yes," the Supervisor said. "Dr. O'Neil will provide you with all the directions and make arrangements."

Apoe found himself embarrassed, wiping away the tears that had magically emerged on his cheeks. He decided that he preferred discussions about program operations.

# CHAPTER 46

Secretary of Defense Brian "Hooknose" Wellsley sat at the front of the conference room table in a secure office buried somewhere in one of the many executive rooms of the Pentagon. In the room with him was his Undersecretary for Intelligence, Dr. John Sores, and the Joint Chiefs Chairman, General Thomas Dickens.

Wellsley knew this meeting would happen when the president signed the new directive and canceled Directive 51. Wellsley had provided his comments and agreed with the final draft, but his outward support did not mean he was not seething inside at the outcome.

"How and the hell could the President leave the DoD out of the final directive? I provided my input and stated emphatically that the DoD needed to be a partner with VLIP!"

The other two remained quiet. Best to let the Secretary rant and rave for a couple of minutes.

"The CIA gets to work closely with the staff at the Los Angeles facility, and we get caught holding the bag."

"Mr. Secretary," the General began. "We still have the Marines at the facility. It was a concession to provide security now that the Agency is working their classified programs. We could use the commander to find out the information about the CIA's efforts."

"Hell, we don't need to spy on the CIA. They are better at it than us. We need an innovative approach." Wellsley stood up and started pacing in the room. "The VP was right about one thing, no one in the World respects us anymore. We used to carry the big hammer, but every country has nukes, and no one will use them unless the Iranians get one, and even then, I bet they'd think twice about it." Wellsley changed direction, "No, not even the Iranians want to see their world destroyed. Despite their beliefs, they are also human and enjoy the finer things this world offers. No, gentlemen, we need the power we saw in those videos, and I don't want the CIA using their assets for more than intelligence collection. The telekinesis power would belong to the US only, and it should be with the Defense Department, not a bunch of spooks. That would push the world balance back in our favor."

"According to the President, congress is going to pass the law precluding the CIA from doing just that," Sores said.

*"Jesus, this guy is naïve,"* Wellsley thought. He liked his Undersecretaries, but they sometimes thought Congress made the rules. Wellsley made the rules; Congress made the laws. There was a real difference. His rules were never broken because they involved loyalty. Congress' laws could be broken when loyalty was required.

Wellsley chose the diplomatic response. He still needed Sores on his team. "That's true, John, but you know Congress. It will take them time to get something through committee. This President will be gone by the time congress gets a bill to the floor that provides controls over the CIA. In the interim, I don't think there will be any laws keeping the CIA in check during the final year of POTUS' administration."

"So, what are our options, Mr. Secretary?"

"Well, General, let's consider the technology needed to put someone in the SOUP and take them out successfully. We have access to Last Memory Reset, so we can put them in at any time that works for our warriors."

"Sir, are we really considering this? I appreciate you bringing us in on the videos, but the three Exited inmates successfully caused havoc during their escape. They tore up the CIA in Las Vegas, are responsible for destroying Site 35, and killed Director Thompson with dozens of his agents. How can we be sure our men that Exit the SOUP won't be the same way?"

"All good points, John. I'll reveal a little more of the puzzle. Roughly three years ago, two people named Alec Richardson and Adelle Hall were reported missing and assumed dead in the middle east. They were researching an article on Syrian Refugee camps or some such thing. I remember this because Alec Richardson had won the Pulitzer in Afghanistan, exposing the government's corruption. His articles created a lot of blow-back for this administration, and we had a lot of ass-covering to do."

"I'm not following, Sir,"

"General, Alec Richardson was also responsible for authoring the articles that informed the public that the SOUP existed. POTUS handpicked him. Alec was one of the few people granted access to the first facility to report what he'd seen. About a month ago, Dr. Gregory and I ran a little test of our own to your point, John, because we needed to know if these powers could be controlled.

As you both know, we sent Marines to the Los Angeles facility. Yes, they had a mission to seize technology if they could but the primary purpose, I can reveal to you both now, was Dr. Gregory and I needed the Supervisor to generate a response to the move. As we hoped, she did, and a man and a woman followed us to a preplanned destination. We saw precisely what kind of capabilities they had. It was amazing to witness. They have telekinetic powers to defend themselves against projectiles and the ability to move objects like paper. Their powers were real, and I first wondered what kind of mess I had signed up for. Then it all stopped, turned off like a light switch."

"And..," Sores asked.

"We had a civilized conversation, and to top it off, the man and woman that night we identified as Alec Richardson and Adelle Hall. Somehow, they were put into the SOUP and brought out with these incredible gifts." Wellsley paused, "And they controlled them."

"So, you believe our top performers can go through the same process? They'll follow orders, carry out our objectives, and not go crazy like the inmates?"

"I do." Wellsley's confidence echoed off the walls.

"And what about the three still out there? Has anyone

accounted for them yet?"

"Who gives a shit, Tom? That's not our problem. Our problem is finding a facility we can use to grow our guys. The Supervisor can track down her convicts. Eventually, they will show up, and when they do, they'll be dealt with. It's not hard to track public paranormal activity. If we can use some of our assets to help the Supervisor find them, that's great for building relationships with the program. Who knows what benefits and technology sharing will come from our help? I know she will be happy to get them off the street and back in the SOUP."

Both subordinates nodded their heads. Sores began, "Mr. Secretary, the technology we need to put volunteers into the SOUP is readily available. I know the CIA shared some exit protocol information to include the frequencies, but we lack the technology to create the free will component. We will need this tech to produce Cause and Effects Scenarios or the Quantum persona. Either way, we must convince our men in the SOUP they need to come out. We lack the technology to do so."

"The new directive keeps the technology in the program. The CIA can use the capability to Exit their assets but will not have the technology to use as they want. We have about three years to figure it out, John, or get the new president to allow us to use it like the CIA," Wellsley said.

"We won't be here then. How do our replacements influence the new president to exit soldiers not authorized by the directive or congress to exist?"

"No president will let assets like that remain in the SOUP. The president will have the program share the technology to get them out."

*"Enough of dealing with Sores' questions."*

"That's the least of our problems, though," Wellsley said, changing the subject. "How are we coming on our facility construction? All this is for nothing if we don't have a facility."

"Not good, Sir. The VP's money allocated for us to build

a facility was pulled as soon as he was no longer a viable candidate to win the nomination. We barely broke ground," Sores reported.

"Someone else, like the Chinese, will figure this out, so how do we start getting our guys into the SOUP?" Wellsley asked.

"Mr. Secretary, I think I have an idea."

"Okay, Tom, let's hear it."

"Mr. Secretary, we provide billions to big firms to build our defense requirements, and some of those firms also...."

The light bulb turned on. Wellsley cut the General off as his excitement grabbed hold of the answer he was looking for from the two executives.

"Say no more. I love it!" Wellsley exclaimed. "Threaten to take away their contracts if they don't provide us access. Or maybe a carrot. You two work the details. We're done here. I have some phone calls to make."

The General explained his idea to Sores, and the two stood and exchanged coordination details until they walked out the door.

Wellsley walked over to a phone sitting on a small nightstand and picked up the receiver.

"Yes, Sir."

"Get me a line to the CEO of SBIC. You should have his secure mobile number."

"I have it right here. Connecting you, Sir."

The phone rang twice, and the CEO answered, "Mr. Secretary," the voice said, "this is an unexpected call."

"Mike, let me get to the point. How would you like a shot at the electronics on the Next Gen 8 fighter?"

"Mr. Secretary," the voice flushed with new excitement. "This is a surprise. Of course, we want the opportunity."

"Okay, Mike. Now I need you to do something for me."

# CHAPTER 47

The Supervisor sat in her office with Dr. Apoe. Both focused on the upcoming report to the committee. The Supervisor was overjoyed with Senator Hurst being re-appointed as Chair. The move by the VP to take the committee from Hurst was the shot from the Supervisor's perspective that started the war. A lot had happened since that day; friends and professionals lost on both sides. So unnecessary, like so many conflicts. The thought of losing UT still caused momentary depression. Thank God for Franklin! He had proven himself loyal and willing to change his life to pursue what was right. Her only concern about the committee was the introduction of the Agency and DoD as ex-officio members. While not officially voting on pending decisions with the original committee members, they would now have information that in the past was not provided, or they had to provide a specific request when Justice took control of the program. The intent was for the DoD and Justice to be separate.

"Let's move through the agenda one last time Franklin," she started, "and discuss the briefing details."

Apoe nodded. "Let's go."

"This administration believes the three escaped inmates caused the death and destruction. They believe they are still at large. I want them to continue to believe this."

Apoe nodded. "Why change their minds? I agree; keep the story going. It places some of the blame on them."

"What about the temporary nature of the powers?" Apoe asked.

"I'm not in a sharing mood about these kinds of details, Franklin. It puts us at a disadvantage if they know everything. Time will answer the questions for them."

"You don't want to share that powers are temporary, and if they are abused...," Apoe hesitated, "there are consequences."

"Not right now. That implicates us and points the finger for the Director's death squarely at us. Some smart guy will figure out that our guys were 'taken away' or ran out of juice and ask questions. It could come back on Alec and Adelle or, worse yet, Grant. I do not want Grant's family to suffer for any of this. He was declared dead by the program's published press release when he entered the SOUP. For now, we continue to support his family as if nothing happened. Later Franklin, maybe we'll tell. For now, we deny any of our involvement."

"I know that's the smart thing to do, but is it right?"

"Smart and right are at odds with each other in DC. For now, we do the smart thing. We ask for help to find the inmates. Eventually, people will tire of finding someone that does not exist."

"What about Lincoln?"

"Lincoln and Sarah have gotten close and told me they wanted to stay on the program. If anyone can change Lincoln's name and give him a new life, it's Sarah."

Apoe nodded his head in agreement. "Next item."

"We need to tell the committee about the Violence Inhibitor technology you and Dr. O'Neil are working on. You two can provide the details and share this freely with the DoD and Agency. I'm sure they'll have some creative uses for the technology, and they will also see this disclosure as something looking to foster cooperation."

"We're on it. Dr. O'Neil and I discussed this very topic. There is no overlapping technology with the Scenario or Persona capabilities."

"Good. Now for a political issue. The SECDEF and Director have a leg up on me. They most likely identified Alec and Adelle. I called both. It's imperative that Senator Hurst not know that Alec is alive. To keep this secret, I promised the Virtual Inhibitor technology. They wanted the scenario information, and I had to leverage future promises and threaten that Hurst would cut their budget if he found out. I also had to threaten another visit from Alec and Adelle. That seemed to get their attention."

"Played a little hardball, did you," Apoe smiled.

The Supervisor was unphased by his comment, "For now, open the Kamona on this effort and tell them everything you and Dr. O'Neil are doing. Share your results. Information and collaboration could be the next great step in criminal reform. Sharing the technology should also keep Alec's secret until Hurst at least leaves office."

"Can you trust them?"

"On this, I have no choice. Wellsley knows that Alec is an Achilles heel for me."

"Speaking of Alec and Adelle. I heard from Alec; they have Addie. He did not say where they were going," Apoe said.

"Can you give me any idea how much longer they will keep their gifts, Franklin?"

"None. It's just the best guess at this point."

"On to the next topic. We need to fix Morrison's voice sometime in the future. I was hoping one of the two could handle it before their gifts ended." she said.

"He may have to wait, which may not be bad," Apoe smiled. "I think Alec and his family want some time away from DC. They have a lot of reconnecting to do. The Program turned their lives upside down."

"Decisions made at the moment. Let's not focus on what was done but on how we can make amends going forward. This brings me to my last point."

"Which is?"

"Right now, most people in this administration knowledgeable about what happened blame me for not capturing the inmates. We know where they are, but as we've discussed, they don't. I have political exposure for the first time while in this program."

"That's true, but this administration is only in power for about another year. Then it's a whole new ball game."

"It's never new. It's only the players that change. I

applaud the president on the new directive, but we still don't know all the program risks."

"Will that ever be possible?"

"Not while trying to figure them out while simultaneously fighting among ourselves."

"So, what are you thinking?"

"I will announce that Dr. O'Neil will take on more responsibility. I will share with Senator Hurst that when you two have finished your VITP prototype, I will be stepping down."

Apoe stared at her. This was new information to him.

"Don't look so surprised, Franklin. The day you walked back into my life is the day I decided to leave this program. I asked myself, 'How do I want to live the rest of my life?' and concluded it was not here."

"Where is it?"

"Any place where I can be with you."

"Have you discussed this with Dr. O'Neil?"

"Yesterday. She's thinking it over, but I believe Dr. O'Neil will accept."

"She's known by many in the DoD. How will you mask her identity, you know, the 'Supervisor thing'?"

"It's time for the Program leadership to be open. The public knows about the SOUP, and each time the administration wants to use its success, Americans will gain more knowledge about what's happening. Masking identities was important when Boyd was building the SOUP under the radar using funding from the different Departments, and no one knew where the money was going. I still marvel at his genius to pull that off. His program was a shocking surprise to everyone, and it worked. Dr. O'Neil was part of that success and should be recognized for who she is. A masked program name is no longer needed."

"What if I want to stay here with the Program?" Apoe asked.

"I guess that would be a wrinkle in my thinking."

Apoe moved close to the Supervisor. She looked up at him, and the two stared into each other's eyes, connecting to their hearts. Apoe and the Supervisor moved closely together, their lips touching, the kiss evolving into a loving bridge, connecting the two at the very essence of their identities. The two parted slowly, not wanting their emotions to cause them to stray from the business topics.

"I guess staying with the program may not be an option," Apoe said. "I knew the day I walked through the door of this building, we would sort something out. We still have time before our work here is complete."

"Leaving the country with the VITP will be one of our major contributions to incarceration reform," the Supervisor commented. "We could tell our grandkids about that."

"Don't forget, getting PD51 revoked. That was no easy walk in the park."

"That came with terrible costs. We'll pass on telling that story at bedtime," she said.

The Supervisor looked deeply into Apoe's eyes.

"What?" he asked.

"When you showed up a while ago, you asked me what you should call me, do you remember?" the Supervisor asked.

Apoe nodded.

"I'm changing my answer. Call me Mary, like you used to."

The two kissed again, assured preparation for the committee meeting was complete.

# CHAPTER 48

A lec Richardson sat on the front porch of his new home about 15 minutes before sunrise. The mountain breeze swept through the porch, just cool enough to need a sweater this morning. While Alec did not feel old, he accepted the rocking chairs as part of the conveying furniture. Each morning he would fix his coffee and, with a mug in hand, make his way to one of the two chairs, ease into its comfortable seat and begin a slow, steady rock. He would fix his eyes on the top of the Rocky Mountains surrounding his paradise in Estes Park, Colorado, and 'be one with the morning.'

Alec used the morning to reflect on all that had happened in D.C.; even now, he had still experienced difficulty separating his virtual memories from his real ones. Adelle and Addie were invaluable to his recovery, helping time slip by for the three of them, and in each moment, the quantum tags from the SOUP and their memories became less recallable.

This morning he was grateful for his family, another joyful surprise in his life. Dr. O'Neil was correct about Addie. She was happy, healthy, and at three, beginning to put together the fundamental awareness of her new life. Her guardians had told Addie her parents loved her and left her in their care until they returned. The guardians referred to themselves as Aunt and Uncle and had built Adelle and Alec into heroes to make the separation easier for Addie when and if they returned. Pictures of Alec and Adelle kept in the living room for Addie's questions, and recognition of her true parents completed the story. When they arrived, Addie had run to them as if they had always been with her. Aunty Jane quickly collected Addie's items, including her parent's picture, and provided them to Adelle. The only awkward moment was the departure, not with Addie but with the four adults. Alec and Adelle could not find the right words of gratitude as Addie jumped into their car, trusting everything around her. Adelle provided hugs to both guardians, and Alec did likewise. The guardians told Alec and Adelle not to be concerned about taking Addie. Another young child was arriving next week. It was what they did and how they provided their 'love to the world.' Addie had been their tenth child in a succession of love-filled homes for young children without parents, regardless of the child's life circumstances.

The new parents could not relax until they had gotten into the car and driven off. Alec and Adelle remarked that both experienced deep, positive feelings for the guardians and agreed they were exceptional people. They declared that they did not know the source of their feelings, but both agreed on their experience and the overwhelming love they felt from the couple.

As to where to start their lives again, Alec and Adelle decided west was where they would go as a family. Adelle researched and found Estes Park, and Alec had agreed that time in the mountains was what he needed. So much had come their way beyond Addie. The Supervisor told them just before departing, they would receive compensation for their time in the SOUP, services recently rendered, and future services as needed. The Program would ensure their financial needs were covered for the foreseeable future. There were more hugs and firm handshakes for this unexpected demonstration of caring.

Sitting in his rocker, he reflected on the guardian's "love to the world' pronouncement. Alec began meditation while alone in the morning during his porch time shortly after moving into the house, and of late, their statement became his focus. Alec fine-tuned his mind to love, and thoughts flowed endlessly with the power of the word.

The door opened slowly, and Adelle joined him and sat down on the other rocker. "Not bothering you, am I?" she asked, holding her coffee between her hands and enjoying the warmth.

"Not at all. I'm glad you got up to watch the sunrise with

me."

The two sat silently, listening to the breeze and the silence around them. Alec looked over at Adelle.

"What?" she asked.

"Do you still have yours?"

Adelle looked down at her wrist. The symbol of the Ankh was still just below the skin. "Yes, and you?"

"Yeah, me too." Alec took a sip of his hot coffee.

"We never talked about this, Alec, what this all means. Dr. Apoe told me it meant our gifts were still active. He said as long as it was there, the Ankh was a sign that we could communicate with the Gods. I think he meant that we would have our gifts."

Alec nodded his head. "He told me the same thing."

"He also told me, Alec, that you," she paused, "that you communicated with them. He said you were the only one they talked to."

Alec listened to Adelle's statement, unsure that he wanted to discuss his experience in the Virginia mountains. Many memories still confused him, and trying to make sense of his experience at Big Meadows made it difficult to ascribe meaning to what happened. But this was Adelle, the woman he loved, asking him, not only for her but her questions might also help him.

Alec answered, "I don't know if I was the only one, but I did talk directly to the Shiny Ones. It was in Virginia, shortly after I Exited."

Adelle became animated and pulled her legs up under her. "Why didn't we ever talk about it?"

"I had, and still have, a tough time sorting out everything they said. They were communicating through what sounded like bible verses and religious language. You know that's not my forte."

"What did they say, minus the bible verses."

"They said they were messengers of the one true message. They provided no detail as to what that meant. Then they told me, I'm trying to remember," Alec paused and put his hands to his ears, trying to recall his memories of the event and then continued as he remembered small parts, "that we had discovered ancient knowledge through the SOUP. We regained the ability to access the higher spiritual – something."

"What kind of knowledge?"

"They said we had healed our pineal glands and opened our third eye."

"How would the SOUP heal our pineal gland?"

"It's because of how the SOUP uses the gland to create part of our virtual reality. By using the gland and our liquid diet, the system healed it. Combined with our technology, we could tap into power out of our reach. I assume he meant the gifts we have. This renewal was something unexpected for them. These gifts were part of how humans existed long ago, acknowledging and interfacing with the spiritual world. Now, our lifestyles prevent our pineal from working correctly. Our advancements in knowledge move us all past legends and mysteries and into science. Our world today is very pragmatic and has trounced the old philosophies that became our religions. We doubt more than we believe unless we can prove it. We've lost our faith in what each of us knows inside." Alec reached into his sweater pocket and pulled out a piece of paper. He handed it to Adelle. "Can you read it?"

"Not really, it's kind of dark."

Alec pulled his iPhone out of his jeans and turned on the flashlight option. "Here, baby, use this," he said, shining the light onto the paper. Adelle read out loud,

"The eye is the lamp of the body. If your eyes are healthy, your whole body will be full of light. But if your eyes are unhealthy, your whole body will be full of darkness. If then the light within you is darkness, how great is that darkness! Matthew 6:22-23. Where did you get this?"

"It's a bible verse. Lincoln gave it to me. He said the eye it mentions is our third eye, opened by the pineal gland."

"It sure fits with what we know. Using the gifts to take

other lives speaks to darkness. But do you really believe that God is involved in the SOUP, Alec?"

"I don't know. That's why I didn't bring this up. I'm still trying to sort out who God is."

Alec felt agitated, not at Adelle, but because he could not connect all the answers to his numerous questions. This part of his life was still in flux, something Alec was never accustomed to feeling. *"Focus on her love,"* he thought. *"She is real, and she is here."*

"I see," Adelle said. "Well, it's out now. We might as well keep talking," she said, smiling.

"Really, Adelle?"

"It might help to get this all out. I'm just as confused as you are and need to talk too. I didn't have the personal experience you did, but I've been waiting for the right time to approach you with this."

Alec looked around at his surroundings. The darkness of the mountains surrounded him, and somewhere, he heard a distant bird of prey crying in the early morning as it circled, looking for breakfast.

"Okay. But it might get a little weird."

"Alec Richardson, tell me how our lives could get any weirder."

Alec smiled. She was right.

"Ready for this next part?"

Adelle nodded.

"So, after Lincoln gave me this, I started, you know," Alec felt uncomfortable but continued, "reading the bible. It seemed the next logical thing to do after everything kept pointing back to it, and I came up with this. I know taking one verse at a time can lead to missing the understanding, but in Luke, Jesus states that 'the Kingdom of Heaven is inside each of us.'

"What do you think that means, Alec?"

"I think it means that God is not in the SOUP. The SOUP is just technology. I believe we have everything we need inside ourselves to be unique, gifts included. Our experiences enabled us to gauge how we would handle our gifts and see the results of our actions. You know, 'if you have ears – hear, if you have eyes – see.' It's all right there."

"What is?"

"We were meant to have these gifts to communicate with something bigger than us – and to use them to make life better for all of us. I believe, Adelle, the stronger we love, the stronger the gifts become. This explanation is starting to sound like mumbo-jumbo." Alec sounded frustrated.

"No, I'm following you," Adelle said, staring at Alec and reaching over to touch his leg, "Then why all the darkness and evil references?"

"Because they told me we have free will. We can make choices about how to use the gifts we have. It's a warning that evil is always present and can corrupt the way we make choices," Alec continued.

"It's much like a decision to leave the SOUP. We decide. We have free will to stay," Adelle commented, reflecting on her experience and choice to leave.

"Our whole lives are supposed to be based on free will. We get to decide who and what we are." Alec sounded more convinced of his emerging belief.

Adelle nodded her head, "But what is evil, Alec? Who decides what is good and what is wrong?"

Alec shook his head, "I think we do. We control our lives, and we have everything inside of us to do it. We have love," he looked at Adelle, "That's an easy one. But we also have greed, revenge, and the lust for power and control inside as well. All the problems we went through were because of ego and hubris with the people we faced. Maybe our ego is the source of evil. I just don't know."

"Did the 'people' you talked with give you any ideas about evil?"

"Yes," he said slowly, "they said that no one can destroy evil or darkness, only defeat it. We need darkness to understand what comes with the Light."

"That makes sense to me, Alec. I am far from being religious or whatever, but I know how I want to live my life, our life now." Adelle waited for Alec to respond. He did so by taking a sip of his coffee.

"Alec, who do you think the Shiny Ones are?"

*"She is really taking me down the rabbit hole with these questions!"*

Alec began, "I think they fit into the big scheme like judges. They don't give us our gifts because they come from another source. The Shiny Ones monitor those that have the gifts. If we misuse them, we and the gifts are taken away. Apoe told me that he and the Supervisor worked together and saw others with gifts like we, have taken away. He said they always heard a voice ask, 'What will you do with the rest of your life?' It sounds like we are always given a choice in our future. We can change and create a new life if we want to and, with change, overcome guilt and other feelings from our past."

The door to the house opened, and Addie emerged. "I heard a party," she said, rubbing her eyes.

"Speaking of changing our life," Adelle said.

Alec reached over and picked her up, placing her on his lap.

"What are we doing, Daddy?"

"Look," Alec said, pointing to his front. "Old man, sunshine is about to start a new day. Let's watch."

The morning sun's rays began their daily creation of a new beginning, shining upward over the mountain peaks and illuminating the clouds above in brilliant orange.

"Will there always be a new day, Daddy?"

Alec looked at Adelle, "Always Addie. The sun will rise every morning, bringing light, and that light allows everything to live and grow, including you! It shines all day, and then like you, goes to sleep at night."

"I like that. I've never seen the day start."

"Most people haven't, Addie," Alec said, looking at

Adelle.

"Alec, don't be so flippant!" Adelle teased.

"*Maybe that was it,*" Alec thought. Each day people were reminded. Each day was a new day to start your life again. 'He who has eyes, let him see.' The sun rose each morning. Could it be that simple? Lives filled with light shone on others and helped them grow. Lives filled with darkness remained within, focused on the self. Both must exist so that people can choose.

The sun reached the mountains' crest and broke over the top. It shone brightly into the small town, its rays lighting up the streets as its beams inched across the houses until reaching the porch where the three sat, content in life, sharing love between them. On the porch, the three were surrounded in light. A new day began.

"It's so bright, Daddy." Addie turned her head slightly and put her hand to her forehead to shield her eyes from the morning glare.

"The light from the sun is always bright, Addie," Adelle said. "That's why we don't look right at it. It will hurt our eyes."

"Why is the light so bright?"

Adelle looked at Alec. It was apparent to him; he would have to provide the answer to their curious three-year-old. Alec reflected on his first recollections of leaving the SOUP and its connections with Plato's cave. The man experienced blindness until adjusting and finding a beautiful and different world illuminated by light. When the man was taken back into darkness, his fellow prisoners would not believe his story and would kill him rather than face the light. One day, when Addie was older, he would tell her this story. For now, it was only important to him.

Alec paused, simplified Plato's story, and said, "Addie, it's bright because it's trying to remind us of who we are and what all of us could be."

# EPILOGUE

A shley Ferguson opened the small envelope from the Virtual Elder Care facility where her mother resided. Ashley always looked forward to receiving the small USB drive every six weeks. The life video contained her mother's virtual life, a menu of experiences on the small plastic device. The envelope always had a brief letter explaining her mother's physical condition, a computer-signed signature of the Chief of Virtual Elder Care Operations for the managing company SBIC, and the standard legal disclaimers in 20 different languages.

At first, Ashley felt she was eavesdropping on her mother's remaining years, but after seeing the first two life videos, she had to admit that she was pleased with the experience her aging mother was living in the final time of her life. Her mother would never remember that she'd been diagnosed with degenerative brain disease five years ago. The doctors said her condition would progress from memory loss to dementia, eventually forgetting most of the people she knew. The situation would also gradually shut down her motor skills until her brain ceased functioning. Ashley had chosen the Virtual Elder Care option, which used the Last Memory Reset technique. Using this technology, the SBIC staff walked her mother back to her early twenties before her family. Ashley was assured the system would care for her mother's body and produce the remaining memories of her life through the fantastic virtual technology. Her remaining life would be happy and without pain, but also without family.

Ashley took the USB drive and placed it into her laptop computer. The video file was immediately recognized and loaded.

"Let's see what we have today."

Ashley pressed play, and a menu of options appeared,

listing the significant events since the last USB. Ashley scanned the list and saw the title, 'Betty Ferguson goes on a date.'

"Mom," Ashley said, slightly shocked. "You go, girl!"

Ashley pressed play, and the video showed her mother sitting alone at a table in a small coffee shop. Her mother's avatar, created by the system, was young and vibrant in her skirt and open blouse, the top button strategically undone, allowing a revealing view of her breast. She was nervously scanning her surroundings, obviously anticipating another person's arrival. She did not have to wait long as an attractive young man, smartly dressed in shorts and a polo shirt, arrived at her table. Her mother sprung up immediately, pulling the young man close and kissing him deeply."

Ashley was shocked by her mother's aggressiveness. "Mom! Jesus, I'm glad dad's not around anymore to see this." Ashley turned up the volume.

"Oh Ray, it's so good to see you again! Even though it was only last night. And what a night it was!" Betty Ferguson said.

Ashley felt her face flush.

"Yeah, it was pretty sweet. That part is always good with us. Especially, 'you know.'"

Ashley knew. She and her mother both blushed.

"Well, I know what Navy men like," her mother said. "You don't live in San Diego and not hear about what sailors like."

Betsy's date sat down at the table, looked into her eyes, and said, "Look, I got some bad news I have to tell you."

"What, are you okay?"

Ashley hoped this was not a big blow-off for her mom.

"Yes, it's just the team needs to deploy for a couple of weeks for some training."

"Where will you be going?"

"Sorry, Bets, you know my job doesn't allow me to talk about these types of things. The Special Operations Command keeps all of our activity classified."

Betsy looked hurt. "I know, but I was hoping I might be able to tag along every once in a while."

"Sorry again, Bets. It's all National Security stuff. I'd love to put you in my bag, but I'd have no room for your picture or my underwear."

Betsy laughed. "Oh, Ray, you're just the best." Betsy looked down at the table, "When do you leave?" she said sheepishly.

"Not for several hours if you want to spend some time together."

"Of course, my Seal always must have something to remember me by. After all," she said, adjusting her bra and providing a peek at her breast underneath, "it's what you're fighting for, right?"

"You are a wizard with words, Bets."

Ashley pushed the ESC key to exit the video. She felt a little angry that her mother was throwing herself at this man, but at the same time felt a little turned on by what she had witnessed and did not need those feelings either, right now.

"Of all the places that I thought I would see this stuff! The last place I ever thought would be my 80-year-old mother's life video."

Ashley felt confused and conflicted by what she saw in the video. "Why couldn't you just go on a trip around the world or something normal, mom?" she exclaimed.

Ashley thought for a moment about people and relationships. Her mother knew, and even Ashley could not deny that the emotions she witnessed were all part of life. Ashley slowly regained her calm.

"I know it's a virtual world," she said, "but hell, mom. Did it have to be a Navy Seal? Those guys will get what they want and dump you. Not a good choice!" She ejected the USB and decided to return to it later.

"Where do we find these guys?"

Ashley always wondered where the other eldercare patients originated. Who, like her, had decided to allow their parents or grandparents their last enjoyment in life by choosing the Virtual Elder Care program. In this case, she would be surprised to know that Lieutenant Commander Raymond Skeets had entered the Virtual Elder Care system less than one year before the video was made. He was 34 years old.

# ABOUT THE AUTHOR

## Tom Dewitt

Tom DeWitt has always been a writer at heart. It began in high school when he tapped into his creative talents by contributing to school plays, the yearbook, the school newspaper, and literary magazines. He drew on his young experiences as part of a military family that transferred from Army base to Army base for most of his formative years. Those years also laid the foundation for his commitment to service, like his father. After retiring from the Army in 1996, Tom poured his creativity into entrepreneurship and co-founded SNVC just two years later. This rich combination of life lessons and late-night discussions with his friends and colleagues, as well as his son and daughter, provided him with the backdrop, plot, and characters behind the SOUP Trilogy. His recent exploration into the works of philosophers like John Locke and Voltaire has given him an introspection that can be seen as he weaves his stories about some of the most complex societal challenges facing humanity today. Evil Walks Among US, his first book was published in 2019. The Nature of Man is the second installment in the trilogy. You may find him on social media on Facebook and LinkedIn, or you may send him an email at tom.snvc@hotmail.com if you would like to have a deeper conversation. Tom graduated from John Handley High School in Winchester and obtained degrees from Longwood College (BS, Biology) and the University of Southern California (MS, Information Systems). He calls Herndon, Virginia home and is a proud grandfather of two.

# BOOKS IN THIS SERIES
*The SOUP Trilogy*

## Book 1: Evil Walks Among Us

Power tends to Corrupt. And Absolute Power Corrupts Absolutely... Great men are almost always bad men." Lord John Acton and others

The Virtual Life Solution (VLS) is a secret government program created to incarcerate the nation's worst criminals by placing them into a virtual reality world called the Special Operational Unfenced Prison (SOUP). Criminals in the SOUP create their new reality in prison by building upon their own memories and sharing others' experiences that share their fate. VLS offers substantial cost savings to taxpayers and transforms every aspect of our incarceration system. It utilizes the newest technology with the potential to create a future limited only by the nation's imagination. It is the perfect solution.

Pulitzer Prize-winning reporter Alec Richardson is selected by the White House to write the story revealing details of the Program to the American people to enhance the sitting president's electability. Richardson, Network Executive Adelle Hall, and DC police officer Jefferson Grant discover there is more to the VLS Program than revealed and find themselves embroiled in action, politics, suspense, and murder as they seek to find the truth behind one of America's greatest achievements.

## Book 2: The Nature Of Man

"Waste no more time arguing about what a good man should be. Be one." Marcus Aurelius

Its two years after the Secure Operational Unfenced Prison (SOUP) is established, and the Virtual Life Incarceration Program (VLIP) has expanded across the country. An earthquake rattles the Los Angeles facility, releasing three of the country's worst criminals with a secret too crucial for the nation's top leaders to ignore. An international incident with China brings the United States to the brink of war. Surprisingly, the escaped inmates hold the key to diffusing the international crisis.

However, with each technological achievement, the Virtual Life Program attracts others that wish to use the Program's secrets and its people to expand and protect their personal power regardless of the cost. Faced with the human and technology challenges of the country's most outstanding achievement, even the Program's leaders and staff are faced with moral and ethical choices as they steer the Program towards a greater America.

Continuing the story from Evil Walks Among US, we find the Program Supervisor, her Chief Scientist Dr. Sandra O'Neal, and the Program's Chief Medical Officer, Mr. UT, racing against time, politics, and murder to prevent the VLIP technology from being exploited and abused by those in power.

## Book 3: A Time To Stand

"Reality is created by the mind, we can change our reality by changing our mind." Plato

A Time to Stand is the last book of the SOUP trilogy. A triad of senior government officials wants the capabilities demonstrated by the SOUP's escaped inmates used to resolve the Taiwan Straits incident. The United States Vice President, acting as a member of the Virtual Life Incarceration Program (VLIP) governance committee, sees the value provided by these criminals as critical to National Security and Intelligence collection. Along with other top administration officials, the Vice President convinces the President to sign a classified Presidential Directive moving the VLIP from the Justice Department to the Central Intelligence Agency. The Supervisor realizes the risks of unleashing the unknown power created accidentally by the SOUP's technology. She and her team oppose the directive and the presidential authority to subsume her program for power and political gain. Each side, believing they are right, pushes for its goals without understanding the consequences of its actions and the impact on the human experience. A Time to Stand paints a contemporary picture of human conflict fueled by the desire to control unknown powers, and the realization that every action has consequences.

www.ingramcontent.com/pod-product-compliance
Lightning Source LLC
LaVergne TN
LVHW051428050326
832903LV00030BD/2972